Save Baseball

Save Baseball
A Prescription for the Major Leagues

Larry Hausner

McFarland & Company, Inc., Publishers
Jefferson, North Carolina

LIBRARY OF CONGRESS CATALOGING-IN-PUBLICATION DATA

Names: Hausner, Larry, 1967– author.
Title: Save baseball : a prescription for the Major Leagues / Larry Hausner.
Description: Jefferson, North Carolina : McFarland & Company, Inc., Publishers, 2024 | Includes bibliographical references and index.
Identifiers: LCCN 2023050223 | ISBN 9781476689920 (paperback : acid free paper) ♾
 ISBN 9781476650661 (ebook)
Subjects: LCSH: Major League Baseball (Organization) | Baseball—United States—Management. | Baseball—Economic aspects—United States. | Baseball fans—United States. | BISAC: SPORTS & RECREATION / Baseball / General
Classification: LCC GV875.A1 H38 2023 | DDC 796.357/640973—dc23/eng/20231122
LC record available at https://lccn.loc.gov/2023050223

BRITISH LIBRARY CATALOGUING DATA ARE AVAILABLE

ISBN (print) 978-1-4766-8992-0
ISBN (ebook) 978-1-4766-5066-1

© 2024 Larry Hausner. All rights reserved

No part of this book may be reproduced or transmitted in any form or by any means, electronic or mechanical, including photocopying or recording, or by any information storage and retrieval system, without permission in writing from the publisher.

Front cover images © 2024 Shutterstock

Printed in the United States of America

McFarland & Company, Inc., Publishers
 Box 611, Jefferson, North Carolina 28640
 www.mcfarlandpub.com

To my children, Riley and Jacob;
they are my world.

Table of Contents

Preface   1

Introduction   13

1. Declining Attendance   19
2. America's Pastime in Recession   51
3. Withering Fan Experience   78
4. Pace of Play   97
5. Generation Lost   119
6. Weakening Youth Participation   135
7. Major League Baseball's Brand   153
8. Labor Negotiation Strife   170
9. Save Situation   181

Bibliography   189

Index   199

Preface

When my son, Jacob, was about to turn 16, I had an exciting plan for this milestone birthday. His 16th birthday was the same day as the Major League Baseball All-Star Game at San Diego's Petco Park. We live in Orange County and we love going to Petco. We typically see about 10 games there every year. I couldn't wait to tell him my idea and see how excited he would be. I mean, come on! The All-Star Game on your 16th birthday, in San Diego no less. It can't get any better.

When I presented this idea to him, I was stunned by his response. "No, thank you, Dad. Baseball is boring," he said.

Huh? I nearly drove off the road. I thought he was kidding. Shockingly, he wasn't. He was serious and said his friends felt the same. While I was stunned, I began to look at this from his point of view and I thought, what is going on here? Looking back, I probably should have been grateful. He probably saved me over $1,000 in tickets, food, souvenirs, etc., at the All-Star Game. What started out as a typical drive in the car with my son became an eye-opening epiphany that led to this work.

What made this all the more shocking was that my son loved the game from an early age. Beginning around the age of three, he would insist on wearing a full Angels uniform to every home game we attended. Throughout the years, the kids and I traveled to see MLB games at Chicago's Wrigley Field and in Arizona, Baltimore, Milwaukee, and New York.

I also coached Jacob's baseball teams, starting in T-ball at age four through Little League. Once he turned 13, I passed him off to the local travel ball team. While it was a tough transition not to have me as his coach, he enjoyed the experience. All of those years were so fun. Playing, coaching, and attending games were such a big part of our lives. Baseball was a huge part of our family.

The research I conducted began as a generational study to learn what my son's Generation Z felt about baseball and if it was the same way as he did. If so, why? While this book does go into detail about this potentially lost generation of baseball fans, the research morphed into so much more.

It led to the discovery that Major League Baseball is in trouble on more fronts than this. I then decided I would highlight these issues but, more importantly, provide solutions to overcoming them.

Issues Facing the Game

To put it simply, Major League Baseball attendance and fan interest are in a free-fall. The future of the game is in jeopardy. The data is concerning, and I will go into detail about the ramifications throughout the book. Issues and concerns are easy to point out. What is most challenging is determining solutions or best practices to solve them. Those in the game are well aware of what I am writing about. Baseball's problems are not top-secret, and while the league acknowledges there are issues, many are stumped as to how best to address them.

The issues are plenty and you will read about them here. A few examples often cited as evidence of the sport's impending collapse are declining attendance, a lack of nationally recognized stars, and poor World Series ratings. What is the driving force behind these problems? Is it pace of play? The fan experience in-venue and away from the ballpark? Is the improved television experience keeping fans home? Is it more choices competing for our time? How about branding or marketing? The answer is yes to all. All of these and more are contributing factors to the erosion of the fan base.

Two initiatives that have the potential to decimate the fabric of baseball across America have sadly come to fruition. The first is Major League Baseball's proposal to contract 25 percent of Minor League Baseball (MiLB) affiliated teams across the country, and the second is the reduction in the number of rounds in its amateur draft. These two initiatives play a vital role in undermining the promotion of baseball and connecting people to the game across the country.

While Major League Baseball and Minor League Baseball are different products, they share a symbiotic relationship. One relies upon the other for success. Without major league teams supplying the talent to minor league teams, there wouldn't be much of a product. Conversely, the minor leagues grow and cultivate prospects and help them bloom into major leaguers (*Baseball America*, 2020).

There is grave concern from those closest to the game about the impact of Major League Baseball's decision to decrease the number of minor league teams and drastically reduce the number of rounds in the draft. Major League Baseball claims to have reasons for both, and as you can imagine they are tied to dollars. However, looking long term, the dollars saved today will be lost tomorrow and so will a future fan base that Major League Baseball cannot afford to lose.

Contraction of MiLB Affiliated Teams

Major League Baseball's decision to contract 42 of the 160 affiliated minor league clubs in 2021 has led to some unfortunate consequences that impacted many minor league teams affiliated with a Major League Baseball organization and their community, as well as the health and advancement of the game.

Mike Palm, vice president of operations for The Circa, The D, and Golden Gate Casinos, said, "This is stunting for baseball. Baseball is losing its place in American sports. I predict in five years baseball will not be one of the four major sports."

These minor league teams were under the control of a Major League Baseball organization through strict franchise rights. Those 42 clubs lost their affiliate status, which drastically changed the future of not only the affected clubs but also the minor leagues as a whole.

While most of the 42 affiliates are privately owned, MLB says it didn't consider pulling the plug on their business, but the loss of their affiliation was a death sentence.

The plan, according to Major League Baseball, was in large part to improve minor league facilities. However, the leadership of these minor league teams said that was far from reality as many teams spent hundreds of thousands of dollars, and even millions, renovating their ballparks to MLB standards only to be told their franchise was being contracted. Some teams that were spared the death sentence were asked to change levels and some of the leagues were reworked.

MLB's deputy commissioner, Dan Halem, told *Baseball America*, "From the perspective of MLB clubs, our principal goals are upgrading the minor league facilities that we believe have inadequate standards for potential MLB players, improving the working conditions for MiLB players, including their compensation, improving transportation and hotel accommodations, providing better geographic affiliations between major league clubs and their affiliates, as well as better geographic lineups of leagues to reduce player travel."

Specifically, reported Jeff Tracy (2020) of Axios: "Each Major League club has about seven affiliates across various talent levels, from rookie ball up to AAA. The parent club pays salaries and buys equipment, while the affiliate pays for travel and other ballpark expenses. Additionally, each affiliate pays its parent club 8% of annual ticket revenue (about $20 million total)."

Tracy added, "The [reduction] reduced MiLB to 120 affiliates, with each big league club choosing which four affiliates it would like to retain. Contracted teams basically had three options: join an independent minor league, transition to a college summer league, or simply fold. MLB took over merchandising, broadcast and sponsorship rights of the remaining affiliates, splitting revenues 50–50 with the MiLB club. The new minor leagues look a lot more like the NBA's G League, which is owned and operated by the NBA and gives them more control over their talent pipeline."

Bill Bavasi, now retired senior director of baseball and softball development with Major League Baseball, had more than 40 years of experience as an MLB executive. He spent stints as a general manager with the California (later Anaheim) Angels and the Seattle Mariners, and his lineage comes from baseball royal bloodlines as the son of one of the game's most well-known executives, Buzzie Bavasi.

The elder Bavasi played a major role in the operation of three franchises from the late 1940s through the mid–1980s. Most notably, he was general manager of the Brooklyn and Los Angeles Dodgers from 1951 to 1968, during which time the team captured eight National League pennants and its first four World Series titles (*Baseball Almanac*, 2022).

While the Bavasi family has served in major league front offices for decades, they also have a history of working for and owning minor league franchises.

One of Bavasi's responsibilities was to oversee the Arizona Fall League (AFL). The AFL is composed of recently drafted players and current minor leaguers. It is an off-season league owned and operated by Major League Baseball operates during the autumn at six different baseball complexes in Arizona. The Arizona Fall League attracts many of the top prospects in Minor League Baseball.

While Bavasi admits that his perspective is from the player development side, he understands that there is a business component to the contraction of 42 teams in Minor League Baseball. However, for the same reasons he makes later in this chapter for having a deep draft, Bavasi believes eliminating teams reduced the number of MLB fans throughout the country.

"Say you're in Davenport, Iowa, and you're the farm team for the Astros," said Bavasi. "That means you have Houston fans, people following the Houston Astros in Davenport, Iowa. How do I see the Astros? I have to buy the mlb.com package. I'll tell you who should be pushing for more minor league baseball, our sponsors, people that are paying for those telecasts," said Bavasi, because those fans will no longer be following the Astros if their affiliation is pulled.

"I really believe that with more baseball there are more fans. We have this minor league system that has all these teams across the country, and you're not just developing players, you're developing fans," suggested Bavasi, and simply put, less baseball equates to fewer fans.

Bavasi adds, "The minor leagues are additionally important because minor league teams promote the game because their fans are first fans of baseball and not necessarily the players on their local minor league club for the simple reason is that the fans don't know the players or have a vested interest in them because the players arrive days before the start of the season."

Jay Jaffe of FanGraphs added, "This [contraction] is an issue. The way that was executed was harmful in terms of growing the game, because you've taken away potential fans from a lot of communities. I grew up in Salt Lake City. I was going to AAA games for a long time. My grandparents lived in Walla Walla, Washington, and I saw Tony Gwynn play at rookie-level ball. So minor league baseball is near and dear to my heart. We take my daughter to more [Brooklyn] Cyclones games than we have Mets or Yankees games so far. It's a cheaper ticket, it's a fun afternoon out. Everything's small scale and it's just easier for a three-year-old or a five-year-old to digest. So, you gotta have those experiences because I think that's how kids fall in love with the game, is getting to see it up close like that and that's important too."

Jeff Lantz, senior director of communications for Minor League Baseball, agrees and said to SB Nation, "A lot of kids might be losing baseball. The real negative here is that the future of the game has been put in jeopardy a little bit."

Lantz told me, "I think it's probably setting a dangerous path for the future of fandom for baseball."

What this really comes down to is losing access to professional baseball in markets that either aren't close to a major league city or would like a more affordable alternative (SB Nation, 2019).

John Blanchette (2020) of the *Spokesman-Review* covers the Spokane Indians in the Northwest League and said of the contraction, "The rich guys will siphon considerable goodwill out of Middle America and throw away more chances to make fans of young people who are giving up on the game."

Also, as one not to shy away from an opinion, former Cincinnati Reds general manager Wayne Krivsky said, "Eliminating 42 minor league teams is ruining the game. It is destroying the fabric of the country. The future fans are in those minor league towns. Saving money? I get it but you've got to be kidding me—at what cost? It is killing baseball."

Krivsky went on to say, "For generations, kids in small towns have gone to minor league games and that is where kids learn to love the game.

They are the ones who grew up and purchase the MLB package, but not anymore. It pains me. It's mind-boggling."

J.J. Cooper (2020) of *Baseball America* weighed in as well. "MLB's goal is that every club will have the same number of minor league affiliates, travel will be more efficient, and minor leaguers will get paid more—it's extremely rough news for employees and fans in the affected markets and the players whose dreams will be crushed as more than 1,000 jobs are eliminated," said Cooper.

To that point, in 2019, 106 Members of Congress signed a letter to Commissioner Rob Manfred calling for MLB to reconsider such drastic measures in the minor leagues. "If enacted, it would undermine the health of the minor league system that undergirds talent development and encourages fan loyalty," the letter stated. Sadly, it fell on deaf ears and did not persuade Major League Baseball from changing course.

The letter was co-authored by Representative Lori Trahan of Massachusetts's Third District, which included Lowell, home of the short-season Class A Spinners. The Spinners were one of nine teams in the New York-Penn League on the chopping block.

MLB's plan fit into what Commissioner Rob Manfred has called his "One Baseball" vision since taking office five years ago. To that point, Wayne Krivsky doesn't agree with the plan. At all.

"If a team wants to have five minor league affiliates, great. If they want 10, so be it. Let the teams decide. The commissioner is trying to clone everyone," said Krivsky.

Dave Ziedelis, general manager of the Frederick Keys, has over 30 years of experience as a front-office executive in both Major League and Minor League Baseball. "Many fans come to a minor league game primarily for reasons other than the game on the field. The minor leagues develop young fans because that's what we are all about," said Ziedelis.

It was frustrating and shocking to him that his Frederick Keys were on the contraction list. He said, "This contraction was not based on how successful we were as a business or attendance or based on our community support because we were a grand slam in all of those areas. We were a team that a lot of other teams tried to pattern themselves after. Our community was very surprised that we were on that initial proposal.

"It is no surprise with this upcoming professional baseball agreement [between MLB and the MLBPA] that it was going to be a little rougher negotiation," Ziedelis said. "We knew MLB wanted to see some changes, meaning facilities changes and standards increased which were put into place in 1992 and haven't changed since. Quite frankly, that's not a difficult ask. Our facility is over 30 years old but since I have been here [2004] it has undergone $6–$7 million in renovations."

Another reason Major League Baseball proposed this change was to reduce team travel. At the time, this wasn't an issue for Frederick, because it played in the geographically condensed Carolina League, but other leagues cover a wider area.

This is a sad example of baseball's shrinking footprint in the sports world, which concerns Ziedelis. "It is very curious that when you look at baseball's total impact and their portion of the sports market is reducing, why would you want to eliminate 25 percent of the teams, especially in many areas that do not have access to a major league team that could be hundreds of miles away? It is a very curious decision," Ziedelis said.

Dave Heller is the president and CEO of Main Street Baseball, a group that owns four minor league teams, three of which—Class A Quad Cities in Iowa; short-season Class A Lowell, Massachusetts; and rookie-level Billings, Montana—were on the cut list.

"We are taking Major League Baseball at its face value," Heller told SB Nation. "We are trusting that they're telling the truth when they say this is really about facilities standards and the 25 percent—their figure—of minor league baseball parks that are not in compliance with MiLB facility standards. All four of my clubs are easily in compliance with that."

In my interview with Heller, he noted, "There are teams on this list that shouldn't be and teams that aren't on it that should be.

"One team not on the list is the Down East Wood Ducks of the High-A Carolina League. The team is an affiliate of the Texas Rangers. The Rangers actually own that franchise and they curiously do not appear on the list," noted Heller.

Heller worries about the impact in small-town America. "It would be horrific for cities like Billings, Montana, to lose professional baseball," he said.

Other MLB teams that own affiliates include the New York Yankees, who own the Tampa Tarpons of the A-level Florida State League; the St. Louis Cardinals, who own their AA-level affiliate in Springfield, Missouri; and the Atlanta Braves, who own the AAA-level Gwinnett Stripers in the International League. None of these teams appeared on the list of clubs to lose their affiliated status.

There was some support for the plan. Several MLB team executives, including Diamondbacks general manager Mike Hazen and Blue Jays President and CEO Mark Shapiro, defended the league's proposal to cut 42 Minor League Baseball teams. They echoed what Major League Baseball previously said in defense of its proposal, which was that cutting 42 minor league teams, mostly in short-season and rookie ball, would free up more money to pay players and improve their working conditions, including food and travel as well as facility conditions (Yahoo Sports, 2020).

These executives say their jobs necessitate developing players efficiently and thoroughly. Chopping 42 minor league teams would have the double benefit of helping reduce overhead so the owners can report higher profits while making their system run more efficiently (or so they think). "So be it if thousands of jobs in towns across the U.S. get slashed in the process," said NBC Sports.

Reducing the Number of Rounds in the First-Year Player Draft

Yet another example of Major League Baseball's shrinking footprint in sports is the decision to slash the amateur draft in 2020 to five rounds, which came after weeks of discussion between Major League Baseball and the Major League Baseball Players Association (MLBPA) as the union was hoping for a 10-round draft. Many were hopeful that MLB would add more rounds in years to come, which they did soon thereafter, moving it to 20 in 2021.

Bavasi says, "[In 2020] the draft so far has been cut to five rounds from 40 rounds, and we're talking about cutting the minor leagues down as well. On the finances, I can't really argue with that. But I will say that the draft really didn't cost you anything, and because you're drafting somebody didn't mean you have to sign them. But we have legislated ourselves into less baseball. If there are fewer rounds in the draft, that's less baseball. If there are fewer affiliated minor league teams across the country, that's less baseball as well."

Bavasi explained the concept of free marketing of baseball through the draft extrapolates. "If there's less baseball, you're cultivating fewer fans. Because if somebody drafts a young man, that father is now a fan of baseball, the mother a fan of baseball, the sister a fan of baseball also. A lot of my thoughts are stuff I've heard over the years, and then I've galvanized together to realize that, wow, we're legislating away fans," said Bavasi.

For comparison, in 2019, the MLB draft had 1,217 players chosen by MLB teams. In 2020, only 160 players were selected, once supplemental picks were added in.

Krivsky, a scout at heart, says lost in all of this is that player development is being marginalized. "It used to be such a joyous occasion to be drafted for that young man. For his family, for his community. That's been taken away from 1,100 players. Reward them. Reward the scouting and the hard work that went into knowing who the players were," said Krivsky.

"Manfred is out to do in scouting. Obviously, with only five rounds you don't need robust scouting to tell you who the top five rounds of prospects will be," reasons Krivsky.

But how Major League Baseball organizations scout prospects has changed. Buck Showalter told me, "We have created a lazy game. We would rather be in front of a computer screen than, for example, get to know a prospect and everything about them like sitting down with their family, getting to know their friends, their teachers, what type of person are they, their character, and what do the people closest to the prospect say about them."

This isn't the first time MLB has cut back on the amateur draft. Until 1986, there were two annual drafts, in January and June. That's right, two drafts per year, and in the June draft there were some teams that drafted 100 rounds. The draft was later reduced to one per year.

Major League Baseball last shortened the draft in 2012, when it went from 50 rounds to 40. Bavasi has issues with reducing the number of rounds. "I'm not a real supporter of us cutting the draft back. We were making fans with deep drafts. At one time we had 100 rounds, and while many of those players were never signed or played in a professional game, those who were drafted became fans of that team, as did their families and friends," said Bavasi.

Blanchette (*Spokesman-Review*, 2020) offers one reason behind this move: "MLB wants to push the amateur draft back to July or August, avoiding the June cluster of getting players still in high school and college seasons drafted, signed, and off to their assignments ... [to] gain an extra year's contract control since the clock will not have started on their playing careers." This prediction came to fruition.

Jeff Passan (June 15, 2020) of ESPN is also concerned about the reduction in the draft. "For a sport like baseball, which is already struggling to attract the best athletes, what sort of a message does it send to shorten the draft from 40 rounds to five and then limit those who don't get drafted to signing for pennies on the dollar? The most troublesome kind: that today is simply more important than tomorrow—and that baseball is impervious to shortsightedness," wrote Passan.

Of course, money is a huge factor in all of this. The money that teams will save as a result of this agreement is significant as it allows teams to delay signing bonuses, with a maximum of $100,000 to be paid within 30 days of a player signing, 50 percent of the remainder due one year out, and the remaining dollars two years from signing. Eliminating the sixth through 10th rounds saved teams a combined $29,578,100 in slot value—nearly $1 million per team and less than $500,000 in actual cash with the new signing-bonus rule. For comparison, in 2019, sixth-round bonus slots ranged from a high of $301,600 to a low of $237,000 (Passan and McDaniel, 2020).

The fallout from the decision could have a significant effect on professional and amateur baseball. The impact on college baseball forced it "to scramble to figure out how to balance its limited scholarships, a potential influx of freshmen and the desires of draft-eligible juniors and seniors," wrote Passan and McDaniel.

"Given the massive falloff in bonus money for comparable talent, scores if not hundreds of players who would otherwise be drafted will flock to junior colleges where they will be eligible to play for one year and re-enter next year's draft," reported Craig Calcaterra (2020) of NBC Sports.

Calcaterra also speculates that other players may leave the U.S. and attempt to catch on in Japan, Korea, or Taiwan. Sadly, many players may give up playing baseball entirely and perhaps focus on another sport. "Regardless of where any specific player goes, this will, overall, reduce the amount of talent in American professional baseball," said Yahoo Sports.

One scenario, and perhaps unintended consequence, in reducing the draft even to 20 rounds is that competition to drive down the bonuses may occur when a team is faced with its last pick in the 20th round and three prospects to choose from. The issue then becomes which one they can get for less as they essentially pit one player against the other.

This is a slippery slope and the fallout may be where players opt out of playing baseball altogether if they don't see the potential to be drafted. In turn, this drives kids away from the game and baseball loses not only a potentially great player but a fan as well.

A deep draft is free advertising for the game of baseball and also fosters goodwill. As for talent, players selected in the sixth through the 10th rounds over the past decade include Jacob deGrom, Dallas Keuchel, Paul Goldschmidt, Marcus Semien, Miles Mikolas, Whit Merrifield, Kyle Hendricks, Brian Dozier, Trey Mancini, and Kendall Graveman—not a bad lineup. Wouldn't it be a shame to miss out on watching future talent because they opted not to play baseball anymore?

I want to be clear that this book isn't about finger-pointing or laying blame as to why these issues are persisting in baseball, although everyone from the owners and players to even the commissioner share responsibility for where the game lies today and where to take it to tomorrow to make it better. While there is plenty of blame and accountability to go around, this book isn't about that. It is about solutions by calling on those with experience, expertise, and an opinion to weigh in on the conversation.

In researching these issues and potential solutions, a few things became clear. When it comes to baseball, there is no shortage of opinions. In fact, most people have passionate, strong feelings about the state of the game. Everyone I interviewed for this book acknowledged the aforementioned challenges the game is facing as real. But more important, they all shared my love for the game and in turn a desire to see it grow, improve, and be sustainable for generations to come. Baseball has that effect upon those of us who love it. We care about the game. As Bob Costas said, "Baseball is one of the things that, looking back, I have always cared about" (Ken Burns, 1994).

In this book I will share those opinions and draw connections to potential solutions. Will we all agree? Hardly. There will be some who make compelling arguments for both sides of a particular issue. Take, for example, the designated hitter debate. My goodness, battle lines are still drawn over the DH, which was instituted in the American League over 50 years ago. We can have a healthy disagreement about what the issues are or are not and the solutions to address them.

Importance of This Work

I believe this work is critically important to the long-term sustainability of the game. I do not profess that baseball is dying as others have, but it might be on life support. Baseball certainly isn't healthy, and if it continues on a steady decline of attendance and fan interest, baseball may not die but it could become nothing more than a niche sport. That would be disastrous. Baseball is at a crossroads and as a fan and one who loves the game, I am concerned and, as you will read throughout this book, I am not alone.

My goal in writing this book is to raise the consciousness of decision makers to implement real strategies for change to help keep baseball at the forefront of the minds of sports fans. This book is a call to action to avert an impending crisis, to offer explanations and a plan of action. Why? Because I love the game and I am worried about its future.

In order to accomplish these goals, I interviewed experts from the baseball operations side of the house to those in the business side of MLB franchises—current and former players, coaches, general managers, a team president, broadcasters, marketing experts, and even fans. Who better to lean on than the people who care most about the game. I believe that the opinions, ideas, passion, and, ultimately, suggestions will point Major League Baseball in the right direction to overcome the steep decline in attendance and fan interest and to secure America's pastime for generations to come as a major sport.

In short, my hope is that I will demonstrate my love for the game and solutions to overcome its issues. This is my opportunity to give back to the game that has given me so much, and as Vin Scully would say, let's see how I come out.

Introduction

"Baseball is Heaven's gift to mortals."—George Will

I'm a baseball junkie. At least that's what my dad called me from about the age of eight onward. I even had a T-shirt made proclaiming that. I was indeed addicted to baseball. From an early age, the game of baseball had a grip on me. My earliest memories are baseball-related. Growing up in Southern California in the 1970s and 1980s and only six miles from Angel Stadium, I recall going to Angels games as early as three or four years old. The images of the bright green, freshly mowed manicured grass and brilliant white uniforms, along with the smell of hot dogs, are forever burned in my memory. Even today, when I walk into a stadium, those memories rush back, and I am a kid all over again. I will never get over it.

Baseball has had this grasp on me throughout my life and has not let go. It's hard to explain where or how this originated, but I felt at peace whenever I played or watched the game. It seemed natural. Although today I am less of a baseball junkie, I nonetheless remain a fan.

While the playing part of the game ended decades ago for me, watching the game is still something I look forward to on television or in person. Even in my 50s when I know that I am going to a Major League Baseball game, I am excited throughout the day. The day takes on a special feeling. I know what awaits me when I walk into the ballpark and become reacquainted with the game I love.

However, my concern is that the youngest generation does not share that same love for the game. Scan the crowd at a major league game today and it's a rarity to see youngsters in attendance. Drive through neighborhoods today and seeing kids playing baseball, as in pickup games, is sadly nothing but a memory. Where have all of the kids gone? I suspect indoors staring into one device or another.

While playing the game was enjoyable, so was growing up to become a fan of Major League Baseball. Consuming Major League Baseball in the 1970s and 1980s was completely different from how it is today. It seems unfathomable to Generation Z and millennials that television consisted of only local, over-the-air channels. Living in the Los Angeles market at that time meant we had a whole seven channels to choose from. The Angels were on KTLA Channel 5, and the Dodgers were on KTTV Channel 11. Typically, fewer than 50 games a year were televised by each team, a far cry from the entire 162 games each team broadcasts on television today.

Information was far from instant. We either watched the late news to get baseball scores and a couple of highlights if we were lucky or waited for the morning newspaper to arrive to read the box scores. The *Sporting News* also led to a weekly run to the mailbox to revisit box scores and features. Even though the box scores were days late, it didn't matter to me. I pored over them as if the game had occurred the night before. Baseball cards also served as a source of information. I began collecting in 1976 and the statistics on the back of those cards are ingrained in my memory to this day.

During the years before cable television, I would race to get the *TV Guide* in the mail every week during baseball season to see which teams were going to be featured on the Saturday *Game of the Week* on NBC. No matter the matchup, I was never disappointed. With Joe Garagiola and Tony Kubek providing the play-by-play and color commentary, the games felt important. They were the voices of my youth on Saturday afternoons in the spring and summer. Thank you, YouTube, for allowing me to go back in time to watch some of those games and become a 10-year-old again.

Cable television didn't begin to enter households in my neighborhood and start to become mainstream until the late 1970s. ESPN's *SportsCenter* did not come on the scene until mid–1979, when sports television changed forever as the sports world became smaller. For a baseball fan, it was a dream come true. Highlights and commentary galore. Until then, the only highlight show was "This Week in Baseball" (or "TWIB"), narrated by Yankees broadcaster Mel Allen, which aired weekly during the baseball season. In addition to highlights from recent games, the show featured player interviews. It was truly one of the only ways baseball fans got to know the players.

As a young fan, I was also blessed to be able to listen on the radio nightly to both Vin Scully, Hall of Fame voice of the Dodgers, and former Dodger and fellow Hall of Famer turned play-by-play voice of the Angels Don Drysdale. I learned the game from them and a passion for it as well. They painted the images in my mind with their words from the ballpark.

Those were wonderful times as a baseball fan. One would think it's better today with every game available on television and the connectivity we have with teams and players via social media. While those are terrific resources, the game back then felt simpler but special.

Baseball has a way of bringing us back to a place and time like no other sport. It is a sport built on memories, history, and tradition. For me, it is remembering watching an outstanding World Series like in 1975 when Cincinnati's Big Red Machine beat the Boston Red Sox or being fortunate enough to attend in person the Anaheim Angels' Game 7 win over the San Francisco Giants in 2002 to secure their first World Series title.

During the research for this book, I had the pleasure of interviewing Dave Ziedelis, who, as mentioned earlier, is the former general manager of Frederick Keys (then in the Carolina League). He also grew up during these years and called this "a time when we didn't have problems and we didn't have responsibilities and we went down to our neighborhood park to play with our friends. We watched our local team and listened to them on the radio. Baseball brings us to a time and place when everything was good. That's what baseball is. That's Americana. That's what we are all about."

A Career in Baseball

Once my amateur playing days ended I transitioned into what I was hoping was going to be a career in baseball off the field. In college I majored in communications: radio/TV/film at California State Fullerton with the goal of becoming a sportscaster. Upon graduation, I knew the job-market would be challenging, so I decided to get a leg up on the competition.

Prior to my junior year, I attended a summer camp where aspiring sportscasters refined their chops, received advice and coaching from those in the business, and also made valuable connections. It did all those things for me but it also fueled a passion for something I knew I could do well even though I had limited experience. From there I devised a plan to gain experience that my fellow graduates would not possess.

First, I developed a relationship with a local cable television company to begin a public access sports television show. In addition, I reached out to Bob Harvey, the radio voice of the San Bernardino Spirit of the California League. Harvey was a major league talent in A ball. I introduced myself via the old-fashioned way of writing him a letter asking to do stats or get coffee, or anything to be up close to a real play-by-play announcer. He graciously invited me into the booth during his broadcasts. The next thing I knew I was sitting beside Harvey for two seasons. As the second season progressed, he gave me the opportunity to do some play-by-play and I was extremely grateful.

After graduation, the strategy paid off as the television show improved over time, as did my on-air talents, and the show was picked up by SportsChannel Los Angeles, Bay Area, and Arizona. In my early 20s

I was hosting a network talk show in addition to doing features for the Angels and Dodgers pregame shows. Pretty amazing stuff indeed. Sadly, it was short-lived as SportsChannel went under after a year of airing my show. I was in transition and I decided to go back to my first love and pursue baseball play-by-play as a career.

The time on the air in San Bernardino led me to become the first voice of the Rancho Cucamonga Quakes. The competition was tough as I beat out over 150 applicants. As the voice of the Quakes, I had the opportunity to be around a professional baseball team every day. It was an incredible experience. While I enjoyed my time covering the Angels and Dodgers for SportsChannel, my role as a host and reporter was on the periphery. In the minors, I was able to see how a manager runs a team on and off the field. I learned the game from Keith Champion, our manager, and coaches like former Major Leaguers Bruce Tanner and Bob Geren. I witnessed how a team weathers the ups and downs of a long Minor League Baseball season. The experience was a baseball junkie's dream. It was fascinating and exciting.

From there I was hired to broadcast in the Hawaii Winter Baseball League for two seasons—the first as the voice of the Honolulu Sharks and the second stint with the Hilo Stars. In between, I spent some time in Palm Springs. I received accolades at every stop along the journey. Hawaii and Palm Springs—not exactly slumming it in the minors at those two stops.

However, while there was nothing I loved more than baseball play-by-play, I was unable to climb the ladder. It seemed there was always someone willing to do the job for less than me and sometimes for free. It also became apparent that those who did move up typically had a contact or a sponsor who helped pave their way. I became somewhat disillusioned and perhaps I should have stuck with it longer. While it was the lowest-paying job I ever had, it was the best one. Instead, I decided to opt for a career in education and that's where I am over 20 years later. However, when each baseball season begins, part of me feels like I should be there. I definitely miss it.

Baseball Is Generational

No matter where I have traveled as a fan, broadcaster, or parent, I have seen evidence that baseball is a game that is generational. It is passed down from one generation to another. Many of our dads brought us to the games just as their father did for them. My parents divorced when I was six, and my dad took my brothers and me to numerous Angels and Dodgers games when we were growing up. He grew up a baseball fan in Omaha, which at that time was the AAA affiliate of the St. Louis Cardinals. He tells stories of selling peanuts at Rosenblatt Stadium as a young kid. His love for the game was transferred to his three sons.

I have also been blessed to become the father of a daughter, Riley, and a son, Jacob. My children couldn't escape my passion for the game and they practically grew up at The Big A in Anaheim cheering on the Angels from about six months of age.

1

Declining Attendance

"If people who love the game and worked in the game for decades don't care anymore, how do MLB moguls expect casual fans to care?"—ESPN

Major League Baseball is hemorrhaging fans by the millions. This might come as a surprise to baseball fans as Major League Baseball owners are enjoying revenue never seen before. However, there is a great deal of evidence to support this claim and my concern is that it signals a free fall of fan support for America's pastime (see Table 1). What can be traced back to 2015 as a dip in attendance figures at Major League Baseball ballparks has become a consistent nosedive and cause for alarm.

In agreement is George Will, an American political commentator and author. He is also a well-known and respected baseball fan who has written extensively on the sport. Will is the author of the best-selling book *Men at Work: The Craft of Baseball*. Will told me, "Before 2020, which threw everything off, I think there'd been four consecutive years of declining attendance. Baseball to me in its strategy in this collective bargaining, to me, resembles a man who goes to a doctor and says, 'I have metastasizing cancer and I want to deal with it. But first I want a knee replacement.' It's absurd. Good God."

Will, when asked about possible reasons and solutions, said, "I know why they're doing this. The owners don't want to talk about changing the rules because when they propose a rule change, the players association will say, 'Yeah, we'll give you that if you give us X.' And it would strengthen the negotiating hand of the players. But the clock is ticking, and time is flying, and baseball's getting weaker and I don't think that's a luxury they can stand."

As Table 1 shows, compared with 2015, Major League Baseball attendance was down 5.2 million fans from 2019, a decrease of 2,146 fans per game. Take that in for a moment. That is a startling decline of over 7 percent. What has been Major League Baseball's response? Would you believe blaming it on the weather because a high number of games were rescheduled due to inclement conditions in 2019?

In 2018, Major League Baseball's attendance dropped 4 percent, resulting in the lowest overall league attendance since 2003. Seventeen of 30 teams had an attendance decrease that season, leading to $93.7 million in lost ticket revenue. The decrease also affected concessions sales. Shockingly, based on the attendance decline from 2017 to 2018, the league estimated almost $50 million in concession sales was lost (T.J. Mathewson, Global Sport Matters, 2019).

Also in 2018, Major League Baseball attendance dropped below 70 million fans for the first time in 15 years. The league cannot use the excuse that the weather was poor year after year. Major League Baseball needs to get serious about this issue and it is in MLB's best interest to determine why attendance is declining.

Table 1: MLB Attendance 2015–2021

Year	MLB Total Attendance	Decrease from Prior Year	Per-Game Average
2015	73,719,340	-	30,349
2016	73,159,044	-560,296	30,131
2017	72,678,797	-480,247	29,908
2018	69,671,272	-3,007,525	28,659
2019	68,506,896	-1,164,376	28,203
2020	COVID-19 Pandemic	NA	0
2021	45,304,109	NA	18,651*

(Source: Baseball-Reference, 2022)
*Attendance was impacted by the COVID-19 pandemic. Capacity was limited for numerous franchises the first few months of the season.

Moreover, just eight years prior, in 2007, Major League Baseball saw over 79 million fans come through its turnstiles, which was an average of 32,696 per game. A little over a decade later, in 2019, only 68 million fans attended games, which was a knee-buckling decrease of 11 million fans equaling a 14 percent decline. Also, in 2019, the per-game average attendance fell to 28,203, a reduction of 4,493 fans per game compared with 2007, or a 13.7 percent decrease (Baseball-Reference, 2022). In that same 2019 season, the league saw 14 clubs out of 30 with attendance declines from the year prior.

According to the *New York Times* (2018), "At the heart of baseball's decreasing attendance is the diminishing appeal of the traditional season ticket and the luxury box. With such a robust secondary market, teams can no longer argue that fans need to buy season tickets so they can guarantee access to the most desirable games and the postseason. Also, getting any person or business to commit to 81 days a year has become increasingly difficult, especially when the risk that the team will be terrible, sometimes intentionally, is higher than ever."

Will Leitch (2018) of *New York Magazine*'s *Intelligencer* suggests in his article "Nobody's Going to Sports in Person Anymore and No One Seems to Care" that the reason attendance in Major League Baseball is plummeting is because it can.

Leitch argues, "Teams don't really care anymore about bringing fans to the stadium—at least not as much as they used to—because they no longer need people in the seats to make money … [due to] expanded partnerships, local television ratings, and its [MLB's] own media-rights deals."

He also reminds us, "This has obviously not historically been the case. Attendance used to be the single driving indicator of a franchise's financial success: It's basically the reason the Dodgers are in Los Angeles rather than Brooklyn and the Giants are in San Francisco rather than Manhattan; by the end of their time in New York, each was averaging about 15,000 fans in stadiums that held more than twice that."

Causes That Factor in Declining Attendance

Professors Mark A. Davis from Troy University and John Miller of the University of Southern Mississippi conducted a 2021 study published in the *Journal of Sport Behavior* related to attendance trends in Major League Baseball.

Their article, titled "Major League Baseball's War on Time: An Analysis of Game Times' Impact on Attendance Using the Theory of Leisure Constraints" (2021), was a study aimed at utilizing the structural constraint of time associated with the theory of leisure constraints to analyze which variables impacted game attendance over the 2015 to 2019 MLB seasons. They define the idea of leisure constraints as any factor that intervenes between the preference for an activity—in this case, attending Major League Baseball games—and participation in it.

The authors assert that it is essential to understand which constraints may impact a fan's ability to attend MLB games that they negotiate regularly. These constraints can also be referred to as barriers and can be broken down into interpersonal and intrapersonal constraints.

Interpersonal barriers are those that are social factors. For example, a fan may choose not to attend if they cannot find someone to come with them. Intrapersonal constraints are individualized factors and examples of those may be motivation to attend a Major League Baseball game—for example, a perceived lack of time. Both of these barrier types, as Davis and Miller stress, impact the decisions of fans to attend games.

Additionally, their study examined how various variables impact attendance. Specifically, they include the length of game, runs scored, runs allowed, home runs, the number of pitchers used, weekend games and night games. The study looked at the 2015 through 2019 seasons.

Their study revealed some interesting and perhaps not surprising results. For instance, game length had a significantly positive correlation with average game attendance. Also, "The number of pitchers used in a game signified a significantly negative relationship to attendance in the day of the game model while revealing no significant relationship to attendance in the seasonal model ... [and] increased number of pitching changes per game has been a matter of contention regarding length of time of MLB game" (Davis and Miller).

Where does that leave the argument that the number of pitching changes lead to longer game durations? Well, Davis and Miller cite research that suggests "pitching changes are not as big of a factor in game length as other aspects of the game, citing a substantial portion of pitching changes happen between innings."

They also conclude that the variables of home runs and runs allowed are significantly related to attendance and, conversely, if your team is allowing more runs than the opposition, there is a negative relationship there and perhaps you would choose not to attend its games.

"The results of this study also indicated that the outcome of attendance at MLB games can be perceived as a function of anticipation or expectation strategies, particularly when teams are offensively proficient," said Davis and Miller. So, teams that put up runs will, according to this study, generate more fans in the seats. Certainly, this is seemingly an obvious outcome of their work.

This aligns with the recent trend in Major League Baseball of teams angling for the big inning courtesy of the home run. The late great Baltimore Orioles manager Earl Weaver, who preached his prescription for winning of pitching and three-run homers, would be proud.

"In other words," said Davis and Miller, "despite the possibility of multiple pitching changes due to offensive output (runs scored) that would increase the time length of a game, the spectators may negotiate items in their work or personal life (i.e., work later or mow the lawn the next day) with staying until the end of the game."

In short, their study validated many things that I contend here as well as their suggestion "that fans may negotiate reasons [for] attending MLB games based on the length of the game, the number of runs allowed, home runs hit, and weekend games" (Davis and Miller).

1. Declining Attendance

As for the declining numbers at the gate, *USA Today*'s Gabe Lacques (August 8, 2019) points out that the 16 teams that did not see declining attendance in 2019 included the "Red Sox, Cardinals, Cubs, Yankees and Dodgers. All sold at least 87% of their 2019 ticket inventory and drew at least 2.6 million fans every season this century. For most of the 25 other franchises, team performance, the economy and the limitations of their stadium can have a far greater impact."

All of those factors certainly play a role in teams drawing fewer fans, and later I will dive deeper into how, or if, winning plays a role in attendance and also how teams are addressing their current stadium amenities and fan experience.

Take, for example, one of the five teams Lacques mentions, the New York Yankees, the most storied franchise in Major League Baseball history. Undoubtedly, the Yankees are one of the most popular franchises in all of sports and one that dwells in the nation's number-one media market—New York City. With a huge market and a history of success on the field, one would assume they are impervious to declining attendance. Well, guess again. The Yankees, with their enormous following, 40 pennants, and 27 World Series championships, are significantly slumping at the gate (see Table 2). In a span of just 11 seasons, from 2008 to 2019, the mighty Yankees' attendance is down over 24 percent. *Shocking* would be an understatement. Who would have predicted this?

Table 2: New York Yankees Attendance

Year	Game Average	Season Total	Percent Decrease
2008	53,069	4,298,655	-
2018	42,998	3,482,855	-18.97%
2019	40,795	3,304,404	-5.11%

(Source: Baseball Almanac, 2022)

How is this possible? It's the New York Yankees, for goodness' sake. Knowing the major-market Yankees are one of many teams suffering declining attendance sheds light that this issue is not a small-market phenomenon. It is a league-wide issue. This should either give solace to other teams that are suffering from declining attendance or terrify every team.

Over the past 100-plus years, baseball has been so ingrained in our culture. America's pastime, right? What has happened to the game that millions of fans are choosing to stay home or spend their discretionary income elsewhere? The answer is far from simple, and the underlying focus of this book will focus on finding the causes of Major League

Baseball's declining attendance and fan interest. However, while causes are not hard to discover, solutions are far more challenging and that is the crux of this book—coming up with answers as to what the solutions are to address these issues.

I suggest that the great American pastime is on the precipice of a crisis, or perhaps it has already begun and I'm not convinced many close to the game are truly acknowledging this as it unfolds before their eyes. Those in positions to do something about it have yet to take real action to stop the bleeding and flatten the curve—or nosedive. While Major League Baseball is not ducking the issue, it doesn't seem that they are overly concerned about it.

If that's true, how can this be? Buck Showalter, who has over 1,500 wins as a major league manager, is currently managing the New York Mets. Showalter is a three-time American League Manager of the Year, and he has an idea. He told me, "For owners, it [declining attendance] is not that big of a thing. Television is. These [owners] are smart people and they don't want to lose money and they are making theirs from television contracts."

Showalter cited the Tampa Bay Rays as an example of a team that has low attendance but is making significant revenue off of its television deal. While the Rays averaged only 9,513 fans per game in 2021, and 14,734 in pre-pandemic 2019 (Statista), they reportedly inked a 15-year television deal with Fox Sports regional network Sun Sports that will pay them $82 million per year, with revenues starting at $50 million for the first year and increasing over the life of the deal. Their previous TV contract paid the Rays about $35 million per season, one of the lowest amounts in baseball.

As I stated in the introduction to this book, I set out to learn from former and current players, coaches, and team executives, along with others who are experts in their field or have a connection to the game in some manner. In each interview, I began with two questions.

First, what are the causes negatively impacting declining attendance and fan interest in Major League Baseball? The issues they spoke of were numerous. Many had theories and passionate ideas as to why these problems are plaguing the game.

The second and more challenging question was, what are solutions to overcome the problems facing the game? The response was typically, "That is a tough question." Initially, most were stumped as to what their responses would be. However, as our conversations progressed, and as we unpacked this question collectively, we arrived at viable and various solutions.

However, David Carter, a professor at the University of Southern California, a national authority on sports business and strategic marketing, and the author of four books about the sports business industry, shared with me possible solutions. "None of these are easy. They are all expensive and not guaranteed to work, but baseball must take the risk if it plans on continuing as a major sport in America," said Carter.

Regardless, Major League Baseball has changed and, many argue, not for the better, and the staggering figures of declining attendance should sound alarm bells throughout baseball that something is wrong and a response is needed—soon.

Can we rely on Major League Baseball as an entity to come to the rescue when they appear to be apathetic about something that seems critically important for the health of the game? I am optimistic that MLB can—and will. Otherwise, why would I spend my time writing this book? But why isn't Major League Baseball taking these issues more seriously?

The answer is simple. As Showalter accurately suggested, Major League Baseball and its clubs continue to rake in money. According to Maury Brown (2019) of *Forbes*, in 2018 Major League Baseball set a new revenue record—$10.3 billion.

In other words, their bottom line is still intact if not healthier than before. Surprisingly, this record-setting revenue was accomplished despite fewer fans attending games. Brown suggests Major League Baseball teams were relying on sources of income that, unlike ticket sales, have little or no dependence on clubs putting entertaining and competitive baseball teams on the field. For example, television revenue. So, what's the concern if the league is setting records for generating revenue? Even when the 2022 World Series and All-Star Game drew the second-lowest television ratings of all time?

However, it is not sustainable. This will eventually catch up with Major League Baseball and its clubs. Former Cincinnati Reds general manager Wayne Krivsky said it best during my interview with him: "It's sad to see what is going on [with the game]. Major League Baseball is not really concerned about these issues. They are giving lip service. The issues are taking a back seat to the bottom line. The value of franchises continues to rise and until the bottom line takes a hit, all we will hear is lip service." When that occurs, it might be too late. If the league isn't concerned, what about teams and their approach to declining attendance figures and the bad optics of nearly empty stadiums. Are they worried?

In trying to find a solution or best practices, Carter said, "It is hard to find exemplars. Most [teams] just throw another bobblehead night at the problem [of low attendance]. They are not innovative. 'We're the Yankees, shouldn't that be enough?' Or the Padres say, 'Come and see our new $50 million player'—who's now hurt. Nothing much, or different, is happening."

Gentry Estes (2019) of the *Courier-Journal* quoted Detroit Tigers beat writer Evan Woodbery, who would agree. Woodbery suggests that the Tigers and other MLB franchises have decided to choose revenue over attendance. Woodbury believes that many teams could increase their attendance if they desired. "They've crunched the numbers and found that they can make more money by maximizing revenue per fan than by maximizing the number of fans," said Woodbery.

He goes on to say, "Movie theaters, aquariums, museums, theme parks are all using predictive algorithms to find the right price and determine the trade-off between revenue and attendance." Woodbery suggests that baseball has been more aggressive in this approach in recent years, especially "as stadium capacities have shrunk and the 'cheap seats' have become considerably less cheap" (Estes).

Obviously, owning a Major League Baseball team is a business venture and the importance of revenues to pay the bills cannot be minimized, but his suggestion that teams are willing to trade money rather than have their fans in the seats and that the two are seemingly no longer connected is startling.

Think about it. Subscribing to Woodbery's assertion means that teams are indifferent to millions of fans *not* attending games. It is true that even though there are fewer fans in major league ballparks, teams are still cleaning up on media rights from local and national deals that are their main revenue sources and attendance has taken a back seat to these streams. The *New York Times* agrees that this trend "make[s] up an uncomfortable truth about baseball in the 21st century. Ticket sales, once the bread and butter for the sport, are no longer the central driver of the business" (Allenduck and Draper, 2019).

David Drea (2019) of Ursinus College, in his paper titled "Bringing Business Back into the Ballpark," added more to the conversation through his research: "It was determined that 'game-to-game factors like ticket discounts, giveaways, or fireworks are overestimated' when it comes to determining attendance, and other factors such as payroll and on-field performance must be considered. Of the overestimated game-to-game factors, giveaways are the most prominent. Bobbleheads and memorabilia promotions are the only giveaways that significantly and positively impact MLB attendance."

Tanking

Another significant issue contributing to Major League Baseball's declining attendance is the notion of tanking. Tanking often refers to the practice of intentionally fielding noncompetitive teams to take advantage of league rules, such as obtaining an early draft pick, that benefits losing teams. The idea of tanking, while a long-standing practice of teams throughout professional sports, has begun to make headlines.

Fans will often hear their favorite teams are rebuilding but in truth many teams are simply stripping their clubs down to the studs with hopes of cutting payroll for a few years and gathering draft picks and prospects through trading off their top talent. The consequences of tanking are significant—certainly at the gate. Fans shy away from noncompetitive teams that lose over 100 games a year. Secondly, fan interest in those clubs dramatically declines in those years as well.

Craig Calcaterra is a writer and editor of the daily baseball, news, and culture newsletter *Cup of Coffee* and the book *Rethinking Fandom: How to Beat the Sports-Industrial Complex at Its Own Game*, and at one time he was the lead national baseball writer for NBC Sports. He weighed in on the topic of Major League Baseball teams tanking.

"One thing that has concerned me, and it's not just the problem itself, but it's what goes into the problem. Everybody talks about tanking," said Calcaterra. "People talk about teams that aren't trying to win, putting a product on the field that is really not major league level. I mean, if you look at what the Pittsburgh Pirates have done over the last few years, that's pretty bad. The Orioles, same situation. At any given time, there are two, three, or four and sometimes as many as five teams that just don't really appear to be trying."

The strategy of teams rebuilding is understandable because over the course of time, most teams will face a roster that is aging or overly expensive to maintain but there shouldn't be room for tanking, and Calcaterra agrees.

"There's really no excuse for not putting out a major league product over the course of a rebuild. You can do two things at once. You can at least try to maybe not win the whole division or win the pennant or something like that but at least be competitive with a major league product while you're trying to rebuild," he said.

Jay Jaffe is a former contributing baseball writer for *Sports Illustrated* (SI.com), the founder of the Futility Infielder website, one of the oldest baseball blogs, and from 2005 to 2012 was a columnist for Baseball Prospectus. In addition, he is a writer for FanGraphs. He told me that Major League Baseball attendance is a problem in certain places for sure.

"I think a lot of that has to do with noncompetitive teams, teams that have decided they're going to take the next two, three years to rebuild, to tank so to speak and are bottoming out," he said. "I think between that and teams that are just in that mode perpetually like the Pittsburgh Pirates, you're going to have areas that are a problem."

Calcaterra added, "The primary root of that is there is a big disconnect right now between what brings revenue to Major League Baseball and winning baseball games. It used to be that if you wanted to make money as a team, you had to draw people through the turnstiles. That was the only way to do it."

A barrier to overcoming this is the fact that MLB owners and the Major League Baseball Players Association rarely agree on much—let alone how to solve this issue. Said Jaffe: "Fundamental in that clash right now are the noncompetitive teams. That is a central issue here—how you incentivize teams to win and disincentivize this route to tanking. We have to come up with some kind of solution there, because I think that's going to ensure that you don't have as many dead markets for baseball. There's always going to be somebody who's the worst team, obviously, but you can do something to reduce the idea that the season is just a complete waste."

Calcaterra told me, "We now have a financial situation in baseball where you can own a baseball team and send it out there to lose 110 games a year, and you're still going to make a profit. The reason for that is because so much of the revenue is locked in over very long periods of time with very long TV deals that aren't dependent on how your team does year to year, or from sources that are completely divorced from the winning and losing of baseball games."

Tanking, according to Calcaterra, is the biggest challenge. "That's been the biggest change. If you talk to people who've worked in the commissioner's office under, say, Bud Selig, or who work there now, I mean they won't tell you on the record, but I talk to these people. That's the biggest change from the business side is there is this huge effort of exploding revenue sources that are not just dependent on how people feel about baseball or how people feel about their team in a given year making it regular. I get that from a business perspective, but what it does is it doesn't cause any penalty for losing. If you don't have an incentive to put a winning team out there, the product suffers. I mean, I'm pretty sure that the guys who own the Pittsburgh Pirates make pretty good money … [But] I know Pittsburgh Pirates fans who have completely lost interest in the team because they don't think the team is interested in winning."

As for a solution, "I don't know what you do about that," Calcaterra admitted. "[Perhaps] some of it's going to be in the labor situation where you penalize teams a lot more for clearly losing over a long period of time, or don't reward them as much for having the worst record in baseball. There are all kinds of nebulous things that you could talk about how to get at that problem. I think that's a huge problem when it doesn't matter if you win or lose. That's not going to be a good thing for the game."

An ESPN article titled "Agent Scott Boras: Tanking, MLB's 'competitive cancer,' led to Atlanta Braves' World Series title" (2021) suggested that the Atlanta Braves' 2021 World Series title was a direct result of tanking by other teams that, out of contention, chose not to compete and unloaded some of their top players for cheap.

This, according to Boras, led to an incentive "for the race to the bottom, because now we have half the major league teams at some time during the season being noncompetitive, trading off their players, making the game and the season very different than what it was intended to be, and that was having an incentive to win every game that you play" (ESPN).

Leitch (2018) actually offered the surprising opinion that Major League Baseball clubs don't necessarily need fans in the seats and had this opinion on tanking: "The tanking epidemic—where teams deliberately sabotage their short-term chances to cultivate a medium-term talent pipeline—has been a boon to lesser franchises, traditionally unable to even dream of championships, and it has largely blossomed, I'd argue, because teams *haven't* had to worry about bringing fans in. The Astros, to take one example, were essentially okay with nobody watching them for three years because they were making enough revenue elsewhere and thus could focus on building for the future. That future just won their franchise their first World Series."

Sadly, that concept of finding revenue elsewhere has led teams to not be concerned about declining Major League Baseball attendance.

However, says Leitch, "Right now the smart money is in all these media contracts, but any sports fan knows that the true iron of lifelong dedication to a team or a sport is forged from the in-person experience; media will change, but the sport itself will not. You need that kid and to have his or her parent, or grandparent, or whoever, take them to the game and make it a part of their lives forever."

That lifelong dedication that Leitch refers to is supported by research. It is true that following and playing a sport as children leads to a greater chance that as adults we will remain a fan of that sport.

Shrinking Stadiums

Speaking of stadium capacities, perhaps you may recall the multipurpose cookie-cutter behemoths that dotted the Major League Baseball landscape in the 1970s before giving way to retro style with modern amenities after Orioles Park at Camden Yards opened in Baltimore in 1992. The immediate success of Camden Yards created a wave of teams following its design model. For example, in the 1990s, the Texas Rangers, Colorado Rockies, Cleveland Guardians (formerly known as the Indians), and San Francisco Giants all followed suit by creating old-style ballparks with modern amenities and, as a result, enjoyed success at the gate.

Another change is beginning to take shape. Gabe Lacques (August 8, 2019) of *USA Today* focused on one approach to declining attendance—shrink the number of seats in the stadium. As a result, some teams are transforming their large-capacity stadiums to smaller ones. *USA Today* points out that the average stadium capacity has diminished significantly. In 1990 it was 54,000, compared with 42,000 in 2019.

Shrinking stadium capacities is an interesting concept. Fewer fans are attending MLB games so instead of trying to draw them back into the ballpark, let's just make the stadium smaller. I suggest this is a reactive, not proactive, response. This hardly seems like a solution to bringing more fans to the ballpark. By reducing seating capacity, it appears teams are simply creating better optics for television—fewer empty seats.

Lacques cited the Tampa Bay Rays, Cleveland Guardians, and others that have modified their stadiums into smaller venues, reflecting a sport where attendance has declined four consecutive years. According to Lacques, another team, the Arizona Diamondbacks, might be next in line for a remodel.

Diamondbacks CEO Derrick Hall said in an email to *USA Today* that their ballpark's capacity is too large and the expectation to fill Chase Field is not realistic. At a capacity of over 48,000, Hall might be right to consider a makeover. As one who has attended many games at Chase Field, I can attest that it's a ballpark with many outstanding amenities and is family friendly. However, even at two-thirds full, the stadium feels empty.

Another example is the Cleveland Guardians. After years of selling out games in the 1990s and setting a then-record consecutive sellout streak of 455 games from mid-1995 to early in 2001, the Indians saw a significant decline in their attendance. Cleveland drew less than 20,000 fans in six of seven seasons from 2010 to 2016. This compelled the team to survey its fanbase and season ticket holders to see what changes the team could make to bring Guardians fans back to the ballpark. The results of that survey, according to Lacques, were the impetus for the Indians to make modifications to the ballpark that included converting unused suites into a family area with baseball-related activities. Also, in an effort to connect with younger-generation fans, the right field corner was turned into a social space complete with a large outdoor bar and gathering area. The right-center field area now opens up to a view of the surrounding city.

Alex King, the Guardians' senior vice president of brand and marketing, told *USA Today* (Lacques) that the responsibility is on them to create a ballpark environment that provides fans "compelling reasons to make that trip. There are no barriers for fans to engage in our game in a living room." King makes a solid point and one that I will explore in some detail later in this book when I cover the fan experience.

Major League Baseball Is Expensive to Attend

Certainly, one cause for fans staying away from major league ballparks is the increasing expense of attending games. With thousands of channels on television, and streaming services like Netflix and Hulu, competition for a fan's time and money has never been more intense. In addition, outstanding in-home sports viewing creates a challenge to get fans to a live sporting event.

This is true of all sports and especially baseball. The advent of numerous in-game experiences enhance the television viewing pleasure, such as watching multiple games simultaneously and statistics galore, including tracking strikes, launch angle, exit velocity, and a host of others that are typically not available at the stadium. Why, then, would a family spend their hard-earned money to attend a live game when these amenities exist on television?

In addition, nearly every Major League Baseball game is easily accessible on television, and if you missed today's game, there is always one tomorrow. Fans growing up in the 1970s and 1980s couldn't have dreamed that this would become a reality. Back then, teams typically broadcasted fewer than 50 games a year and the All-Star Game, playoffs, World Series, NBC *Game of the Week*, or *Monday Night Baseball* provided the only national exposure.

So, what does it cost to attend a Major League Baseball game? If you haven't been to a game in a while, more than you might think. Considering teams play 81 home games, one would assume they would be affordable to attend.

Jay Jaffe agrees that "the ticket costs are a problem. Especially at the entry level, ticket costs are a problem. The so-called fan index of what it costs to take a family of four to a game, those kinds of metrics have not been good for a while."

An article from the *International Journal of Applied Sports Sciences*, "Applying the Concept of Sport Affordability to Professional Sporting Events: The Case of the Major League Baseball Games," by Sangkwon Lee and Chi-Ok Oh (2016), suggested, "The cost of attending professional sporting events has been increasing steadily but the median household income has been relatively stagnant over the last three decades. As a result, sport consumers are now required to spend a higher portion of their income to attend professional sport games."

Lee and Oh's research also revealed that "attending professional sporting events has become a bigger financial burden even to middle income groups that represent a majority of the US population," and one reason, they surmise, that may contribute to this issue is the worsening economic inequality in the United States.

The results of their study showed that the sport "affordability index" has become "polarized among major league baseball teams. For 21 teams, the study showed that their sport affordability indexes have been deteriorating steadily over time but the trend was different for the other eight franchises."

Lee and Oh suggest that a majority of the latter franchises are either in small markets or were expansion teams that joined Major League Baseball in the 1990s. The results of the study confirmed the idea that equity between the owners of professional franchises and sport consumers is a concern that is escalating.

Interestingly, the authors feel that future research would be of benefit to understand underlying reasons why "the polarized pattern may be more conspicuous in MLB than other professional sport leagues, which can be partially attributed to a lesser degree of a revenue sharing policy and the lack of a salary cap."

The concept of revenue sharing and a salary cap will be discussed later in this book. Lee and Oh draw the conclusion that "the absence of such policies are likely to make it hard for small-market and/or expansion teams to compete for a good record, leading to lower revenues, tighter budgets, and then bad records again in a vicious cycle."

Their study also concluded, and not surprisingly, that as prices of major professional sporting events increase, the average sport consumer is driven away from stadiums, ballparks, and arenas.

"While ticket prices have increased at a rate that substantially exceeds the inflation rate of the economy, sport consumers' ability to attend sporting events has weakened relatively due to stagnant income growth," Lee and Oh wrote.

The Team Marketing Report is one resource that examines not only the price of tickets but also other related costs of attending live sports, and it has for several years published a Fan Cost Index (FCI) (see Table 3). This index looks at what the cost for a family of four to attend a Major League Baseball game might look like. It includes:

- Four tickets
- Four hot dogs
- Four small soft drinks
- Two small beers
- Two game programs
- Parking
- Two adult-size caps

1. Declining Attendance

Table 3: Fan Cost Index (FCI) (2015–2021)

Year	2015	2016	2017	2018	2019	2020*	2021
FCI	$209.05	$217.06	$224.55	$230.63	$234.38	NA	$253.64
% +/-	-	3.8%	3.5%	2.7%	1.6%	NA	8.2%

(Team Marketing Report, 2019)
*COVID-19 Pandemic

The FCI from 2015 to 2021 shows an increase of over 21 percent to $44.59 per game for a family of four, but is the Major League Baseball product on the field improving at the same rate? Most would say no.

Brown (2019) says while Major League Baseball attendance has been down, Minor League Baseball enjoyed an attendance increase of 1,053,740 from 2018 to 2019.

"If we're going to look at one reason why fans may be opting to go to MiLB [Minor League Baseball] games over MLB games, that reason is likely cost … reducing the number of games they might otherwise attend," said Brown.

Table 4 shows the most-expensive average ticket costs in Major League Baseball in 2021. There are not too many surprises in the top five most-expensive tickets. However, looking back at the Fan Cost Index indications for a family of four, these teams would far exceed the 2019 average of just over $234 per game. The Red Sox would surpass that amount with just tickets alone. Factor in the other expenses and families would easily be spending over $300 to attend just one game—and remember, these are for average tickets, not front-row, feet-on-the-dugout seats.

Table 4: Top 5 Most-Expensive Average MLB Ticket Prices 2021

Major League Baseball Team	*Average Ticket Cost*
Boston Red Sox (Lost American League Division Series)	$75
Atlanta Braves (Won World Series)	$59
Los Angeles Dodgers (Lost National League Championship)	$54
Houston Astros (Lost World Series)	$51
Milwaukee Brewers (Lost National League Division Series)	$48

(Source: TickPic, 2021)

When examining Table 4, two questions come to mind. First, as I am a baseball fan who actually enjoys the in-person experience, are any of the teams I frequent on the list of the top five most-expensive tickets? Second, is it worth paying those prices to see the product that the team puts on the field? In other words, is it worth paying $75 a ticket to see the Red Sox? If you're a diehard Boston fan, you might say yes and perhaps at any price because they typically field a competitive team and it may also be tough to put a price on attending a game at iconic Fenway Park.

For me, the answer to the first question is thankfully no. While I typically attend a couple of Los Angeles Dodgers games, I would not consider that frequent. Two teams my kids and I do frequent are the Los Angeles Angels and the San Diego Padres. We consider the Angels our home team, as Orange County has always been our home. Even though the Big A could use a makeover, and the Halos are not always competitive, we always enjoy being at the ballpark, especially that one, and watching Mike Trout and Shohei Ohtani is also exciting.

My family and I also love Petco Park, home of the San Diego Padres. It is truly unique and one of the most beautiful stadiums in all of sports. Unique in that the stadium was built around the Western Metal Supply Co. building in left field and the building is actually part of the ballpark. Beautiful because it is in downtown San Diego and boasts spectacular views of the city and harbor. San Diego calls itself America's Finest City for a reason. While we love the ballpark, the team has made the playoffs only once since 2006 and quite frankly over some of those years their roster resembled more AAA than major league–caliber players. In short, in terms of a baseball product, the Padres have not always been worth the most expensive ticket, but even the cheap seats are excellent at Petco.

Some could argue that the five teams in Table 4 were among the best value in terms of fielding a winning team, and while they were the most expensive tickets, they all backed it up by making the postseason. All made the playoffs and, except for the Brewers, made it to at least their respective league's championship series.

To further the point, the Atlanta Braves, Milwaukee Brewers, and Houston Astros each won their respective divisions and the Los Angeles Dodgers, who earned a wildcard berth, won an impressive 106 games, finishing one game behind the division champion San Francisco Giants.

The Braves were the 2021 World Series champions and the Los Angeles Dodgers won the title in 2020. While their tickets are not cheap, do these World Series champions provide excellent value for their fans? I'd say so. A number of teams are quite honestly terrible and their ticket prices may be less expensive, but do you want to watch your team struggle? The Arizona Diamondbacks, Baltimore Orioles, Texas Rangers, and Pittsburgh Pirates all lost more than 100 games in 2021. All but Texas (26,052 average per game) also had dismal results at the turnstile. In 2021, Arizona (12,876), Pittsburgh (10,611), and Baltimore (10,161) were near the bottom of MLB attendance averages.

Ben Langhorst (2014) has a PhD in materials science and engineering, works as an engineer, and has a love for the game. He authored a research article for the *Baseball Research Journal* in the spring issue that year titled "What Do Your Fans Want? Attendance Correlations with Performance, Ticket Prices, and Payroll Factors," where he went a little further with his study.

Langhorst estimates that teams such as "Philadelphia, Boston, and Chicago Cubs earn 50% or more of their revenue from ticket sales, while Tampa Bay, Arizona, and Cleveland earn less than 20% of their revenue from ticket sales," and he suggests that Major League Baseball teams can directly manipulate various factors in an attempt to improve attendance patterns that will impact those revenues.

His research showed that most Major League Baseball "fan bases are as individualized as their cities and many of their attendance patterns are strongly correlated with factors that can be directly or indirectly controlled by team management." Some organizations should consider investments in their team with a reasonable confidence that their fans will attend more games when their team wins more games, has a higher percentage of elite players, and has a higher team payroll.

However, that cannot be applied to all major league teams. Those other organizations, Langhorst found, had fans (such as the Milwaukee Brewers) who surprisingly "appeared to respond weakly to changes in team performance, team payroll, and individual performance."

Are Winning and Attendance Linked?

We just took a look at teams that had the highest ticket prices, and as it turned out, at least in 2021, those teams performed quite well on the field. That leads to another question. Is there a correlation between fielding a winning team and having robust attendance? Build a winner and they will come, right? Perhaps surprisingly, the answer is not necessarily. Think back to the example earlier in this chapter of the New York Yankees. They have a winning tradition but their attendance is plummeting.

Rick Schlesinger, Milwaukee Brewers president–business operations, told me, "I'll start out by saying the best solution to drawing fans is to have winning teams, and that doesn't guarantee it but it certainly helps tremendously.

"I think at the end of the day, it certainly helps if the team performs well. And I think that's true in sports in general. And obviously in Milwaukee, when we have very good teams on the field, we have strong support and in the last few years we have been in the postseason, so that certainly is helping to generate close to three million in ticket sales. Even when we have not had strong teams, we still have managed to draw very well."

Looking at data from 2017 to 2021 (excluding the COVID-19-impacted 2020 season), Table 5 suggests that winning on the field doesn't necessarily mean winning at the gate.

Table 5: Best Winning Percentage and Top Average Attendance 2017–2021
*2020: COVID-19 Pandemic

Best Winning Percentage 2017	*Top Average Attendance 2017*
Los Angeles Dodgers .644	**Los Angeles Dodgers 46,492**
Cleveland .623	St. Louis 42,567
Houston .622	San Francisco 40,785
Washington .593	Toronto 39,835
Boston .566	Chicago Cubs 39,554

Best Winning Percentage 2018	*Top Average Attendance 2018*
Boston .676	Los Angeles Dodgers 47,042
Houston .629	**New York Yankees 42,998**
New York Yankees .611	St. Louis 42,019
Oakland .595	San Francisco 38,965
Milwaukee .590	Chicago Cubs 38,793

Best Winning Percentage 2019	*Top Average Attendance 2019*
Houston .650	**Los Angeles Dodgers 49,065**
Los Angeles Dodgers .647	St. Louis 42,967
New York Yankees .632	**New York Yankees 41,827**
Minnesota .612	Chicago Cubs 38,208
Oakland .595	Los Angeles Angels 37,321

Best Winning Percentage 2021	*Top Average Attendance 2021**
San Francisco Giants .660	**Los Angeles Dodgers 34,625**
Los Angeles Dodgers .654	Atlanta Braves 29,490
Tampa Bay Rays .617	San Diego Padres 27,061
Houston Astros .586	St. Louis Cardinals 26,281
Milwaukee Brewers .586	Texas Rangers 26,052

*Attendance was impacted by the COVID-19 pandemic. Capacity was limited for numerous franchises the first few months of the season.
(Source: Spotrac, 2022)

In 2017, only the Los Angeles Dodgers fielded a winning team and were in the top five in attendance. In fact, they were tops in both. In 2018, again only one team, this time the New York Yankees, was in the top five in winning percentage and attendance. In 2019, two of the top five winningest teams, once again the Dodgers and Yankees, were also tops in fans coming through the turnstiles. Finally, in 2021, again only the Dodgers were featured in both columns. Shockingly winning teams aren't drawing fans into their ballparks to the degree one would expect. For example, the Houston Astros, who had their third straight 100-win season, drew 1,500 fewer fans per game in 2019 (Baseball-Reference, 2022).

What is going on here? Well, again, that's the point of this book: to uncover the numerous issues that are impacting the game, including declining attendance. Some of those I have covered in this first chapter, and others are still to come.

Is Major League Baseball Concerned?

Research by David Drea (2019) suggests that "Commissioner Rob Manfred has expressed deep concerns for these statistics [of declining attendance] and has drawn the conclusion that 'the length of games, preponderance of defensive shifts, and reliever usage' are the reasons for the decline."

Based on these assumptions, said Drea, Commissioner Manfred has implemented rules that he believes will remedy the length-of-games issue through initiatives centered on pace of play.

"The hope is that these rules will result in quicker games and therefore attendance will no longer be affected by the game's length of time," said Drea. However, he notes that his study found that it is clear that the recent pace-of-play rules have been ineffective in addressing the problem.

Nonetheless, said Drea, "The record-breaking revenues for the league and star-studded, youthful rosters would lead one to believe that baseball is stronger than ever. However, the seats remain empty. The league has attempted to address this problem with pace of play rules that avid fans feel question the history and integrity of the game."

Most of the people I interviewed for this book say that Major League Baseball is not as worried as it should be. For example, Carter says, "Of all the major sports leagues, baseball does not seem to have the moorings to remedy this [decline in attendance and fan interest]. They have an aging fanbase and revenues are leveling off. In regard to being high tech, baseball is slowest to adapt. They need to reinvent it as a family sport."

However, as Buck Showalter told me, "Those of us who love the game are concerned. It's a problem that scares a lot of people."

The data don't lie. Major League Baseball's attendance is plummeting. Noah Garden, MLB executive vice president for business and sales, said of ticket sales in a 2019 MLB press release: "It isn't going to die. But it's going to change. There are going to be a different number of people that want to purchase tickets a different way" (Love, 2019).

There already are. In the next chapter I will share innovative practices that many teams have implemented to meet the needs of today's MLB fan.

In terms of the sheer number of fans attending major league games, the league says that Major and Minor League Baseball combined to draw nearly 110 million fans in 2019. Garden points to baseball's overall popularity as a sign that it thrives in these uncertain times. As MLB's executive vice president of business and sales, he noted that over 41 million people attended Minor League Baseball games in the 2019 season—a 2.6 percent rise year over year. Sadly, with the contraction of 20 percent of minor league teams, or 42 team affiliations, that number has declined.

The problem is Major League Baseball's attendance decline, not Minor League Baseball. Minor League Baseball is growing. MLB acknowledges these issues, but it's not enough. Recognizing a problem and taking action are two different things. I think MLB cares but to what degree is debatable. Again, until the financial bottom line is impacted, the status quo is here for the duration. Those closest to the game are the ones most frustrated by the lack of a real plan. Perhaps the most glaring response is that of baseball fans who are simply not showing up.

Baseball writer Calcaterra told me, "I am in complete agreement that self-identified baseball fans and people who can or would in the past, in the normal course, sustain the sport is going down pretty precipitously."

He continued: "I think that's concerning because all of us probably want more people to love baseball and care about baseball. I don't know that Rob Manford or the people who run Major League Baseball, if they're being honest, are particularly concerned. However, because I think they have decided based on everything I've seen about the business decisions, they make that they are perfectly content to have the number of baseball fans go down as long as they can more effectively monetize those that remain. Baseball, and a lot of other entertainments, but baseball in particular has decided 'we're okay with becoming a niche sport as long as we remain lucrative.' I think that's a future that they're charting out for themselves," said Calcaterra.

If that is true, it is certainly concerning for those of us who love and care about the game of Major League Baseball.

In every chapter of this book I will investigate problems facing Major League Baseball but, more important, offer solutions and next steps to overcome them. I will highlight what I believe are best practices and ideas that Major League Baseball should consider as it relates to its attendance problem. The issue of declining attendance is spurring teams to think up innovative ways to get both hard-core and casual fans to attend games.

In this section I will introduce you to a small-market team that is a box office and attendance smashing success. I will also share innovative ticketing options and successful strategies from minor league teams that can be applied to Major League Baseball. I will also offer MLB's response to this issue and its plan to address it.

Small-Market Success— Lesson from the Brew Crew

Earlier I stated that this crisis is not exclusive to small-market teams, and the Milwaukee Brewers are an exemplary organization in a small market that has enjoyed success on the field and at the turnstile. They made the top five in terms of best ticket value (see Table 5) as they offer the 10th-cheapest ticket cost in MLB, along with their place as a regular playoff contender. In 2018, they were the Central Division champions, and in 2019 and 2020 earned Wild Card playoff berths. Since 2017, they have consistently put a winning team on the field, and millions have come through the turnstiles to support their efforts.

The Brewers are a true outlier. Theirs is a success story and one that other teams can learn from and replicate. In 2019, Sports Media Watch (SMW) ranked the 114 U.S.-based franchises in the "Big Four" sports leagues (MLB, NFL, NBA, NHL) by Nielsen market size. According to SMW, Milwaukee ranked as the 35th-largest sports market with only 875,000 homes. In terms of Major League Baseball markets, only Cincinnati ranks smaller at 37th on the list with 828,000 homes. Despite being in MLB's second-smallest market, Milwaukee fans have a great relationship with management, said Tyler Barnes, the Brewers' senior vice president of communications and affiliate operations. Barnes told Eddie Moran of Front Office Sports, "When we deliver on our promise to offer an entertaining experience for them, the support is unmatched."

That fan experience has led to Milwaukee finishing recent seasons with impressive attendance figures (see Table 6). Consistently drawing over two million fans per season to Miller Park (American Family Field as of 2021) and a per-game average of over 30,000 fans is quite impressive.

Table 6: Milwaukee Brewers Home Attendance 2011–2019

Year	Game Average	Season Total
2011	37,918	3,071,373*
2012	34,955	2,831,385*
2013	31,244	2,531,105
2014	34,536	2,797,384*
2015	31,390	2,542,558
2016	28,575	2,314,614
2017	31,589	2,558,722*
2018	35,195	2,850,875*
2019	36,091	2,923,333*

(Source: Baseball Almanac, 2022)
*Exceeded National League average

The Brewers finished seventh in all of Major League Baseball attendance in 2019 and finished 10th in a truncated 2021 season. In both 2017 and 2018, the club finished 10th best in each of those years. In 2021, the Brewers won the National League Central Division title.

Small market or large market, this is impressive considering the Los Angeles Dodgers, New York Yankees, and Chicago Cubs consistently rank in the top five. That doesn't leave much room at the top for the rest of the teams in Major League Baseball.

Certainly, when Milwaukee's Miller Park opened in 2001, it provided many amenities that could not be found at the Brewers' former home of County Stadium. In turn, the Brewers' attendance rose accordingly. Ballparksofbaseball.com (n.d.) detailed the amenities: "A Brewers Hall of Fame, children's area, brew pub, open air patios and walkways are throughout Miller Park. Fans can enjoy dinner and a ballgame at T.G.I. Friday's Front Row Sports Grill that is located in the left field area known as The Front Row. Kids can enjoy the Miller Park Kids Zone, an 8,000 square foot interactive play area that includes a replica of Bernie the Brewer's slide."

There is little doubt that the stadium has lived up to everything the organization had hoped for when it opened in 2001, and as one who has been to Miller Park a few times, I have to agree. It's a fan-friendly, beautiful, modern ballpark and the food choices are incredible. It is also true that Brewers fans have a passion for baseball whether their team is winning or losing. They always come out to support them at American Family Field. So how is this small-market team an attendance-generating juggernaut?

That question led to an interview with the team's president-business operations, Rick Schlesinger. The Brewers have established new records in nearly every aspect of the organization's business during Schlesinger's tenure. In 2019, over 2.9 million fans attended Brewers home games, marking the 12th time in the past 13 seasons that the organization surpassed 2.5 million in attendance.

When asked how he accounts for the Brewers' success at the gate, Schlesinger said, "There's a number of strategies we've undertaken and implemented to generate strong attendance. It's embracing things that are sort of unique to Wisconsin. It's affordable, it's making the ballpark experience great, and obviously, paramount is having a successful team on the field."

He went on to say, "Those aren't necessarily magical but they are integral and I think they each carry weight in how people decide whether to come to the games."

As for their home park of American Family Field, Schlesinger said, "We spent a lot of time investing in the ballpark, cleaning it, and making it affordable, which is really important. We make no bones about it, we make no apologies for it, but our average ticket price is one of the lowest in Major League Baseball. We think that that is a direct correlation to attendance because even though baseball is generally affordable, if you're talking about a family of four and you add parking and concessions, every dollar matters."

The investment in American Family Field has led to a richer connection to the baseball and ballpark experience for Milwaukee fans. Schlesinger suggests, "First of all, we have invested a lot of money into American Family Field into that experience and in terms of everything from new fan amenities to upgrading concessions, to upgrading the scoreboard, to spending money on customer training, training for all of our events staff to really make it a great atmosphere. That's important because all the logistic components of actually getting people and going to a game as opposed to sitting in front of your television or your smartphone and consuming the game that way are challenging."

Those successful strategies may seem simple, but they are not; otherwise, all Major League Baseball teams would implement them. They demand resources, including time and money, but also take a vision and commitment to making their product worthy of their fans' time, money, and attention. While not easy or inexpensive to implement, other major league teams should consider learning from their model of success.

Innovative Ticket Options

One unique idea for increasing attendance and gaining traction is an innovative ticket option that began as a pilot program in Major

League Baseball in 2015 to help teams fill their ballparks. It has evolved into a practice that is redefining the ticket-selling business in MLB—the Ballpark Pass. The Ballpark Pass is a subscription option where fans pay a monthly fee to have in-venue access to attend their home team's games.

The Ballpark Pass, according to John Lombardo (2019) of the *New York Business Journal*, has been a success, as more than two-thirds of Major League Baseball teams have plans that are similar—all designed to drive attendance and to attract younger fans who prefer plans that are flexible and can be accessed in a mobile manner.

Noah Garden, executive vice president of business and sales for MLB, was behind the Ballpark Pass in 2015. In 2019, 18 of the 30 Major League teams had some type of subscription option, which varies in price from $30 each month for standing room only to $125 for a guaranteed seat.

"We have to sell 81 home dates … and it's a hard job and it forces us to be very open-minded and take a very broad view at the industry as a whole," Garden told the *New York Business Journal*. He added, in terms of attracting younger generations, the approach is how "are they consuming sports and what is the best way to attract them."

With the in-game experience so key to building fan loyalty, wouldn't it behoove teams to fill up empty seats at discount prices? The subscription model is no longer aimed at poor-performing teams playing in front of half-empty stadiums (Lombardo, 2019).

According to the *New York Times*, "While it has not been enough to reverse the downward trend in ticket sales, baseball executives believe it is attractive to younger fans, who are used to paying for subscription services like Netflix and Spotify."

MLB reports that one million tickets were purchased with the Ballpark Pass in 2019, up from 150,000 in 2016, which was the first full year of the program (Lombardo, 2019). The following are some examples of how the subscription-like service is providing a unique option for Major League Baseball ticket purchases and helping close the gap in declining ticket sales.

Oakland Athletics

The Oakland Athletics play in one of baseball's most outdated stadiums. Year in and year out, the A's are typically at or near the bottom of attendance. They needed a boost. From 2015–2019, the A's averaged 1.5 million fans each year while the American League average over the same time was 2.2 million. The A's launched their subscription option, called A's

Access, in 2017. From 2017–2019, the A's attendance increased by 200,000 fans.

It was such a success that it is now their only season ticket option. In 2019, they were the only major league team that took the model that far. Subscriptions cost between $33 and $75 a month. The cheapest option grants fans standing-room-only access to all 81 games and a guaranteed seat for at least 10 games, with the option to purchase a seat for additional games (Lombardo, 2019). A's Access members receive general admission entry to the entire ballpark for every regular-season home game, a flex or set seat, 50 percent off concessions, $10 prepaid parking, and 25 percent off merchandise (MLB).

"We're now seeing a rapidly growing group of fans that want something completely different," Chris Giles, Oakland A's chief operating officer, told Jim Tierney of Clarus Commerce (2019). "They want something more flexible and something more social. They liken it to a food tour or bar hopping."

New York Mets

For $77 per month, the Amazin' Mets Pass subscription includes a mobile ticket to regular-season home games. It is a guaranteed standing-room ticket to most every game, including weekend games. The standing-room option is typical of these subscriptions, and Citi Field offers numerous outstanding vantage points from which to watch the action.

The Mets plan also offers the option to upgrade to a ticketed seat for games Monday through Thursday. Like other plans, there is the ease of delivery via the MLB Ballpark app. Fans simply scan their ticket at the gate directly from their phone. Also, they offer a nice feature in that fans can forward their Amazin' Mets Pass to family or friends beginning four hours prior to each game, also via the MLB Ballpark app.

Miami Marlins

One team that is desperately in need of an attendance boost is the Miami Marlins, who drew less than 1 million fans in 2018. In 2019, the team tried to be innovative with ticket offerings when it unveiled its new Marlins Membership, which is basically a season ticket benefits package. It's a 365-day membership with added benefits and incentives including ticket exchange, savings on food, additional ticket savings, and savings on parking, merchandise, fan experiences, and memorabilia.

The Marlins have also tried to make the ballpark experience more affordable. One example is the value menu options located throughout the stadium where fans can purchase food and beverage items for under $5. I have attended games at the Marlins' LoanDepot Park and I experienced firsthand that the food choices are affordable and the variety is spectacular. There is truly something for every palate.

Milwaukee Brewers

Not surprisingly, the Brewers are part of this innovative approach to ticket sales as they implemented the Ballpark Pass + starting in 2016. For just $38, Brewers fans gain access to home games at American Family Field. Tickets are delivered digitally via mobile device, and seats will vary from game to game. Unique from other teams is that the Brewers' Ballpark Pass includes an actual seat—not just a standing-room-only ticket. That's a terrific option as many fans may not want to stand for the entire game. Seat locations include Terrace Box, Terrace Reserved, Loge Bleachers, and Loge Outfield sections.

Lessons Learned Down on the Farm

Major League Baseball should be looking everywhere for solutions to its issue of declining attendance. I suggest MLB should be learning from Minor League Baseball and its success with over 41 million fans coming through its gates in 2019, which was an increase of 2.6 percent over 2018. Also, 2019 was the 14th consecutive year that Minor League Baseball has drawn more than 40 million fans.

Minor League Baseball president Pat O'Connor told *Baseball America* (2020), "Our attendance numbers, while they may fluctuate, have been fairly stable. You can count in a shaded area between 40 and 41.5 million and we're likely to land in that spot."

Impressive to say the least. So, what can Major League Baseball learn from its kid brother, the minors, in terms of bringing in fans to ballparks? The answer is that MLB can implement numerous strategies. Some will be described here and others when I dive into the issue of the MLB fan experience.

As a former minor league radio play-by-play announcer, I was part of two successful teams that others have tried to emulate. The first was the San Bernardino Spirit, the Seattle Mariners' California League Class A Advanced affiliate. The Spirit played at raucous Fiscalini Field, or better yet, Spirit Land, from the late 1980s to 1992. Most notably, future Hall of Famer Ken Griffey, Jr., was once a member of the Spirit.

What stands out to me about those warm summer nights in San

Bernardino, California, was how the fan experience began the second the fan approached the gate. The smell of the food, the outstanding friendly customer service, and the freshly mowed green grass just feet away lured the fan into another world. In addition, the between-inning promotions were incredibly enjoyable and added to the family-friendly atmosphere. Spirit Land set the bar high for affordable, wholesome family fun.

In 1993, the team relocated to Rancho Cucamonga 24 miles to the west and became the well-known and popular Quakes. I was fortunate to be their first radio play-by-play announcer, and what an experience it was!

Their ballpark is known as the Epicenter, a beautiful $20 million stadium that included amenities such as luxury boxes and affordable ticket choices. The Quakes drew over 5,000 fans per game (which was quite impressive for A ball) and shattered California League attendance records in the process as the team drew over 331,000 fans that first season. The franchise cut its teeth in San Bernardino and upped its game in Rancho Cucamonga with a spectacular stadium, an official mascot—Tremor, a captivating dinosaur that became known nationally—and an atmosphere that was indescribable.

Another franchise that has enjoyed success at the minor league level is the Frederick (Maryland) Keys. It previously was a Carolina League Advanced Class A club and an affiliate of the nearby Baltimore Orioles before it became an MLB Draft League team. For over 15 years, Dave Ziedelis served as Frederick's general manager. His responsibilities included sponsorships and advertising sales, marketing, and public relations and enhancing the fan experience through game presentation. Additionally, he was responsible for increasing season ticket sales. Ziedelis also has major league front-office experience as the San Diego Padres' public relations manager, where he directed community events.

As a successful baseball executive, along with being a lifelong baseball fan, Ziedelis is passionate about the issues facing the game at the major league level and how Minor League Baseball can serve as an exemplar. "MLB has to figure out that they have become a lot more corporate and expensive. The average family cannot afford to attend that many games. That's a big issue. That's an issue we [Minor League Baseball] certainly don't have. We are very affordable. We have fun, crazy promotions. Our motto is every time you come to the ballpark we want you to see something you have never seen before. We are all about the families. Major League Baseball's marketing needs to take that into account and I know from my experience working in Major League Baseball they are [mostly] about seeing the best players play the game," and not necessarily the fan experience.

The minor leagues are far from being defined strictly by baseball. In some ways, it's as much about the fan experience at any given game than the on-field product. Minor League Baseball says families with children under 12 years old spend just two and a half innings actually watching a game they attend. That's a lot of time to fill with activity not between the foul lines. This creates an incredible challenge for Major League Baseball but one that the minor leagues seem to have embraced and successfully overcome.

At a minor league game, there are numerous activities for fans of every age to participate in. For example, the Quad Cities River Bandits of the Midwest League have amusement park rides—inside the ballpark. While the family plays, the adults can keep an eye on the kids and the game. I'm certainly not advocating for Ferris wheels at MLB stadiums, but adding some hands-on, fun activities should be a part of the MLB in-venue experience.

The Minor League Baseball experience has a different feel to it—one that harkens back to the earlier times of baseball. Entertaining activities between innings to keep fans excited and entertained are something that MLB seems to have co-opted from MiLB. The Presidents Race at Washington Nationals home games or the Legends Race at Arizona Diamondbacks home games can trace their history back to the minors. Fans at minor league games are accustomed to getting involved in these contests. These are engaging activities that major league teams should be creating to make the ballpark experience more fun, which in turn should increase ticket sales (Traveling Mom, 2022).

Earlier in this chapter we learned that the cost for a family to see a Major League Baseball game can be prohibitive, but the minor leagues have made the game affordable. It's hard to justify spending hundreds of dollars to see an MLB game in person that you can watch at home on television for free in air-conditioning. This is where Minor League Baseball really shines (Traveling Mom, 2022).

MLB's Response

Where does Major League Baseball stand with the issue of declining attendance? What does it see as the primary need to overcome it? Garden says that the league's focus is on the changes with season ticket holders. While he estimates that single-game ticket sales are up double digits compared with 2018, season tickets have generally been on the decline. How to address this trend is something Garden says MLB is intent on—and he believes it can help the league's future.

"I think the one step that we have taken on the subscription products has helped address that in a small way [and] is growing exponentially," Garden said. "I think we need to still figure out ways to combat that drop in season tickets generally. It's challenging, but we will solve that as well." I'm curious as to what Major League Baseball's plan entails.

Solutions

This chapter has provided some solutions to the issue Major League Baseball is facing. The findings in this chapter reveal some factors that positively affect both attendance and team financials. As I stated earlier, this entire book will be filled with solutions that will connect directly and indirectly and bring more fans to the game of baseball, be it in person or away from the stadium. Here are some solutions that Major League Baseball could implement—now.

Understanding Constraints

Earlier, the study by Davis and Miller (2021) revealed that constraints, or barriers, have an influence on attendance at Major League Baseball games and noted that the "pace-of-play initiatives may make the games' flow more appealing in the long run, but with no conception of the constraints being placed on fans in their everyday lives."

The researchers added that the "implications of this study indicate that fans may be willing to negotiate work or personal elements for more excitement at the MLB game. Decreased attendance of major league baseball games because of constraints may threaten the potential sustainability of the sport. This study underscores that MLB should try to understand the elements of constraints that will assist a fan's negotiation to attend a game."

Payroll and Winning with Offense

Drea's (2019) study leaned on research that may sound somewhat obvious but is clearly not subscribed to by Major League Baseball teams: "The teams that spend the most money on total payroll also have the highest average attendance."

Additionally, asserts Drea, winning matters, as "on-field performance is paramount to the determination of attendance since fans prefer to watch in-person a winning team or a team with enough talent to give off the impression that it will win consistently."

This leads to the suggestion that teams should genuinely rebuild and not tank, which as super-agent Scott Boras says, is a huge issue and one that I contend is bad for Major League Baseball.

Given the significance of winning percentage as it relates to attendance, suggests Drea, it is then essential to understand what are the most significant factors that influence it. His research found that "on-base percentage (OBP), slugging percentage (SLG), and batting average (BA) are the most impactful significant factors in contributing to winning percentage."

Specifically, his study found that home runs are an effective means of stimulating attendance. Drea (2019) concluded, "If baseball wishes to bring business back to the ballpark in the near future, it will look towards its most entertaining aspect, the home run. Teams should focus on offense and strive for rosters that focus on home runs." As you will read later, "this suggestion may be interestingly in contrast with how former players and front office executives feel about how the game is played today."

Also weighing in is Craig Edwards of FanGraphs (2019). He suggests that "teams that are doing well this season … had active winters or just won a bunch of games. The sport needs to do whatever it can to cultivate new fans and to get them out to the ballpark because without them, the television money that has made baseball less dependent on attendance will eventually dry up as well. Generating excitement about a team, through wins and activity in the offseason, is the best way to get more people to buy tickets."

Ticket Subscriptions

There is no reason a major league team should not be offering a subscription-based ticket option to their fans. One million Ballpark Pass tickets sold should be reason enough. That's a tipping point and a significant number. Kudos to Major League Baseball for initiating and supporting this innovative option. Teams that have not jumped on this may think it will cheapen or devalue their product. Nonsense. This is meeting fans where they are in this digital, fast-paced world. Darn near everything is a subscription, from the television content we consume to gym memberships.

Another concern may be the message it communicates to teams' season ticket holders. After all, they spend thousands of dollars on their ticket packages. Again, this is a nonissue because the Ballpark Pass fan is typically not a hard-core fan and without this option they might not come to a game ever. All one has to know is the major-market New York Yankees offer their Ballpark Pass for $49 a month. If the Yankees are onboard, everyone should be.

There is one drawback, however. Teams can sell only a limited number of Ballpark Passes. They sell out quickly. My suggestion to major league teams' ticket departments is to track the number of fans who are using the pass every game and consider increasing the allotment—especially on weekends.

Follow the Brewers' Lead

The Brewers clearly have the secret sauce on so many levels. They are a small-market team that is crushing it at the box office year after year. Their best practices, which teams should implement, include offering an affordable product for their fans. Affordability means more than tickets. It includes parking, concessions, and souvenirs.

In addition, their ballpark is amazing and fans recognize that the moment they drive into the stadium parking lot. Their stadium offers amenities such as numerous open-air social spaces. My favorite is the field-level bar in the right field corner. The vantage point of looking through the fence while enjoying one of Milwaukee's cold adult beverages is second to none. Any closer to the field and you'd be playing right field for the Brew Crew.

Finally, when fans are spending their hard-earned dollars, they want to feel welcomed and appreciated. The customer service at American Family Field sets the standard. As they come through the turnstiles, visiting fans, as well as Brewers fans, are greeted with a smile and friendly welcome. MLB teams should connect with the Brewers about their hugely successful customer service training.

Minor League Lessons

Again, we learned that minor league games are affordable. Empty seats generate zero dollars in revenue. I am not suggesting giving away tickets by the truckload, but major league teams can find creative ways to make their product more affordable. Just like in the minors, for weekday games during the summer there is no reason the entire upper deck of major league stadiums cannot be filled with thousands of summer camp kids. Get them in for $1 and provide them a voucher for another game.

In the past, major league teams would snicker and roll their eyes at the thought of having the same fun and crazy between-inning promotions that minor league fans have enjoyed for decades. However, in recent years we have seen MLB teams starting to have some fun at the ballpark. Wholesome family fun is starting to creep into major league stadiums. Teams should embrace this and go deeper. Let loose and focus on the family. Dave Heller, the president and CEO of Main Street Baseball and majority owner of four affiliated minor league baseball teams, said of his franchises, "The goal is to have a great time every time at the ballpark and to leave with memories of a lifetime." Not a bad goal for Major League Baseball teams to strive for as well.

2

America's Pastime in Recession

"I can't believe that I am disinterested in baseball."
—Scott Karl, Former Major League Pitcher

In addition to declining attendance, another major issue plaguing Major League Baseball is declining fan interest. In chapter 1, I highlighted in detail the current state of declining attendance in Major League Baseball—by the millions of fans not attending games. I believe that while baseball is still popular in some cities, it may be on the way to becoming a fringe sport in places not named Los Angeles, Boston, St. Louis, or Chicago.

In this chapter, I will cover the lack of fan interest as it relates to baseball's appeal, its television ratings, the impact of the steroid era and the recent cheating scandals, and the competitive imbalance of MLB's teams. I discovered in my research that there is not one silver bullet that can be applied to this issue. However, I will provide solutions that begin to tackle the problem and increase fan interest in Major League Baseball.

What Is Your Favorite Sport?

Since you are reading this book, I will assume that you are a baseball fan and most likely it is your favorite sport as it is mine. Unfortunately, while we love the game, its popularity is diminishing.

Gallup (Norman, 2018) conducted a poll asking fans, "What Is Your Favorite Sport to Watch?" (See Table 7.) The leagues of the four major sports (NFL, NBA, MLB, and NHL) finished in the top five. The Gallup poll also included sports such as tennis, golf, auto racing, and boxing. It is no surprise that the National Football League continues to reign supreme in terms of watchability.

Table 7: What Is Your Favorite Sport to Watch?

	2017	2013	2008	2007	2006	2005	2004
Football	37%	39%	41%	43%	43%	34%	37%
Basketball	11	12	9	11	12	12	13
Baseball	9	14	10	13	11	12	10
Soccer	7	4	3	2	2	3	2
Hockey	4	3	4	4	2	4	3

(Source: Gallup, 2018)

Interestingly, soccer has grown in popularity and has surpassed hockey as America's fourth-favorite sport to watch, and heads-up baseball, soccer is closing in on you. From 2013 to 2017, soccer's popularity nearly doubled while baseball's fell by a shocking 35 percent. An annual poll that surveys baseball fandom conducted by HBO *Real Sports*/Marist (2019) showed that only 31 percent of respondents said baseball is a large part of what people talk about or follow during Major League Baseball's season. An additional 42 percent reported the subject of baseball is sometimes part of the conversation, and close to one in four, 23 percent, says baseball is not part of the water cooler discussion. It appears that baseball isn't much of the sports talk conversation even during its own season. That should be cause for concern.

What's most surprising about baseball is that it has virtually no competition from other major sports during the summer months. The NFL is conducting training camps and the NBA and NHL seasons are on hiatus during the summer. Major League Baseball should dominate the market for the exception of Wimbledon or other one-off events (though other sports are working to fill any void).

But it's not so, said George Will. "When you and I were young, baseball had the undivided attention of the country from the first of April until Michigan played Ohio State. Today, there's six, seven weeks, I think, between the last NBA championship game and the first NFL preseason game. The competition for the sports fan's attention, of the sports fan's dollar, the time and space on sports pages and sports radio and all the rest is the competition is severe. And baseball right now is not competing," said Will.

Additionally, that 2019 HBO *Real Sports*/Marist poll found that 56 percent of American adults do not follow professional baseball at all. That number rises to 67 percent among ages 18 to 37, whom the HBO *Real Sports*/Marist Poll deemed millennials plus Generation Z fans. Only 28 percent of U.S. adults say they are very interested in baseball or somewhat interested in Major League Baseball.

The proportion of Americans who say they are baseball fans matches its lowest in nearly 10 years. Only 44 percent of Americans currently say they watch baseball a great deal (7 percent), a good amount (8 percent), or a little (29 percent). A majority (56 percent) do not watch America's so-called pastime at all. The proportion of baseball fans is down from 50 percent in April 2016. In 2009, 44 percent of U.S. residents were baseball fans.

Older Americans (51 percent of those age 45 or older) are more likely than younger Americans (37 percent of those under the age of 45) to say they are baseball fans. Racial differences are also present. Forty-eight percent of white Americans and 43 percent of Latinos, compared with 35 percent of African Americans, say they are fans.

Americans who live in the Northeast (52 percent) and Midwest (51 percent) are more likely than those in the South (39 percent) and West (39 percent) to call themselves baseball fans.

Is Baseball Losing Its Appeal?

The Gallup and HBO *Real Sports*/Marist polls indicate that baseball is losing its appeal, which is alarming. However, Major League Baseball would disagree, as it stated, "More people identify themselves as MLB fans than at any time in the past 25 years according to research conducted by SSRS/Luker on Trends Sports Poll. A total of 167.9 million people aged 12 or older identified themselves as MLB fans, the highest number for MLB in the history of the poll."

Jay Jaffe of FanGraphs suggests, "The on-field problems for baseball, the way that the game has evolved over the past two decades towards more strikeouts and fewer balls in play, is a problem."

SSRS/Luker also conducted a poll in 2020 asking fans which sport they're most interested in today. Not surprisingly, coming out on top was the NFL at 23.1 percent. However, Major League Baseball was only 14 percent. Why such a low response for baseball?

Theodore Sprencel (n.d.) of Suite 101 suggests, "Today's fans and consumers desire entertainment that is blatant and straightforward, that asks little more of audiences than to sit back and be amazed. That's why baseball, which to be enjoyed requires more than just surface-level observation, is losing appeal."

New York Times writer Juliette Love (2019) asked "How Popular Is Baseball, Really?" The *New York Times* cites evidence such as declining attendance, poor World Series ratings, and a lack of nationally recognized stars of the sport's impending collapse. As we learned in chapter 1, it's well documented that attendance at Major League Baseball games has been declining since 2007. About 68.5 million fans attended major league games during the 2019 regular season, down from a peak of nearly 80 million in 2007 (Statista, 2022).

Peter Panacy (2013) of Bleacher Report, in his piece "How Major League Baseball is Losing its Appeal in the Modern Era," wrote, "Baseball is slowly being relegated to just something sports fans can watch between spring and late summer. It is a pretty simple analysis: Baseball requires the knowledge and patience of fans much more than any of the other major sports. It also lacks the fast-paced and action-packed intrigue compared to other sports as well."

Former major league pitcher Scott Karl told me, "Baseball is not instant. It never has been and as far as other sports are concerned, it's slower."

"This is not to say that baseball is boring and lacks the action of other sports," says Panacy. "It also does not state that baseball employs more or less strategy and preparation than football, basketball or hockey do. Rather, baseball fans, typically, have to know and understand much more than the casual fan. They have to be more patient too, something that is difficult in this day and age. In reality, baseball is becoming a victim of its own game play."

Jaffe added, "I think part of the problem is the increased amount of time between pitches and the lack of balls in play. I think those two things make for a very static viewing experience that if you're not fully engaged in the game, you could certainly see it as boring. If you're not thinking along with the pitcher, thinking along with the manager, thinking along with the hitter, if you're not engaged in some way, it's going to seem boring."

Is Baseball Unwatchable?

Has the game on the field changed for the worse? Some, even those who played it, would say sadly yes.

Karl told me, "I can't believe that I am saying this, but I don't like to watch baseball because of its style today. I can't believe that I am disinterested in baseball. It's like beer league softball. It is either a home run or strikeout."

Fans also believe that the game of baseball that they grew up with is "lost" with meaningless statistics, instant replay appeals, home runs or strikeouts, and pitchers being practically strip-searched for foreign substances—after each half inning.

Case in point, Barry Svrluga (2021) of the *Washington Post* said, "The game itself is wounded. In 2021, major league hitters collectively produced a .244 batting average. When I buy a seat and sit in the stands or flip on the television and plop down on the couch, how much action is there?

"The last time major league hitters produced an average as low as .244 was 1972. The last time the average fell below that was 1968, when Bob Gibson, Luis Tiant, Denny McLain and others defined the year of the pitcher as MLB posted a .237 average. We know what happened then: MLB lowered the mound to a uniform 10 inches and shrank the strike zone to make sure hitters weren't overpowered," wrote Svrluga.

Hall of Fame slugger Mike Schmidt added, "Hitters [are] being led astray by information: Hitting the ball in the air is better than on the ground, striking out is only one out, and a high velocity off the bat and perfect launch angle makes a great hitter.... The decline of hitting today lies directly in the hitters' inability to hit the high fastball and the lack of accountability for striking out."

World Series–winning manager Joe Maddon told me, "I don't think we will see a Triple Crown winner again. It's not even being discussed."

But this is solvable, says Karl. "The onus is on the owners and players. It begins with the players. It falls on their shoulders to make the game better. Hit against the [defensive] shift, be better, and pitchers pitch."

Major League Baseball defines the shift as "a term used to describe the situational defensive realignment of fielders away from their 'traditional' starting points." Think of it as loading one side of the field with players to defend where the percentages suggest a batter will most likely put the ball in play.

Thankfully, in September 2022, MLB announced the rule change that there would be a limit on defensive shifting. Beginning in 2023, "The defensive team must have a minimum of four players on the infield, with at least two infielders completely on either side of second base. These restrictions are intended to increase the batting average on balls in play, to allow infielders to better showcase their athleticism and to restore more traditional outcomes on batted balls."

Karl actually enjoyed watching the World Series champion Washington Nationals in 2019 because, as he said, "They actually pitched. Yes, they threw hard but they hit the corners and *pitched*."

In terms of the shift, "I go back and forth on it," said Buck Showalter. "What we used to think was a hit—traditional ball hit to the right side between first and second was a hit. Today, the crowd lets out a groan when the ball is hit into the shift and it's an out. Guys are now taught differently. Don't blame the players. They are not being paid to hit the other way. It's not their fault. It is the skill set [hitting home runs] the people are now embracing."

Former Cincinnati Reds general manager Wayne Krivsky, who has spent 41 years in the game, concurs. "Every night it is a strikeout, walk, or home run. It is home run derby. It is sad to see the damage done to the game.

"We need to get back to basics with the game. There is too much technology. Also, technical verbiage such as launch angle and exit velocity—it's garbage to me. We are too carried away with it. It's confusing to the fans and it is taking away the enjoyment of the game. We are complicating the game," added Krivsky.

To their point, during the 2021 season, more than a third (35 percent) of all major league plate appearances ended in one of the three true outcomes—a home run, walk, or a strikeout—which was the highest rate of all time. This makes for a boring product on the field.

Interestingly, while balls in play have decreased, home runs and strikeouts have dramatically increased. Strikeouts are significantly on the rise over the past decade. Who could imagine that strikeouts would become an acceptable norm in the game?

Table 8: Strikeouts on the Rise

Year	MLB Total Strikeouts	Percent Increase/ Decrease	Percent of Plate Appearances
2010	34,306	-	18%
2015	37,446	9.15%	20%
2019	42,823	24.8%	23%
2021	42,145	-1.6%	23%

(Source: Baseball-Reference, 2022)

There is a correlation between the lack of action and fan interest. For example, balls in play have significantly declined.

George Will told me, "In the last 25 minutes of that most-watched game of 2020, the ball was put in play twice. Baseball of the three true outcomes—walk, strikeout, home runs—is boring. We have the stupendous athleticism of people like Nolan Arenado and Javy Baez and Lindor and all the rest and the ball's not put in play. Baseball players spend a lot more time with leather on their hands and with wood in their hands and most of the time they're just standing there. If baseball doesn't change, baseball is well on the way to becoming, as has been said, a niche sport like boxing."

During the 2018 Major League Baseball season, only 120,320 balls were in play compared with 125,565 in 2015 and 129,279 in 2010. That is a decrease of nearly 9,000 balls in play, or 7 percent, in just eight seasons (Baseball-Reference, 2022).

Buck Showalter told me, "Walks, home runs, and strikeouts are not entertaining. Don't blame the players. They are getting rewarded for playing the game this way. It won't change until they are rewarded for playing differently"—such as hitting against the shift.

I contend that players are also not being held accountable for that failure and there is seemingly no accountability for not hitting against the shift.

In addition to a lack of action on the field, bad play itself and the idea that, according to *Forbes*'s Maury Brown (2019), numerous teams are choosing not to be competitive either before or during the season as eight teams lost 95 or more games and three teams finished the 2018 season with more than 100 losses.

As for bad baseball, Brown pointed out that strikeouts outpaced base hits for the first time in the history of Major League Baseball, which was the 11th straight season that strikeouts increased from the previous season. The league batting average, said Brown, was .248, the lowest since the 1972 season. A year later, in 2019, strikeouts again exceeded hits.

Showalter added, "The game has moved more toward efficiency over entertainment. That's the problem. We have also lost the shame of failure in our game. Striking out is no longer a big deal. [In turn] we have embraced things that are artificial—the home run—with things [analytics] that are more efficient. It's a beautiful game but until the players develop [and get rewarded for] new skills it won't change."

Analytics

To Showalter's point, numerous people in the game have indicated to me that today's Major League Baseball managers are controlled more by the Harvard graduates in the front office.

Baseball sense may be a thing of the past for some franchises as they rely more heavily on analytics. Has it ruined the game? Improved it? Is there too much focus on launch angle, exit velocity, etc.? The game has always been driven by stats, but the human element is being marginalized.

Maddon said, "The game is scripted and controlled by the front office. From the top down. Teams have spent a lot of money on their analytics departments and while I support a balance [of analytics and scouting], these [analytics] people don't have much to do so they spend their day finding things."

Jay Eddings has served as a pro scout for over 20 years and currently is in that role for the Texas Rangers. He also played in the Chicago Cubs system from 1987 to 1990, and as someone who has been in the game for nearly 40 years, he feels that analytics is missing the human element. Not every situation, or player for that matter, can be quantified in a statistical analysis.

Eddings said, "Analytics are being forced upon the scouts and a lot of coaches at all levels in baseball do not like the Harvard analytics people. For example, they are obsessed with OPS."

"One of the issues," continued Eddings, "is that many owners and the analytics people speak the same language. They have a formula to tell them if a guy is good or not. Owners like this because they want a definitive answer before paying a guy $5 million," and analytics, in their mind, gives that answer.

Additionally, Eddings said, "The computer takes out the upside, and the potential of a player. Kids develop at different stages. We [baseball] are losing guys, athletes, because the analytics people either say they are good or not good today but what about their potential?

"Sometimes kids are moved off a club. Perhaps they are released because of a roster situation and sometimes they need a change of scenery, a different voice of a coach. So the question is, is the formula [analytics] right in those situations?" asked Eddings.

Also, let's be realistic. Recently, patience is not a strength of the industry.

Indeed, it appears that there's no contingency for potential player growth. If baseball is simply using the formula to decide whether to sign, resign, or release a player, it seems dangerous as that presents a slippery slope to losing great athletes to other sports.

The Instagram account Vintage Bubble Gum (2022) said, "Before the heavy use of analytics in baseball, managers relied on their instincts, prior knowledge from years in the game, and even quirky superstitions to make critical decisions." Guess what? It worked.

However, not many managers can or choose to use those instincts, and as it relates to accountability, it seemingly lets managers and general managers off the hook when they don't succeed in their decision-making. They can simply blame the analytics when things do not work out: "The analytics said to leave him in."

Vintage Bubble Gum added, "With the rise in analytics in baseball, the number of stolen bases has declined significantly."

It noted that the number of stolen bases in 2021 was the lowest of the expansion era, which began in 1961. "Only a few decades ago speedsters such as Rickey Henderson, Vince Coleman, and Willie McGee were impacting games with their prowess on the base paths. It was not uncommon for the top baserunners to steal over 50 bags in a season," said Vintage Bubble Gum.

With the lack of base stealing, Showalter asked, "How do you evaluate good baserunning [today]?"

Today's game is station to station and waiting for the home run.

Showalter also told me, "I don't find launch angle or spin rate entertaining. The game is not won with spin rate or launch angle. Until the value of a home run changes, I don't care if a ball scrapes off the fence for a home run or it goes 500 feet. It doesn't matter to me."

Jerry Reuss, who pitched in the major leagues for 22 years, thinks differently about spin rate. "I think it's a great measure," he said. "I would have loved it when I played. I would have been able to understand why it is important and also improve it."

Baseball has always been a game of statistics and analytics, however. "We have used analytics since I broke in," said Showalter. "I know what you're going to do before you do it. Everyone is chasing an edge and we are all looking at the same stuff [data]. So, what is the separator? We don't have as many boots on the ground [scouts] today so it is the organization that evaluates better, drafts better, gets those pieces, and the sixth tool, which is their makeup—mentality, emotional maturity, and stability. These tools cannot be analytically evaluated but are critically important. We are looking at things too robotically, but these are not robots. They are human beings."

Showalter added, "What you choose to weigh in your organization gets attention. For example, in New York [with the Yankees] in 1989, Gene Michael and I decided to focus on on-base percentage long before it was popular."

The Fallout from the Steroid Era

Scandals in baseball that tarnish the integrity of the game have been embedded in the sport since the beginning, and here is one issue concerning Major League Baseball that perhaps you haven't thought of in while—steroids. Almost 20 years later, does the fallout from the steroid era of the late 1980s to early 2000s still impact fan interest? Surprisingly, it does. Apparently, time does not heal all wounds, as baseball's popularity took a hit then that still lingers today. Some fans have never forgiven the players, owners, and the league itself who, in their mind, cheated the game.

In 2009, 60 percent of those surveyed in a CBS News/*New York Times* poll (n.d.) said it matters to them "a lot" if baseball players use steroids or other performance-enhancing drugs. Of the rest, 29 percent said it matters to them "a little." Only nine percent said it matters "not at all."

The poll also asked, "If it is proven that an athlete used steroids at the time he or she set a major record in a sport, what do you think should happen to that record?" The responses: 32 percent said the record should be eliminated; 47 percent said that it should be kept but with a note saying it was set when steroids were in use; and 18 percent said it should be "kept like any other" record.

Lifelong baseball fans such as University of Southern California professor John Roach thinks baseball has not recovered from the steroid era, and there may be something to this notion. Roach cites declining attendance and a drop in national TV playoff and World Series ratings coinciding with the outings of some players and admissions by others of taking steroids. Baseball has a storied past and long tradition and history of records. Many of those records are sacred, and steroids obliterated a fair number of the seminal ones—and some would say it tainted the game. This turned off many fans who have not returned to the game (CBS News/ *New York Times*, n.d.).

Though steroids have been banned in MLB since 1991, Major League Baseball did not implement leaguewide performance-enhancing drugs (PED) testing until 2002. Throughout those prior years, the lack of testing meant it was unlikely players using PEDs would get caught.

The Major League Baseball's Joint Drug Agreement (JDA) between MLB and the Major League Baseball Players Association first agreed to a testing program in 2002, which called for survey testing in 2003. In 2004, penalties were then introduced and since then have increased in severity. For example, initially first offenders were given a 10-game suspension, but it has since transitioned to 80 games for a first offense. Players are randomly tested for banned substances all year, even in the offseason, when the agreement is in place (Associated Press via ESPN.com, 2022).

Under the JDA, all MLB players are subject to at least three random tests per year for PEDs. Also, within 72 hours of a positive test, Major League Baseball then reveals the name of the guilty player and that player is immediately suspended without pay. The length of the suspension depends on the individual's number of previous positive tests as well as the type of substance (Cisik, 2020).

However, the agreement was suspended for the first time in 20 years during the 2022 lockout, which raised concerns centering on the idea that players could have used PEDs knowing that most likely they would not be detected before the collective bargaining agreement was in place—at which time the agreement would be restored.

PEDs originally became a focus in the wake of power-hitting surge.

According to ESPN (2012), "During the 1990s, [MLB] experienced an increase in offensive output that resulted in some unprecedented home run totals for ... power hitters of the decade. While just three players reached the 50-home run mark in any season between 1961 and 1994, many sluggers would start to surpass that number in the mid–90s. The home run onslaught captured the attention of the country and helped to reclaim popularity for the league four years after a strike had shortened the 1994 season."

ESPN noted that in 1998 Mark McGwire and Sammy Sosa shared the "Sportsman of the Year" honor from *Sports Illustrated*. During the 1998 home run chase, McGwire had admitted to using androstenedione, a substance that was banned by the National Football League and the NCAA. Androstenedione was not illegal at that time in Major League Baseball, however, which had yet to institute a testing program for many substances.

One former major leaguer who played during the height of the steroid era spoke to me on the condition of anonymity. He told me that during the steroid era it was clear that owners, players, and even fans knew steroid usage was rampant. After the strike-shortened season of 1994, baseball was dismissed by many fans, but the offensive onslaught at the hands of steroids brought the sport back. The excitement was there. There were home runs galore as the ball was flying out of stadiums across the league. We knew the reason but we loved the results.

Steroids and the laissez-faire attitude of Major League Baseball to police behavior was an egregious example of a lack of accountability that turned off many fans. While not illegal in baseball, players who used steroids in the 1990s and early 2000s traded padding stats for the consequences of a tarnished image.

But what has been the ultimate impact of steroids on the popularity of Major League Baseball? A study by Jeffrey Cisyk (2020) from the *Journal of Sports Economics*, "Impacts of Performance-Enhancing Drug Suspensions on the Demand for Major League Baseball," took a unique look at the fallout.

Cisyk's study found that PED-related suspensions have two major impacts on the demand for baseball. First, there was on average an immediate 9.3 percent reduction in the television audience of a suspended PED player's team.

Second, the study noted that the "magnitude of the effect gradually decreases over time yet remains negative and significant for a period of 37 days or approximately 33 game-broadcasts. This is the first study to link PED use to an adverse reaction by consumers in a systematic way using television audience while controlling for the change in team quality caused by removing the suspended player from the team."

Cisyk noted a 2005 poll found that 86 percent of Major League Baseball fans say PEDs are either "a serious problem" or "ruining the game" while only 5 percent think PEDs "make [the] game better."

As illustrated by Cisyk and Courty (2017), news of a PED announcement results in a loss of close to $743,000 in forgone ticket revenue to the PED player's team.

That study also found "there is no effect on television audience when the same players are removed from their teams due to injuries, suggesting that consumers are responding solely to the PED announcement."

The researchers contended that "consumers do care about PED use in sports. While PEDs are said to be a potential benefit (greater chance to see an exceptional athletic performance) as well as a potential hindrance (loss of consumer support) to the financial integrity of sports, this study certainly points to the latter."

Cheating Scandals

While not officially cheating, many fans still debate over steroid users being crowned "cheaters." However, one recent issue that has fans united over cheating is the controversy involving sign stealing, most notably by the Houston Astros and Boston Red Sox, which won the World Series in 2017 and 2018, respectively.

In the *Marquette Sports Law Review*, Walter T. Champion's (2020) piece titled "The Commissioner Goes Too Far: The Best Interests of Baseball Clause and the Astros' 'High Tech' Sign-Stealing Scandal discusses "Astros employees in the video replay review room [accused] of using live game feed from the center field camera to attempt to decode and transmit opposing teams' sign sequences."

Champion (2020) went on to say, "The Commissioner held both General Manager Jeff Luhnow and Field Manager A.J. Hinch were personally responsible for the conduct of the team. They were suspended from baseball for one year and subsequently fired by Astros owner Jim Crane. The Commissioner argued that the smartphone/trash can machinations raised questions about the game's integrity.

"These employees would communicate the sign sequence information by text message which was received on the Apple watch of a staff member on the bench. The center field camera is (was) primarily used for player development. After decoding the sign, a player would bang a nearby trash can with a bat to communicate the upcoming pitch type to the batter," said Champion.

The commissioner forfeited the Astros' regular first- and second-round selections in the 2020 and 2021 player drafts. The club was also ordered to pay $5 million, "which is the highest allowable fine under the Major League Constitution." In short, suggests Champion, the commissioner went too far in forcing the Astros to forfeit four top draft picks.

I disagree. I offer that Manfred did not go far enough. These were coordinated efforts using live video feeds homing in on the opposing catcher's signs.

As we just learned, the Astros would then bang a trash can to relay to the hitter that a breaking ball or some other off-speed pitch was coming. The Astros were also involved in another scheme using the team's replay room to help decode catchers' signs to the pitcher. As for the Red Sox, in their home ballpark of Fenway Park in Boston, there's a replay room a few steps from the dugout that managers can use to figure out whether they want to challenge plays, which means they have footage of the catcher signaling the pitcher. The Red Sox were accused of having players slip into that room to analyze catchers' signs to help decipher them (*MassLive*, 2020) in real time.

Fast-forward to 2022. Prior to that season, New York Yankees general manager Brian Cashman, in an interview with The Athletic (2022), disputed the notion that the Yankees were in a prolonged title skid and cited the 2017 team that lost in the American League Championship Series to the Houston Astros, who were eventually sanctioned by Major League Baseball for illicitly stealing opposing teams' signs.

"The only thing that stopped [the 2017 Yankees] was something that was so illegal and horrific," Cashman told The Athletic. "So, I get offended when I start hearing we haven't been to the World Series since '09. Because I'm like, 'Well, I think we actually did it the right way.' Pulled it down, brought it back up. Drafted well, traded well, developed well, signed well. The only thing that derailed us was a cheating circumstance that threw us off."

The Astros defeated the Yankees in seven games in the 2017 ALCS before beating the Los Angeles Dodgers in the World Series.

"I'm past it now," Cashman told The Athletic. "But it does bother me when it comes up. We built something that—I can't tell you we would have won. I can't tell you we would have beat the Dodgers. But I do feel pretty confident that that team [the Astros] wasn't stopping us, if it wasn't for those advantages. That's all."

"Sign stealing, in and of itself, is not a violation of our rules," Major League Baseball commissioner Manfred said. "It has been a part of our game since Lassie was a puppy" (Castillo, 2020). That's concerning to hear. Sign stealing by trying to outsmart the opponent is relatively common in baseball and not illegal. However, the use of technology to steal signs is.

Consequences were levied against both teams. Here is a recap of the discipline:

Houston Astros:

- Fined $5 million, the maximum allowed under MLB's constitution.
- General Manager Jeff Luhnow suspended for one year. Luhnow was then fired.

- Manager A.J. Hinch suspended for one year. Hinch was then fired.
- Former assistant GM Brandon Taubman suspended one year.
- Forfeit first- and second-round draft picks for two years.

Boston Red Sox:

- Minor penalties to the team and a replay operator.
- Manager Joey Cora was given a year's suspension for his contributions to the 2017 cheating scandal of the Houston Astros.
- Cora was then relieved of his Red Sox managerial duties.
- Red Sox have to forfeit a second-round draft choice.

Surprisingly, no Houston Astros or Boston Red Sox players were punished for their sign-stealing. Players had been given immunity in exchange for information about the schemes. It was simply a practical thing, Manfred claimed. He reasoned that the league office would not get cooperation from players if they were at risk of punishment. Moving forward, future penalties will include suspension without pay and without accrual of service time.

Regardless, I believe the commissioner's office should have gone further by imposing two-year bans on participating in the playoffs for both the Astros and Red Sox, akin to the NCAA postseason bans on programs that are found guilty of rule violations. That consequence would hurt the franchise and players in more ways than one.

Not only were fans upset with these cheating scandals, but some players were also furious. Players' reaction to sign stealing was at times scathing. Former Atlanta Braves outfielder Nick Markakis voiced one of the strongest responses regarding the Astros scandal.

"It angers you, especially from a guy who has played the game the right way his whole career. No shortcuts. I know how hard this game is, I know how hard preparing for this game is," said Markakis. He added, "To see something like that is damaging to baseball. It's anger. I feel every single guy over there [Houston] needs a beating. It's wrong" (The Athletic, 2017).

Brandli Stitzel, Ryan Mattson, and Rex Pjesky (2021) investigated the efficacy of the cheating scheme employed by the Houston Astros during the 2017 Major League Baseball season, in which they won the World Series. Their paper appeared in the *Economics Bulletin* and was titled "The Trashy Side of Baseball: An Econometric Analysis of the Houston Astros Cheating Scandal." They presented evidence "that the cheating scheme profoundly affected player performance and increased the number of wins the Astros accumulated in the 2017 season."

As I recapped prior, the authors summed up the scheme this way: "The Astros positioned video cameras in center field of their home stadium and trained them to steal the opponent's catcher's signs to the pitcher. They then conveyed this information in real-time to an operator behind their team's dugout who used decoding software and audible signals to communicate the pitch information to the batter in time for him to react to the pitch."

They added, "Knowing the pitcher's intended pitch and location is an enormous advantage for the batter. The batter no longer needs to discern between pitch types and can then predict the pitch's eventual location relative to the strike zone based on relative movement tendencies of different pitches. The value of this is high because the act of deciding whether or not to swing at a pitch, and the ability to hit it, happens during an extremely short time frame, as short as 375 milliseconds."

Their study answered the question, Would the team have won the World Series or even made the playoffs without cheating? While answering that question, keep in mind that the 2017 champion Astros had the most prolific single-season offensive output at the time.

"Despite the potential benefits and scope of cheating, Major League Baseball did not expunge or even place a qualification on the Astros' championship season" said Stitzel, Mattson, and Pjesky.

They suggested, "Therefore, the league did not think the cheating had a decisive impact on the season. In contrast, this paper presents evidence that the cheating scheme had a profound effect on player performance and increased the number of wins the Astros accumulated."

In the *Atlanta Journal-Constitution* (2020), Los Angeles Dodgers pitcher Trevor Bauer, who is rarely unwilling to share an opinion, stated, "I'm not going to let them forget the fact that they are hypocrites, they are cheaters, they've stolen from a lot of other people and the game itself. We're all pissed."

Colorado Rockies third baseman Kris Bryant simply said, "It's really a disgrace to the game."

Bryant's former teammate, San Diego Padres pitcher Yu Darvish, provided another perspective: "In the Olympics, if players cheat they can't have a gold medal. But they still have a World Series title."

MLB on Television

How popular is baseball on television? Locally somewhat popular. Nationally, it's a different story, and that is negatively impacting the game.

In 2019, 12 of the 29 (41 percent) United States–based major league teams were the most popular prime-time broadcast in their market. Although baseball's national television ratings lag far behind those of other top sports, local broadcasts are unquestionably popular. Also, Major League Baseball teams are beginning to purchase part or all of their own television network to generate additional revenue.

Solid local ratings and an added revenue stream sound promising. However, local MLB broadcasts should be the number one show on their regional sports networks as Major League Baseball doesn't face much competition for the attention of sports fans during the summer months.

Nationally, Fox, ESPN, CBS, and NBC own the national broadcasting rights for National Football League games, giving broad exposure to the league's best teams and stars. Baseball's broadcasting model is much different. Individual teams sell exclusive rights for nearly all of their games to either regional branches of these national networks or to local stations (*New York Times*). While individual team revenues have been substantial, this is mainly due to the aforementioned local television contracts.

For example, numerous teams, including the Los Angeles Dodgers, Texas Rangers, Los Angeles Angels, Seattle Mariners, and Philadelphia Phillies, have signed long-term, multibillion-dollar deals with regional sports networks in recent years. Also, in 2019 the Tampa Bay Rays agreed to a new 15-year television contract worth a reported $82 million annual value (Dusenbury, 2019).

While the money is enormous for local and national contracts, with games being aired locally every day, the national ratings just aren't there. It's no longer special to watch a national broadcast. The days of NBC's MLB *Game of the Week* in the 1970s and 1980s are long gone. Those games felt significant no matter who played.

Even with those aforementioned examples, not all teams are big winners in their regional TV deals.

T.J. Mathewson (2019) of Global Sports added, "One franchise sets the example of how to profit big off of the deals. After signing a new television deal in 2014 with Spectrum Sportsnet LA worth $8.35 billion over 25 years, the Los Angeles Dodgers, who are the majority owner of the regional sports network, made $204 million in revenue off of TV money alone in 2016.

"Only one other team, the Los Angeles Angels, collected more than $100 million ($118) in TV revenue in 2016. The after-effects of these types of contracts are massive," wrote Mathewson.

Another issue is Major League Baseball's blackout rules relating to MLB.TV. MLB.TV is a streaming package that enables subscribers to view out-of-market MLB games live and on demand online on computers and supported mobile and connected devices. The key phrase "out of market" differs from one market to the next.

Jay Jaffe of FanGraphs weighed in on the subject of blacking out games. He said, "It's a complicated thing that has to do with the regional sports networks and the owners and the national broadcasting contracts. The blackout rules are a very common complaint. Historically teams had such reservations about televising games and they were worried. And you look back, I mean this is a stone age in terms of marketing and you look back at the paltry attendance figures from then, and it's like obviously this stimulates interest rather than detracts from it."

Jaffe thinks this issue impedes access to Major League Baseball's product. "Baseball has to make itself easier to consume. I think MLB.TV is a wonderful thing. I can get games out of market and watch the Dodgers every game or whatever if I want to, but I need to be able to stream the Yankees or the Mets on my device at home as part of my cable package or whatever or as an alternative to my cable package. When you've got the blackout rules that prevent somebody in Iowa from watching six teams and watching—I think the number somebody kept track of was 37 percent of all Major League games are blacked out if you live in certain pockets in Iowa or Nevada. Baseball needs to do a better job of making it easier to watch their games. If you're six hours away from a major league ballpark, maybe you're going once a year, maybe you're going twice a year. To black somebody out from those games is idiocy."

As a subscriber to MLB.TV, I also think it is a good product, but it does infuriate me that I cannot watch (and support) my local teams by watching their games live. MLB.TV would counter that I can watch in-market games 90 minutes after their conclusion, but who wants to stay up until nearly midnight to begin watching a game that was played earlier that evening? Not many, I suggest.

Postseason Television Ratings

Meanwhile, according to MLB, fees from baseball media rights are growing at a much faster rate. That explains how revenue can soar while attendance plummets. Baseball's television agreement with Fox (through 2028, seven years, $5.1 billion) included a 39 percent increase over the previous deal and the contract with Turner Sports is a 40 percent jump (through 2028, seven years, $3.29 billion). TBS will continue to air one League Championship Series, two Division Series, and a Wild Card Game each season, but its regular-season inventory will shift from Sunday afternoons to weeknights (Wagner, 2018).

However, George Will told me, "The canary in the coal mine is local broadcast revenues. And the canary would be if viewership declines because the great driver of baseball's current prosperity has been the very rich local broadcast rights sales. The problem is, I believe you'd have to check this, but if memory serves, the current commissioner once told me that the average fan watching a baseball game watches 50 minutes and goes away. Now, whoever's selling commercials for the remaining two hours and 20 minutes of the game is going to notice that. And that will cost them."

Along with the World Series and the All-Star Game, Fox retains the rights to one League Championship Series and two League Division Series during the playoffs as well as its Saturday doubleheader throughout the regular season.

Collectively, these agreements are a mind-blowing $8.1 billion. However, this appears to be a false narrative suggesting that, since MLB is getting enormous revenues from television deals, there isn't a problem with ratings and declining interest.

While ratings for regular-season local broadcasts are strong, the ratings for postseason Major League Baseball haven't measured up. Major League Baseball posted its lowest U.S. television ratings in at least a decade for the Division Series round of its postseason in 2019, despite having three of four series extend to a maximum five-game length. The league averaged 3.04 million viewers per game during the Division Series round for 18 total contests aired on TBS, Fox Sports 1, and the MLB Network. The figure is down from 3.2 million viewers per game in 2018, despite four fewer games being played in the 2018 Division Series round (Paulsen, 2020).

A stark example of declining ratings: the five least-viewed World Series in the past 50-plus years are (in order) 2012, 2008, 2019, 2014, and 2018, according to Baseball Almanac. Looking deeper, from 2000 to 2010, the average World Series rating was 11.7. From 2011 to 2019, it fell to 9.2. That decline represents a significant decrease of 3.5 million fans on average—for the World Series, no less.

World Series Game Times

While matchups may play a role, one significant problem I see contributing to poor ratings is the starting times for not only the Major League Baseball playoffs in general but, more important, the World Series. Memo to MLB: the World Series is your moment to shine. This is the opportunity to show the world your incredible product on the biggest stage. However, the television networks' demand that World Series games be played during prime time precludes fans from enjoying the action. How?

For instance, most World Series games start after 8:00 p.m. Eastern

Time and often end close to or past midnight. Of the 13 longest nine-inning World Series games this decade, six came in the 2019 Fall Classic between the Houston Astros and Washington Nationals. Game 3, a 4–1 Houston victory, took four hours, three minutes, which, according to Baseball-Reference, was the first time a game lasted over four hours that didn't go into extra innings and had five or fewer total runs scored.

As a result, fans living east of the Rockies probably have difficulty staying awake for games that end at 1 a.m. on the East Coast and are being played close to an hour longer than regular-season games due to added commercials and numerous pitching changes. Also, if your favorite team isn't playing in the series, it is difficult enough to get you to watch. Couple it with a ridiculously late start time, and it's no wonder World Series television ratings have plummeted. How can kids, the future fans of the game, stay up late to watch these games?

One network baseball play-by-play announcer shared a story on the day of the 2019 World Series Game 7, which he said was an epiphany as it relates to late World Series start times and the popularity of the game for younger-generation fans.

On the morning of Game 7, he asked his high-school-aged son if he was excited about watching Game 7 of the World Series that evening. He replied, "Dad, it's on too late [they live in the Eastern Time Zone]. I can't stay up. Plus, I have school tomorrow." The stunned network announcer acknowledged, "I realize there are rights fees involved with the networks and they want the biggest audience, and that's prime time," he said.

He added, "Day game during the World Series, well, that ship has sailed. However, couldn't they start them one to two hours earlier? This would help overcome the lack of a young audience. The way it currently is [8:00 p.m. Eastern start time] is not good for young people and not good for the future of the game."

Speaking of day games, when did World Series games become scheduled only at night? Since 1984 there has been only a single day game in the World Series: Game 6 in 1987. That game between the St. Louis Cardinals and the Minnesota Twins was scheduled for a 3:00 p.m. local start (Central Time) on ABC. In 1985, with ABC taking over the broadcast from NBC, all seven games had first pitches in prime time.

"It certainly was considered," former Fox Sports president Ed Goren said in an MLB.com (2019) article about moving back to at least some games having afternoon starts. "And the commissioner [then Bud Selig] has certainly expressed his interest in it. But it gets back to economics: What I do know, from our research people, is that if we played Saturday afternoon, viewership would be 30 percent lower. And there would be an economic impact to that." It is hard to see his point considering that the World Series prime-time viewership ratings are in a nosedive. Isn't it worth a try? The current model sure is not working.

Former MLB Commissioner Bud Selig said, "This really is a reasonable hour. Young fans were one of the reasons we wanted to do it, but, again, our goal was to have the largest possible audience. This is a real change for us, in a very positive way—something I have had very strong feelings about for a long time." I disagree with the former commissioner. He said young fans matter, but MLB didn't change to earlier game times. In other words, money today mattered more than the game tomorrow.

Maybe there is hope with current major league commissioner Rob Manfred, who is also aware of this issue. Manfred stated, "We are cognizant of the fact we are trying to serve those fans [on both coasts] as well. I understand game times can be difficult. It's hard when games finish late. By the same token, when you start games at 5 o'clock Eastern, it's in the middle of the workday in L.A. We're trying to strike a balance and get the window where we can give the most people in the country a meaningful opportunity to watch the game" (Sheinin, 2018).

Perhaps there is a compromise somewhere in all of this.

Another factor playing a role in poor World Series ratings in recent years is again the local popularity of baseball. "Fans may be unlikely to sit through a series between two teams they have rarely seen play and ... players ... they may barely recognize," said Juliette Love of the *New York Times* (2019).

Importance of Regular Season and Competitive Balance

Also impacting fan interest are the importance of the Major League Baseball regular season and the competitive balance of teams. MLB and the Major League Baseball Players Association should strive to ensure the regular season has more meaning, as many teams are out of the race as early as June. Later in this chapter, I will discuss ideas on how to add importance to a lengthy 162-game schedule and also thoughts on teams rebuilding while fans suffer through 100-plus-loss seasons.

Driving the issue of competitive balance, according to Spotrac, is that baseball remains the only major American sport not to employ a hard salary cap.

"Professional basketball, hockey and football all have set salary caps in place that help ensure teams in small markets can remain competitive. While all that cash does not guarantee championships, it certainly puts teams in a better position to win them," said Spotrac (2022). I also suggest it helps keep fans interested and engaged longer during the season.

A salary cap has value not just by allowing franchises to outbid other teams for top free agents but by also making it easier for teams to retain their own talent instead of seeing them seek large contracts elsewhere (Spotrac, 2022). A salary cap in baseball would promote competitiveness because small-market teams would have the same opportunity to attract and retain top players as the rich teams.

Instead of a hard cap, Major League Baseball currently employs a luxury tax, or as MLB calls it, the Competitive Balance Tax. "Each year, clubs that exceed a predetermined payroll threshold are subject to a Competitive Balance Tax—which is commonly referred to as a 'luxury tax.' Those who carry payrolls above that threshold are taxed on each dollar above the threshold, with the tax rate increasing based on the number of consecutive years a club has exceeded the threshold. A team's Competitive Balance Tax figure is determined using the average annual value of each player's contract on the 40-man roster, plus any additional player benefits. A club exceeding the Competitive Balance Tax threshold for the first time must pay a 20 percent tax on all overages. A club exceeding the threshold for a second consecutive season will see that figure rise to 30 percent, and three or more straight seasons of exceeding the threshold comes with a 50 percent luxury tax. If a club dips below the luxury tax threshold for a season, the penalty level is reset. So, a club that exceeds the threshold for two straight seasons but then drops below that level would be back at 20 percent the next time it exceeds the threshold" (MLB, 2022).

Clearly, the so-called luxury tax isn't penalty enough for large-market teams like the New York Yankees and Los Angeles Dodgers to pull back from spending big in the free-agent market year in and year out. Something needs to change.

Sam Yardley, Two Circles' senior vice president of consulting, told Front Office Sports (2019) that he thinks that the one real remedy to lack of fan interest is better competition. With the talent gap between baseball teams seemingly widening, Yardley believes that this has hurt the sport—and it shows in the latest attendance numbers. "The competitive balance of the league is not where it once was," Yardley said. "I think that has harmed ticket sales because the product put on the field is less and less interesting for fans of teams that are already 30 games back by mid–July."

One interesting study by Humphreys and Miceli (2020) was published in the West Virginia University Working Paper Series, titled "Outcome Uncertainty, Fan Travel, and Aggregate Attendance."

The authors focused the study on the development of "an alternative model based on a standard expected utility model of fan behavior which incorporates fans' decisions to travel to away games and aggregates decisions across local and visiting fans."

Their research noted that "attendance tends to increase at games or matches with uncertain outcomes, and decline at those with more certain outcomes, including when the home team is thought to be very likely to win: the 'tighter' the competition, the larger the attendance."

Based on that research, I contend as the baseball season progresses, the difference between the better and midrange teams grows exponentially and therefore, to the author's point, fans are less inclined to attend games where they expect a team is (tanking, trading players, etc.) likely to lose.

Perhaps obviously, the study tells us something we already assume. However, it also offers a nugget that we might not have otherwise considered: surprisingly, the authors suggest that the opposite is true as well. "A pennant winning team that wins 80 percent of its games will attract fewer patrons than a pennant-winning team that wins 55 percent of its games," said Humphreys and Miceli.

That is seemingly shocking but the authors added, "In each case, consumers of a specific good, live sporting contests make decisions about consuming the good when the actual consumption experience, the game, season-long, or postseason contest, has an uncertain component."

It seems counterintuitive but the authors argue that "according to this hypothesis, fans prefer to attend games in which the outcome is uncertain—that is, the contest itself, independently of fan loyalty to a particular team, is a component of preferences."

"The model includes direct costs of attendance and travel costs, and includes attendance by both local fans and fans of the visiting team. The key insight is to … consider the aggregated preferences of both home and visiting fans for a particular contest," said Humphreys and Miceli.

Solutions

In this section, I will highlight what I believe to be solutions from a number of sources that Major League Baseball should consider as it relates to its lack of fan interest. In fact, every chapter about solutions will directly or indirectly focus on declining fan interest.

In terms of tackling this issue, David Carter, sports business expert, told me that one challenge facing the game is that "MLB has a different view of itself than fans have of it." Some, as you will read later, would say arrogance.

Carter went on to say, "It is time for Major League Baseball to look in the mirror. It won't be pretty but it must be done, and best of all there's hope." The idea here is that MLB rarely is honest about its challenges or actually addresses them.

The Game Is Unwatchable

Recall in chapter 1 that former MLB pitcher Scott Karl said baseball is unwatchable and he is surprisingly disinterested in the game. The good news is that Karl believes the issue is solvable.

"The onus is on the owners and players. It begins with the players. It falls on their shoulders to make the game better," said Karl.

In terms of the game resembling a home run derby and the constant defensive shifts, Karl's message to current players is, "Hit against the shift! Be better, and pitchers, pitch." He admitted that he enjoyed watching the 2019 World Series Championship won by the Washington Nationals because they actually pitched. "Yes, they threw hard [like most major leaguers today] but they hit the corners and pitched well."

Also frustrated with today's game but optimistic is former Cincinnati Reds general manager Wayne Krivsky. "We need to get back to team baseball. The game is beautiful if it's played the right way. The little things, hitting behind the runner—fans appreciate it. It's the beauty of baseball," said Krivsky.

Along those lines, former Kansas City Royals manager Trey Hillman said, "Get back to basics and what is best for the game and what's best for the fan, the players, the owners. Baseball is entertainment. It's show business."

Expand the Playoffs

Thankfully, Major League Baseball made the decision to expand to 12 teams beginning with the 2022 season. Each league now has three division champions and three wild cards. The teams with the two best records in each league receive a first-round bye. The other four clubs play a best-of-three wild-card round. Baseball isn't the first sport to expand the number of teams qualifying for postseason play. It has successfully worked in the NFL and the NBA.

During the 2020 season, shortened due to COVID-19, Major League Baseball expanded the playoff format to include eight teams from each league. The 2020 expanded playoffs consisted of all first- and second-place teams in the six divisions qualifying, with the division winners slotting in as each league's top three seeds. The three second-place teams in each league also qualified, and the seventh and eighth seeds went to the remaining teams in each league with the best records. Tiebreakers were set up so that no additional games were necessary.

The first-round matchups were a best-of-three series with all three games played in the higher seed's ballpark. From there, things picked up as usual, with the division round a best-of-five and the League Championship Series and World Series both best of seven.

In many years numerous teams are out of the race in June, and while MLB has done well by adding the wild card, more of an effort is needed to bring more teams into postseason play. This is definitely something that MLB should consider moving forward. More teams making the playoffs and more teams in contention, without watering down the postseason, will increase fan interest. Any new plan may not go into place until the 2022 season after the new collective bargaining agreement is hopefully ratified.

Some traditionalists might have a problem with this but there is evidence of other leagues, such as the NFL, that have increased their number of playoff teams and have enjoyed success as a result. From the *New York Post*, Joel Sherman (2020) weighed in on this idea. "So if you do not like the playoff format that the commissioner's office is mulling please don't hide behind purity, unless you also think players should stop using mechanical pitching machines because Ruth and Gehrig never had that and players should be forbidden from the best in modern medicine, nutrition and workout regimens because Cy Young never had an option for Tommy John surgery, Willie Mays never had protein powder in his smoothie and Ted Williams never did Pilates."

As Sherman suggests, not surprisingly, the move to add additional teams is driven primarily by money, which is true, but let's also hope that increasing fan interest—which equals more revenue—is also at the heart of this proposal.

Adding Meaning to the Regular Season

A result of deepening the playoff pool is that it will add relevance to a long baseball season and there will be more incentives for teams than just finishing first or playing out the string after clinching a playoff spot.

Sherman asserts that the additional playoff spots may lead to teams spend, which should improve attendance by virtue of more contenders in the mix.

World Series Game Times

This is one issue I am truly passionate about. Earlier I discussed the later start and end times of the World Series and other postseason games.

Major League Baseball should recognize the obvious: that the World Series is the game's moment to shine. It is the league's opportunity to showcase the game, and currently half the nation is asleep or tuned out because their team isn't in it.

I suggest MLB consider a couple of compromises to the idea of moving the game times earlier. One, move the weekend games to a daytime start like the NFL does with some of its playoff games. If you think your product is great, stand by it. Put it up against Saturday afternoon college football or the NFL's regular season. It's the World Series, for goodness' sake. Two, for the weekday games, at least move them one hour earlier to 7:00 p.m. Eastern Time. Two, I shared in this chapter that television ratings are already plummeting, so why not try to make the games more accessible to fans?

Former Angels and Mariners general manager and current MLB executive Bill Bavasi agrees with moving some games to a daytime start. "It seems to me that if you lost some viewership because you played more day games, wouldn't you get more viewership if you had all those kids or people that are watching back east or are not watching currently? More children would have a shot to watch it."

Right. What a concept, ensuring that kids who are the future fans of the game are thought of as important. Building lifelong baseball fans begins at an early age.

Increase Social Media Presence

One area in which Major League Baseball claims to be making progress is in its digital footprint. This is an excellent start to build and sustain fan interest. The suggestion to MLB is to keep pressing, deepen the offerings, and invest more into its digital platform, primarily to target the young Generation Z fans. I will dive deeper into how this generation is consuming Major League Baseball content in chapter 6.

According to Major League Baseball, "Baseball fans are increasing their use of MLB digital products to watch and follow their favorite teams and action across the league. In 2019, MLB.TV, the league's out-of-market streaming service, increased by 15% in paid subscriptions. The MLB At Bat app featured an 18% increase in app starts over last year and surpassed 2 billion starts this year. As a result, MLB digital platforms across mobile and web ranked number one in all of U.S. sports and sports media for Average Minutes Per Visitor from April through August of 2019. In addition, MLB At Bat ranked number one among all U.S. sports and sports media apps in Total Minutes Consumed and Average Minutes Consumed during that same period."

Also encouraging was MLB's first season of exclusive game broadcasts on YouTube and YouTube TV in 2019. This innovative way to reach fans included a 13-game package produced by MLB Network that began after the All-Star Game that season and generated 1.2 million live average views per game.

Salary Cap Proposal

Major League Baseball is the last holdout of the major sports leagues to implement a salary cap. The suggestion here is to strongly consider it, as it could improve fan interest.

Sheryl Ring (2019) of SB Nation suggests, "Every team in Major League Baseball should be required to have a player payroll of not less than $120 million." In other words, a salary floor. It's an interesting idea. Typically, when considering a salary cap, it's the ceiling, not the floor, that garners the most debate. While that is still part of the conversation, the salary floor idea is gaining traction. In fact, the NBA has had a salary floor for years with relative success.

Major league manager Buck Showalter agrees. He told me, "We have a soft cap now with the luxury tax. But we should consider elevating the floor [minimum amount each team should spend]. For example, make it $100 million per year that a team must commit to salaries. The players [MLBPA] would go for that. Right now, for example, the Yankees are paying these clubs and they don't know where the money is going. With the floor that would help with that [accountability]."

After researching the NFL's, NBA's, and NHL's salary floor percentage, Al Yellon (2019) of Bleed Cubbie Blue proposed the NHL's salary floor of 74 percent as a place to start for MLB. He chose 74 percent because that was the lowest salary floor of the other three big sports. "What form a cap should take would, of course, be up to MLB and MLBPA negotiators. Maybe they'd have a hard cap like the NHL, which would appeal to owners wanting cost certainty. In that case I think players would want a floor higher than 74 percent of the cap," said Yellon.

Tanking teams, those who claim to be rebuilding year after year but never seem to really do so, would then be forced to spend more and in theory become more competitive. Players would most likely be on board with this as it would guarantee more money in their pockets. Ring suggests that teams would spend more and win more, and winning is fun and fun brings fans and dollars into the ballpark.

Also, Major League Baseball could reduce tanking, and teams stripping their team down to nothing and becoming an unwatchable product for a few years, by having a draft lottery like the NBA where the worst team isn't guaranteed the number one pick. What a fun television event that would be for baseball. It would definitely generate interest.

Yellon (2019) believes that "baseball needs a salary cap with a salary floor to bring it into line with the other major sports, and to force teams refusing to spend to do so."

Ring's (2019) final take on the subject was, "Every MLB team should be required to spend enough money to field at least a competent team. It's good for the sport, good for the players, good for the fans, and good for the owners in the long run. It's also long overdue."

3

Withering Fan Experience

"Gambling might save baseball."—Wayne Krivsky,
Former Cincinnati General Manager

This chapter focuses on the issue of Major League Baseball's stale and fading fan experience—but more important, what MLB can do to improve it. Recapping our discussion: in chapter 1, we noted that MLB is hemorrhaging fans by the millions in terms of attendance, and in chapter 2, we discussed how fan interest has declined over recent years. The fan experience has not evolved in many ballparks and therefore has contributed to these two overarching issues. For major sports brands, such as professional sports franchises, to foster loyalty among fans, they must consistently deliver a compelling entertainment experience that fans feel vested in. Major League Baseball needs to step up its game in this area.

Throughout this chapter, I will answer what is contributing to this issue and also uncover some solutions that may seem unconventional at first glance but I believe have the potential to positively impact the in-venue and out-of-venue fan experience for MLB diehard and casual fans alike.

In many Major League Baseball ballparks, teams continue to roll out the same tired promotions in hopes of attracting fans. This is not a successful strategy for improving the fan experience, and if I see one more bobblehead, I'm going to lose it. Teams are resting on the assumption that the game itself will be the experience, and as we will see, that's not the case.

However, there is good news in that some MLB teams are providing their fans with an outstanding experience and are exemplars. These teams continue to evolve and innovate, and their best practices have a track record of success.

In this chapter, we will learn what those teams are doing to provide a great experience that can be replicated throughout the league. First, these MLB teams have listened to their fans, much like retailers listen to their customers. The input from fans focused on in-venue spending, which encompasses the whole fan experience, including tickets, transportation, parking, food, beverages, and, as we will see soon, even more.

As for that in-venue experience, Zachary Rymer (2020) of Bleacher Report suggests, "Stadiums must ultimately be judged on the experience they provide for fans. Location and accessibility matter, as do the park's aesthetics. Further, it definitely doesn't hurt if a stadium offers fun activities and tasty food and drinks."

It is apparent that fan attendance is essential for organizational growth due to the revenue teams generate through ticket sales. Major League Baseball teams should be driven to attract as many fans as possible to purchase game tickets or their products. Davis and Miller (2019) conducted another study pertaining to Major League Baseball's attendance. This article, "A Fan's Choice: An Application of the Theory of Consumer Choice to Major League Baseball," provides a foundation for Major League Baseball teams to gain insights into the reasons (and choices) their fans consider for attending games.

The study cites research that, not surprisingly, supports the notion that Major League Baseball teams need to be able to produce results on the field or they will not attract fans to the park, which may lead to the failure of the team.

One club, the Tampa Bay Rays, while enjoying success on the field, has struggled bringing in fans through the turnstiles at their home park—Tropicana Field. In 2021, the Rays' attendance average was a dismal 9,396, which ranked 28th of 30 MLB franchises.

As a result, they proposed a unique solution. Riding the momentum of the desire to bring Major League Baseball back to Montreal, they had planned to split their home schedule with the Canadian city.

One team in two cities was an innovative and creative suggestion. However, the idea was scrapped by Major League Baseball officials in early 2022. Rays owner Stuart Sternberg called it "flat-out deflating" (Gonzales, 2022).

Alden Gonzales (2022) of ESPN added, "Rays officials had spent 2½ years hyperfocused on what was called a 'sister city' proposal, believing it to be the best path toward increasing revenue without permanently relocating the franchise. Now they must pivot, either by revisiting Tampa Bay-area-stadium talks that had previously stalled or by exploring a new city altogether."

The Davis and Miller (2019) study found that winning percentage had a significantly positive relationship with attendance. Moreover, batting average and runs scored also had a significantly positive relationship with attendance as a percentage of capacity. This suggests that while it is obvious that fans want to see a winning product, they will also turn out for a winning team that puts up strong offensive numbers. Apparently, a corollary to the old adage that pitching and defense wins championships is that a well-built offensive team will mostly lead to an increase in attendance.

However, they did find research to support that "outstanding pitchers boosted attendance at MLB games by 8%–9% representing an additional 2,000 to 2,500 fans per game." This I can relate to as a youngster attending California Angels games in the 1970s. While the team was often at the bottom of the standings, when future Hall of Famer Nolan Ryan took the mound, the Big A saw consistent near-capacity crowds. Forty-plus years later, similar phenomenon still rings true.

For the MLB teams that are excelling on the field but seeing a decrease in attendance, it speaks to the need to adapt the ballpark experience. There needs to be an experiential experience for the fan. An experiential marketing campaign increases brand loyalty by forging an emotional relationship between a brand and its customers. Unfortunately, many teams are failing to make that connection. The focus puts the needs of the customer first. What does a customer want from a brand as opposed to what a brand wants from a customer (Trade Group, 2022)?

The goal for MLB should be to create an impression on fans, to convey the importance of the fan experience through actual tactile measures, and to cement that brand loyalty. This has been a challenge for Major League Baseball. After all, going to a game is already an experience. However, baseball fans have come to expect much more than just a competition between two teams when they head out to a ballpark (Trade Group, 2022).

Creating an experiential activation around the sport, whether at an actual game or not, can help MLB connect with fans and potential customers (Trade Group, 2022). The only way Major League Baseball and its teams will be able to reach consumers is knowing what appeals to them and what their needs are.

Experiential Marketing at Sporting Events

One example of an experiential experience began in 2021 when Major League Baseball paid tribute to the film *Field of Dreams* by holding a game on the field where the classic movie was shot in Dyersville, Iowa. Now an every-year occurrence, the game is played on a temporary 8,000-seat ballpark built exclusively for the event. In fact, attendees of the "Field of Dreams Game" reach the contest by walking along a pathway through the cornfield. It is the biggest experiential activation by the MLB to date (Trade Group, 2022).

Trade Group also said that MLB "is not alone in scheduling unconventional games to generate interest and boost attendance. Since 2008, the National Hockey League has held 'The Winter Classic,' a regular-season game that's played outside on a rink set up in a football or baseball stadium (the 2014 event set a new NHL attendance record of 105,491). Also, since 2008, the National Football League has taken its show on the road with a series of international games held primarily in Mexico and London."

The *Field of Dreams* game, while not being played at one of the 30 major league ballparks, is undoubtedly a step in the right direction in creating an innovative fan experience that will most likely increase interest in the sport.

Option Overload

Undoubtedly, the competition for sports fans' attention is at an all-time high. Maury Brown (2019) of *Forbes* suggests one issue impacting attendance and the in-venue experience is the bottomless entertainment options that threatens the game externally. He calls it the "option overload" factor.

"With thousands of channels on television, streaming services like Netflix and Hulu, gaming platforms, and mobile devices, the ability to retain interest is hyper competitive," said Brown.

Baseball is losing the fight for the customer's attention and dollars as well. As Chris Hine (2020) of the *Minneapolis Star Tribune* wrote, "Sports are in a dogfight, competing for your time and money. From television to digital streaming to other competition for consumers' interest, the context on why interest is up or down can be complex. Certainly, attendance of live sporting events is part of the entertainment landscape, and how the game fared at the gate has been a hot topic of discussion."

Mark Hyman, veteran journalist, professor, author, and lawyer, says that the television experience keeps getting better and therefore reduces the incentive to attend games in person. "Fans are paying $150 to attend one game in person but on television the product is superior. There is Pitch Tracker and the K zone. There is also a graphic showing how far the runner is off first base with their lead and the data on their stolen base success rate. The access to information [on television] is excellent," said Hyman.

Hyman, who covered the Orioles for the *Baltimore Sun* for decades, added, "The challenge is for MLB teams to market the in-game experience. I suggest adding some of those to the venue." I couldn't agree more. The ballparks that provide a plethora of information—for example,

Milwaukee—connect that data to the game and make it more meaningful and engaging. Another suggestion would be to add an in-venue app so fans could track all of that data right on their devices, which some might pay more attention to than the game itself.

While the game on television has improved greatly over the past decade or two, the in-person experience is what draws fans.

"Each game I've been to is its own memory—what great players I saw, who won the game, where I was in my life at that time, and, most important, who I went to the game with," said Will Leitch (2018) of *New York Magazine*'s *Intelligencer*.

He continued, "Getting out to the ballpark is the foundation of this … [and] the reason we care in the first place. Teams and leagues might not think they have to worry right now about the fact that fewer people are doing that than they have in recent years. But they should probably start."

David Carter, sports business guru, suggests, "The venue experience [for MLB] needs to become more contemporary. Younger and hipper make sense. Teams are adding craft beers perhaps aimed at the 40-something fan. Right now, the MLB game is uneventful. It's not cool."

Compounding this issue, says Emily Cosler (2020) in her research paper from the Marketing Department of Texas Christian University, titled "An Analysis of the Decline in MLB Stadium Attendance and the Marketing Techniques That Can Be Utilized to Reverse It," is that Major League Baseball competes daily with a multitude of competitors.

She contends, "This number will only continue to rise as consumers demand additional options. With a premium price tag, MLB games should be advertised as a superior product to other options. With a chance to be outdoors, socialize with friends, watch athletes with unmatched abilities, eat incredible food, and enjoy hundreds of drink options, baseball games check the majority of boxes consumers are asking for."

Interestingly, Cosler asserts that Major League Baseball games uniquely combine many "of the other options available into one package, but they are not always seen this way. Often, games are advertised for the baseball aspect alone, but updated stadiums have changed this. One can argue that those who dislike baseball can still enjoy themselves at an MLB game because of the diverse offerings the stadium brings."

Specifically, she points to the examples of Chase Field, the home of the Arizona Diamondbacks, which has a pool in right field; Yankee Stadium, which has a museum highlighting its storied history; and the Tampa Bay Rays' Tropicana Field, which offers fans the opportunity to pet live stingrays as ways to draw in additional fans above and beyond the game on the field.

"With restaurants, bars, live music, and also a baseball game happening all in one place, teams need to advertise the offerings they have outside of the game itself. Recommendations include spotlighting unique food offerings, selling cheap standing room tickets that give access to the amenities within the stadium, and using the ballpark for team sponsored events outside of game days," recommends Cosler.

Fan Experience Exemplars

Bird Land—a Case Study

Orioles Park at Camden Yards— Baltimore Orioles

At the top of most fan experience polls and surveys, you'll typically see the Baltimore Orioles and Orioles Park at Camden Yards as the benchmark for providing an outstanding fan experience. What are the best practices that makes the Charm City's team the one to emulate? Considering that the answers to that question are numerous, the Orioles and their success are worthy of a deep dive.

I spoke with Greg Bader, the Orioles' senior vice president, administration and experience, who said the Orioles are "committed to providing the most family-friendly experience in Major League Baseball." With that as the team's foundation, he was able to provide some insight into how the O's breathe life into their mission.

What Makes OPCY Different?

Camden Yards is without question one of the jewels of the league. Even though the ballpark opened in 1992, it still holds up as a must-see for any baseball fan and it's the stadium other teams have strived to emulate.

"Oriole Park at Camden Yards is a tremendous ballpark and what it stands for. What it means to baseball cannot be understated," said Bader.

The community interacts with the ballpark in a downtown area that has been revitalized. It creates a closeness common to ballparks in the 1940s and 1950s. Bader said, "In our ballpark, there is a connection between the player and fan. It also has more amenities. For example, there are areas to socialize. It appeals to the diehard fan who is there to see every pitch and it appeals to the casual fan who is there to create a memory."

He continued, "The ballpark is beautiful as it has the warehouse and skyline. We also offer diverse food offerings, shorter lines, affordability, and diverse music. We focus on the experience. We want the fan to enjoy every aspect, in a safe, family-friendly stadium. We want them to feel their money was well-spent and Baltimore in the summer, there's no better place to be."

Business Administration and Baseball Operations Relationship

Throughout the research for this project, the concept of the importance of a solid relationship in a Major League Baseball team's front office between the business side of the house and the baseball operations side was considered paramount for success. If both sides work with synergy, a great deal can be accomplished.

Bader agrees that this relationship is critically important, and in Baltimore, they have a model of success. "In 2019," he said, "we went through a restructuring of the organization with five positions. A senior leadership team was established including Mike Elias, the team's executive vice president and general manager. This brought the baseball ops and business admin together. The result is that our communication has been streamlined. Then Michael can sell that to the players by sharing with them what we are doing. It works both ways. It is true that our fans want more authenticity and open communication," and the Orioles' restructuring has led to that.

Digital Voice

Later in this book, I will discuss the importance of Major League Baseball and its teams having a strong social media platform. This is considered an off-venue component of the fan experience and is a contemporary vehicle to successfully engage with the fanbase. The Orioles recognize this and are constantly retooling theirs.

Bader said the team has made a concerted effort "to revamp and deepen our digital voice. We have done a better job centralizing our dialogue through Twitter, Instagram, Facebook, and YouTube. These are real ways to engage with our fans. Our social platforms are authentic, real, fun, and created by people doing creative things. It is clearly not corporate. No matter where you are, you can experience Bird Land. They can take their fandom anywhere."

O's at Home

The COVID-19 pandemic was a tipping point for many sports teams in terms of marketing and connecting the games, which fans couldn't attend in person, and team information to their fans. The Orioles were no different.

"The challenge [during the pandemic] was what to do to engage with our fans and our fans to feel connected to the team. As a result, we established O's at Home, which allowed the fans to watch the games on television and feel connected through different avenues," said Bader.

The O's at Home was an innovative way to create unique content for your Orioles baseball viewing experience. Fans download the Ballpark app and enable push notifications so they can participate in exclusive offers and earn points toward experiences including live look-ins and a sneak peek at batting practice and meet and greets with players (Orioles.com, 2022). Improvements Coming

For decades the Orioles have received accolades and high marks in fan experience surveys. One would think the Orioles have found the secret sauce and can rest easy. Not true. Bader and his team are not complacent. Instead, he sees the next phase of what Orioles Park at Camden Yards will look like.

"We need more social spaces to allow for our Generation Z fans to connect with the team and each other. We don't expect Gen Z fans to sit and stay in the same location for multiple hours. We want to provide them the opportunity to be mobile with different places of interest showcased through social media. Our plan is to create an environment with more of those spaces," said Bader. For example, the upgrades include an upper-level bar that is more casual and a high-end bar in another location, both providing the fan a unique angle of the game, as Bader says, "to create mini moments."

Interestingly, the idea of creating more social spaces is one teams should consider and one the commissioner has touted as well. Commissioner Manfred said stadiums are beginning to create more social spaces for fans to congregate and experience the game atmosphere without being glued to their seats for nine innings.

I agree with Bader when he says today's younger fans are not hanging on every pitch. It's about being a part of the crowd. These days people like to feel like they belong to something. More on this in chapter 6.

Game Times

In an effort to draw more fans, the Orioles have also planned to start some games earlier, which is another strategy teams should implement. The Orioles shifted home game times to 6:35 p.m. for all weeknight games prior to Memorial Day and after Labor Day. The earlier start time allows families with children to enjoy more games on school nights.

Once again, the fans weighed in and their voices were heard. "The earlier start time for select weekday games is based upon extensive feedback from our fanbase as we continue to explore efforts that can enhance the Oriole Park experience for families, children, and fans of all ages," said Bader.

The New York Yankees, Cincinnati Reds, San Diego Padres, and Los Angeles Angels have also shifted some home games to earlier starts such as 6:35 p.m. and 6:40 p.m. local time. They join several others, including Arizona, Milwaukee, Cleveland, and Colorado, that have experimented with early start times and are developing plans for similar efforts for seasons moving forward.

Eric Fisher (2017), of the *New York Business Journal*, explained that "executives with several of the involved clubs said the moves were a result of fan opinion, attendance data, and other analytics. The Yankees will start seven weekday home games in April, games likely to be among the club's lowest draws of the entire season, at 6:35 p.m. … in a move to improve the fan experience."

"We did a lot of surveying and looked at our turnstile data, and found that our fans … were coming earlier and leaving earlier," Karen Forgus, senior vice president of business operations for the Reds, told the *New York Business Journal*.

Along with earlier game times, the Orioles continue to offer many popular family- and kid-oriented initiatives. Kids Cheer Free allows parents to bring children ages nine and younger to the ballpark free of charge with the purchase of a regularly priced upper-deck ticket. Oriole Park at Camden Yards also features the Kids' Corner, an activity area for children of all ages, and a variety of specially sized and priced concessions items, along with one of the most flexible food and beverage policies in professional sports (Orioles.com, 2022).

Honorable Mention

In addition to the Orioles, other teams are providing fans an engaging experience. Each of these ballparks is unique and offers something different to those who visit them, and they deserve some recognition.

Petco Park—San Diego Padres

One of my favorite stadiums to visit is Petco Park, home of the San Diego Padres. From my house to home plate was a 75-mile drive, and worth it even in Southern California traffic. The stadium sits in the East

Village area of downtown next to the iconic Gaslamp Quarter, which is essentially the heart of San Diego's nightlife scene. The ballpark is gorgeous and incredibly family-friendly. My children practically grew up in Petco's Park in the Park. I fell in love with the area and later moved next to Petco Park. That 75-mile drive was reduced to a three-minute walk!

"Located outside the outfield wall but inside the Petco gates, the Park at the Park is a grassy area of approximately 2.7 acres. It contains a mini little league infield diamond, trees, a statue of Tony Gwynn, and lots of area to sprawl out to picnic and play," said Petco Park Insider. Bring your blanket and watch the game from the grass and enjoy the vibe.

Another feature of the ballpark is that it allows fans easy access to a number of social areas with great sightlines. For example, Petco Park is basically built around the Western Metal Supply Company building. The building is actually part of the stadium and has a luxury-box level, another level with a bar overlooking the field, and a rooftop experience—all providing great views of the game and the city.

"Petco Park itself, meanwhile, boasts one of the more fan-friendly seat maps in the majors, and the field isn't the only thing that draws one's eyes. Want something to eat? Well, Petco Park probably has whatever it is you're craving. And if it's your whistle that needs wetting, The park's craft beer selection is one of the best in the National League," said Rymer (2020).

Oracle Park—San Francisco Giants

Also a favorite ballpark of mine, and others as well, is Oracle Park, home of the San Francisco Giants since 2000. Oracle Park is located in the South Beach neighborhood of San Francisco. Oracle Park is an excellent place to watch a baseball game. The stadium offers gorgeous views of the San Francisco Bay and China Basin, which sits alongside McCovey Cove.

Oracle Park is one that every baseball fan should see, Ballparks of Baseball (2022) agrees. "Of the 30 ballparks in Major League Baseball, that should be on every baseball fan's bucket list. Oracle Park's charm, character and breathtaking views can only be rivaled by few other ballparks in the country."

Rymer (2020) also rates Oracle high. "There isn't a bad seat in the house, and the park itself is marked by its marvelous architecture, wondrous views and quirks. It's also a good idea to arrive at Oracle Park with an empty stomach. You're going to want to fill it with some of the park's outstanding food—Gilroy Garlic Fries!—and maybe one or two of its many beers," reported Rymer.

PNC—Pittsburgh Pirates

A lot of what makes PNC Park, home of the Pittsburgh Pirates since 2001, such a great ballpark is the Roberto Clemente Bridge and the Allegheny River just beyond the outfield, and beyond that is an entirely unobstructed view of downtown Pittsburgh (Rymer, 2020). The reviews of PNC are unanimous.

"Inside PNC Park, Pirates fans are treated to captivating retro design. This ... is the Holy Grail of ballpark views," said Rymer.

Ballparks of Baseball (2022) said, "Whether you walk across the Roberto Clemente Bridge from downtown Pittsburgh entering the ballpark through the outfield entrances or enter at the home plate entrance, PNC Park looks like a classic ballpark from a bygone era."

Said Baseball Pilgrimages (2022): "With the city's buildings, rivers, and bridges starring as the perfect backdrop, PNC doesn't disappoint upon entrance. The unique rotunda in left field is a great place to catch a few innings, while the world-famous Primanti Brothers have concessions on each level."

Rymer adds, "It also helps PNC Park's cause that attending fans are charged neither an arm nor a leg. The Fan Cost Index put the average cost for a group of four during the 2019 season at just $182.42. That was the fourth-lowest mark in the majors."

Sports Betting

In researching for this project, I was surprised in particular by one possible solution to improving the fan experience and, in turn, increasing attendance and interest in the game: sports betting. This unconventional idea has tremendous potential to improve the fan experience both in-venue and out of venue and, as we will see, has the support of Major League Baseball.

The Arizona Diamondbacks now have Caesars Palace Sports Book. I was in attendance for their grand opening and, while you would not confuse it with a Las Vegas sportsbook, it does provide numerous amenities, such as every game being displayed on televisions throughout the two-story property, upscale decor, a fine menu, and a 30-second walk to Chase Field.

Wrigley Field, home to the Chicago Cubs, also received approval to build a two-story sportsbook on its premises.

As baseball writer Craig Calcaterra told me, even before these retail sportsbooks began springing up in arenas, they had already made a financial impact on the game. "These gambling deals that they're making with casinos, I mean, if you're the house—and increasingly teams and Major League Baseball are the house—you make money no matter what the outcome is. There has been an explosion in those kinds of business partnerships with Major League Baseball since Rob Manfred took over," said Calcaterra.

One of the most well-respected authorities on the subject is Mike Palm, the vice president of operations for The Circa, The D, and Golden Gate Casinos in Las Vegas, Nevada, and also a regular host on the Vegas Information Sports Network (ViSN).

While sports betting is not legal in every state across America, Palm told me it's coming. "It is funny how the big states are struggling with it [legalizing sports betting]. There are some roadblocks, but eventually we will get there. In about three or four years we will see over 42 states with legalized sports betting," said Palm.

Palm suggests the perception of sports gambling has changed, and the activity is now a part of society and a growing component of the sports business. "Sports betting creates an increased level of fan interest because of the financial component and it helps all sports," said Palm.

When asked how sports betting could improve the fan experience, Palm said to look at mobile betting options. "This idea benefits the in-venue game experience. For example, fans will stick around when it's a 9–2 blowout in the fifth inning because they may have bet the totals [the combined number of runs scored. It keeps them in their seats," said Palm. He reasons that with money wagered on the game until its conclusion, fans will not leave the stadium as early and this would increase sales of concessions and merchandise.

Hibai Lopez-Gonzalez and Mark Griffiths (2018) wrote a paper for the *International Review for the Sociology of Sport* titled "Understanding the Convergence of Markets in Online Sports Betting" in which they suggest that the online sports betting industry is a solid and rapidly growing sector of the global economy.

The reasoning, according to Lopez-Gonzales and Griffiths: "The proliferation of online sports betting has run in parallel to at least four cultural converging processes, namely the development of constantly available, ubiquitous and affordable personal communication technologies, especially mobile devices."

They added, "The business of betting has moved irreversibly into mobile platforms. Many major operators have noted in their annual reports the unprecedented prevalence of mobile betting over other forms of access," which relates to the idea that baseball fans can make wagers in real-time, at the ballpark itself.

They add that "in-venue betting operators have proactively reacted to such technological innovation by expanding its online betting functionalities. Likewise, the in-stadium gambling experience has also gone digital."

The authors make the point that it "situates live in-play betting at the heart of the betting experience and further facilitates the interactions between mediated sports consumption and wagering. The picture it arguably portrays is that of a fan who bets on sports while watching it live on television (or in person) or streaming it online. In just a few years, in-play betting has arguably become the preferred way of placing a bet among most types of sports gambler.

"For online sports betting to become a prominent cultural artifact, journalism will have to play a big part in spreading and normalizing it. A number of examples illustrate the extent of the normalization of betting in everyday sports media."

This is already occurring as fans have seen an increase in more analytical statistics than previously imagined. In addition, depending on the network, on-screen statistics and betting odds of all sports—but increasingly Major League Baseball—have become commonplace. The Chicago White Sox, for instance, air the current odds to win the World Series during every broadcast. No one would have believed this would occur even a few years ago, but it is now endorsed by Major League Baseball.

Also, in 2022, baseball television viewers saw Apple TV+ join in the airing of Major League Baseball games. They offered an engaging component—live, real-time stats in the lower right of the screen that had not been seen before. For example, when a batter is at the plate, the viewer can see in real-time that as the count changes, so do the odds of the batter driving in a run or striking out. Also, NBC Chicago displays not only the velocity of the pitch but also what type of pitch was thrown.

However, not everyone is a fan of this shift. World Series champion Manager Joe Maddon told me that the increased use of analytics leads to a decrease in emotion.

He said, "Gambling has led to less competitiveness and a subtraction of passion because it is all about the data."

The National Basketball Association jumped on this in 2019. The NBA and William Hill, one of America's leading sportsbook operators, announced a new partnership that made William Hill an authorized sports betting operator of the league. As part of the agreement, William Hill has the right to use official NBA betting data and league marks across its mobile platforms and in its sportsbooks throughout the United States (NBA Communications, 2019).

Additionally, the NFL and NHL all have teams that have partnered with sportsbook operators through similar marketing deals. The Denver

Broncos were the first NFL team to sign with a sportsbook company, in 2020.

As for Major League Baseball and its future with sports betting, Palm believes Commissioner Manfred sees it as another revenue stream and it appears the Detroit Tigers are the first in the pool. In 2020, the Tigers became the first Major League Baseball team to sign a sportsbook deal when they paired up with PointsBet, signing a multiyear agreement to be the official gaming partner of the Detroit Tigers.

According to Matthew Waters (2020) of Legalsports.com, PointsBet is "the first sportsbook to land a Major League Baseball team sponsorship. The exclusive agreement includes in-stadium signage visible on TV, including on the primary scoreboard and the right-field wall at Comerica Park. The brand will be visible on the team's digital platforms as well as the Detroit Tigers and MLB Ballpark apps." Online sports betting in Michigan became legal in 2020.

Interestingly, it appears MLB is on board as well. Waters said, "PointsBet also agreed with the MLB to be an authorized gaming operator. That lets the sports betting operator use official MLB data and trademarks within its sportsbook."

Korea Baseball Organization

Here's an unconventional place to look for solutions to the challenge of building a better fan experience: Korea. Baseball in Korea is akin to religion, so why not take a page from the Korea Baseball Organization (KBO) and turn the MLB fan experience into what makes the KBO fan experience one to emulate—the game as an event. The KBO in-venue experience is second to none.

Many of us were introduced to the KBO during the spring of 2020 when Major League Baseball was on hiatus during the COVID-19 pandemic. While the MLB season was silent, the KBO was a lifeline for those of us starved for baseball. It didn't matter that there weren't any fans in the stands. No one cared. There was baseball on television, and while it wasn't to Major League standards, it was professional baseball.

What makes the KBO unique is the fan experience inside the ballpark. Jeeho Yoo of Yonhap News Agency told me, "The fan experience is vastly different compared to the major leagues. From the first pitch to the final out there is constant cheering, singing, dancing, and chanting the players' names. It seems that the KBO fans relate to the players and they have a bit of a connection with them because of their walk-up songs."

Leander Schaerlaeckens (2020) of Yahoo Sports said, "Each player doesn't merely pick his own walk-up song—no no. Special theme songs are composed for them and they're amazing. The atmosphere, above all else, is generated by the crowd itself, rather than being orchestrated by a PA system as spectators are tamely shepherded through whatever fan engagement is expected of them."

Yoo added, "Teams have their cheering squad on the stage, which is the dugout, and lead the fans in song and dance. The fans learn the lyrics to the players' songs and dance moves, the rhythm of the clapping. All of this builds a connection with the players. This is going on from start to finish."

As one KBO fan said, "No matter who's playing, it's the most fun you can have at a ballgame."

An expatriate and university professor added, "MLB is like an opera. KBO is rock and roll."

Mark Lippert, U.S. ambassador to South Korea and a huge baseball and KBO fan, sums up the experience as "KBO is where baseball meets college football."

Trey Hillman, former Kansas City Royals and former KBO championship-winning manager, told me the KBO fan experience is incredible and Major League Baseball could learn from it. "MLB should consider more music. I am a big advocate for it. Every player has a song for them and the cheerleaders are on the dugouts. It's an engaging fan experience especially for kids because they aren't going to watch the entire game," said Hillman.

What is also interesting is that the KBO caters to the casual fan as well and no one leaves early. Yoo said, "They do not leave early to beat the traffic. Even in a blowout. They are there until the final out." MLB teams would love to see their fanbase stay to the end of the game, which would increase concession sales all while fans are having a great time.

"Many casual fans go to the games for just that experience," said Yoo. "They have a blast singing and dancing with other fans working off their stress from their workday. Going to a KBO game is a great excuse to have some fun on relatively cheap beers. Their concessions are cheap compared to the local restaurants or bars. You can even bring in your own food. You can actually grill food in some of the ballparks in the outfield," said Yoo.

The KBO games offer an exciting atmosphere for all types of fans. "There are some people who go to the games and perhaps they are in the outfield or upper deck and not paying that much attention to the game but they enjoy the time with their family or coworkers. They have a good time because there is constant music playing and it is kind of raucous. It is like an outdoor club but it is a lot less expensive," said Yoo.

The KBO didn't always enjoy this type of success. Like today's Major League Baseball issue of plummeting attendance, the KBO was having its own struggles to draw fans around 2002. KBO executives knew a retooling was needed in order to save the league. They focused on improving the in-venue experience for fans, and the games became more of an event.

Yoo shared what also happened. "Some games drew less than a thousand fans per game. Then, a couple of years later individual teams began to market toward women to increase the fanbase," said Yoo.

The strategy paid off. "Women started coming to the games and bringing their boyfriends or husbands. There were a lot of female fans who took up an interest in the KBO and you'll find many female fans at the KBO games to this day," said Yoo.

More Lessons Learned from the Minors

Earlier I shared the strategies that make Minor League Baseball the king of baseball fan experience. Their formula is successful and uncomplicated: create a safe, affordable, fun family atmosphere and they will come. What it boils down to is innovation. Innovation and creativity drive fan interest and keep them coming back for more.

I spoke with Jeff Lantz, senior director of communication for Minor League Baseball, who said, "Minor League Baseball employees are some of the most creative people in sports and there's a constant flow of ideas coming through." They have the evidence—41 million fans in 2019—to back that up. Minor league attendance is on the rise while MLB's is plummeting.

Former MLB general manager Bill Bavasi, who is part of one of the first families in baseball history, knows this firsthand. "The minor leagues do a better job of promoting the game than we do because they always have to promote the game and not players because they don't know what players they are going to get. But somebody's watching the players, so they have to promote the game itself and they promote how fun the ballpark is."

It bears repeating: Minor League Baseball is known for customer service and customer needs, which are paramount for a successful fan experience. Also, chief among those factors are promotions, with numerous studies showing that giveaways and sponsored off-the-field activities at games can increase gate receipts (Langhorst, 2014).

Fans are drawn to their minor league team to watch the people, eat good food, drink, be around friends, feel a sense of belonging, and to watch the sports contest. The fans expect to enjoy themselves in a fun, clean, and hassle-free environment (Langhorst).

Innovative Ticket Options

As I also discussed in chapter 1, fans can now binge-watch their favorite team live and in person—if their team offers a ticket subscription service, that is. Offering this option to fans definitely provides an innovative experience for fans.

As Chris Giles, the Oakland A's chief operating officer, told Jim Tierney (2019) of Clarus Commerce, "Baseball is at a crossroads as far as what fans are looking for in their experience." He said that going to 81 games a year is a massive commitment for someone who wants to buy a season ticket, and many fans are seeking more practical alternatives.

Robbie Kellman Baxter, a customer loyalty expert who created the popular business term "membership economy," told Tierney (2019) the trajectory of the subscription loyalty model is a winner.

"Subscription services are exploding now, and technology is enabling it," she explained. "Companies love subscription models for recurring revenue…. Subscription services are also appealing to consumers, who appreciate the value of being packaged differently."

Solutions

In short, let's recap the solutions to improving the fan experience. You're on the clock, MLB.

Davis and Miller (2019) suggest that fan attendance "is essential for organizational growth due to the revenue it generates. Due to such reliance on a team's ability to draw a crowd to its home games, it is only reasonable for professional baseball organizations to understand the relationship between attendance and any variables that may affect attendance to their fullest ability."

Davis (2009) further contended that "an above average team that was 20 games over a .500 win-loss record could improve home attendance by an estimated 15,200 spectators."

Also, Davis cites Glass (2003), "who indicated that when a team increased its win-loss record by a 16 wins per season, attendance also increased by an average of 6,347 fans per game," and Domazlicky and Kerr (1990), who "stated that an increase of one run per game, particularly in the American League due to the designated hitter rule, related to an additional attendance of slightly more than 2,200 spectators per game."

It could also be assumed that an increase in offense could be perceived as being more exciting and engaging to fans, thereby providing a crucial reason for increased attendance.

In short, to drive attendance, Major League Baseball should be striving to put competitive teams on the field that are offensively strong.

Another solution, offered by Cosler (2020): "Movie on the field, anyone? Group workouts up and down the stadium seats? How about watch parties for the city's other professional or college sports teams? MLB teams have done these events successfully and continue to build team loyalty and enthusiasm."

Let's Go, O's

Just as the Orioles have done in their ballpark, MLB teams need to create more social spaces for fans with views of the game and city. In addition, the O's have focused on providing an affordable, safe, family-friendly experience for their fans.

Earlier Game Times

With games dragging on sometimes well past three hours, it is a tough ask to expect fans to come to a game that starts after 7:00 p.m. and ends after 10:00 p.m.—especially on weeknights. Simply put, start games no later than 6:40 p.m.

Digital Voice

Again, the Orioles seem to be the clubhouse leader in this area of fan experience. For example, they have seen success with O's at Home. Other teams are creating a digital voice to connect with their fanbase. As stated earlier, I suggest an in-venue app for fans to track stats in real time. Also, it is important for teams to keep in mind that the fan experience away from the ballpark is just as important as the one inside.

Sports Betting

Sports betting has become legal in numerous states and, with MLB's support, clearly acceptable in American culture. Teams should do as the Tigers have done and embrace sports betting and, better yet, increase their marketing revenue by creating a partnership with one of the sports betting entities.

KBO

I am not sure where you stand, but after researching and watching the KBO, I suggest a trip to Korea should be on a baseball fan's bucket list. Isn't that idea of moving from opera to rock and roll appealing? MLB teams should consider having real cheer squads leading the fans in cheering and song. Sounds like a blast.

Ticket Options

Again, offering fans innovative ticket options such as the subscription model is working, with over one million sold in 2019. This is low-hanging fruit, MLB teams—create your ticket subscriptions. Your fans want it and it will be successful.

4

Pace of Play

> *"I can't watch these games anymore. It's not baseball. It's unwatchable. A lot of the strategy of the game, the beauty of the game, it's all gone."*
> —Goose Gossage, Hall of Fame Pitcher

In an HBO *Real Sports*/Marist Poll (2015), 40 percent of respondents said they believed the length of a Major League Baseball game has something to do with why children don't gravitate toward the sport. The game has gotten progressively longer over time, and as games consistently average over three hours, younger fans are turning away. Currently, it is nearly impossible to contain a game within a three-hour television-friendly window.

According to Gabe Stutman (2016) of Vice, "Pace of play efforts have been a top priority of Commissioner Robert Manfred's administration. Quicker baseball games became an official priority for the league when Manfred's predecessor, Bud Selig, created a committee to study the issue in 2014."

"I hate the phrase 'pace of play,'" said Jay Jaffe of FanGraphs. "But pace of play is probably the shorthand that works. It just has to do with more pace of action is more what I would say. You [fans] want more action. The lack of action in the game, whether it's because of the delay between pitches or because of the dearth of balls in play, I think all of those things lend themselves to a growing disinterest."

To Jaffe's point, what does the pace of play actually refer to? We often equate the pace of play with time—the length of a game. The typical hallmark is anything over three hours is considered too long. I suggest that is the wrong way to define pace of play. Does it really matter how long the game is? Pace should equate to the action, the excitement, and the fans' level of engagement in the game. The issue is certainly polarizing as there are passionate opinions about the attempted and proposed initiatives of Major League Baseball to overcome this issue.

Andrew Billings, a professor and director of the University of Alabama Program in Sports Communication, told Cameron Easley (2018) of the Morning Consult in his piece "Past Time for the Pastimes? NFL and MLB Lose Ground with Gen Z—NBA and MLS are growing in popularity," "It's not just the length of the game, but the length you can count on. While fans can reasonably expect basketball and soccer contests to clock in at around two hours, the length of baseball games are fickle."

Craig Calcaterra told me, "I think to the extent we need changes and to the extent we can, to use your term, find a solution for some of these problems [impacting the game], it's tied up in the timing and the pace of the game and how long between pitches and things like that. That is where I think the real substantive work needs to be done. I think it would address so many of the sorts of criticisms about the game being boring. Because baseball can be boring."

Baseball, from a fan's perspective, does not move along, but of course those who play, coach, and manage may disagree because baseball is a fun game to play and coach, so to them the game moves along just fine.

However, former major league pitcher Scott Karl falls into the Goose Gossage camp. Karl said simply, "The game is boring."

Rob Flippo, the Miami Marlins bullpen coordinator, told me, "There are long commercial breaks throughout the game. Sitting for nearly four hours, well, it's tough to be engaged. If we get a three-hour game, that's a great day."

In my interview with Buck Showalter, he said, "When I was managing the Orioles, we were on a charter flight heading west around 3:00 a.m. after a game. I was watching an old game from the 1970s. My pitching coach was sitting across from me and he was also watching the same game. I asked him, 'What's different between today's game and the game we are watching from the 1970s?' It was clear. The players played faster."

Showalter summed up the pace-of-play issue by stating, "We have lost the rhythm and tempo of our game."

I had the chance to visit with major league manager Joe Maddon, who added, "The game is now based on efficiency, which is awful to watch. There's no art in baseball, all at the expense of data."

A prominent network play-by-play announcer told me, "Old-school and some new-school players, executives, and scouts say the fans don't care about the length of the game. That's clearly a disconnect and they are not watching the metrics. MLB is not doing something right. We [the networks] see a decline."

Not all of this has fallen on deaf ears. In 2019, Major League Baseball commissioner Rob Manfred made a spring training swing through Arizona and he acknowledged pace of play is one trend that the league watches carefully. "We're thinking we can make small changes in what is still the greatest game in the world," Manfred told reporters, "in order to make our entertainment product more competitive" (Goldman, 2019).

Representing the other side is Los Angeles Dodgers All-Star third baseman Justin Turner. On the pace-of-play argument, he told me, "It's a gimmick about local and network television contacts. They pay for a three-hour window. If the game is faster by like twenty minutes, more fans won't come. It's a load of crap. It's about the quality of play—the game."

To Turner's point, will a game that is a few minutes shorter really bring in more fans? If so, how many minutes? He feels it's the product, the game itself, that matters most and those who are baseball fans don't care if the game is over three hours.

With the length of games, like in all sports, you can have a game that lasts well over three hours and it feels like it flew by, and conversely, a three-hour game can feel like slow torture. It truly depends on the action, or the flow of the game.

George Will, baseball author and political commentator, added, "What I consider the greatest game ever played was the seventh and final game of the 1960 World Series. The Pirates beat the Yankees 10 to 9. The game was about two hours and 25 minutes long and there were zero strikeouts in that game. None. Now, that's partly because one pitcher was five-six and another was five-eight, Elroy Face and Bobby Shantz. But still, just as the games have been becoming longer, longer games with less action is not a recipe for entertainment, and baseball is in the entertainment business."

Some recent approaches to improve the pace of play appear to be haphazard and have fallen flat despite support from players and managers alike. Major League Baseball seemingly only tinkers with the pace of play. One example from 2015 was the rule that no longer were baseball fans subject to watching a batter stepping out of the box, adjusting his batting gloves, taking a practice swing, spitting a couple of times, and then repeating the entire routine between each pitch (*Los Angeles Times*, 2015).

Then Los Angeles Dodgers manager Don Mattingly told the *Los Angeles Times* he was "all for us playing at a better pace. The dead time in between pitches, cut out some of that. I think it will be good for the game."

Chris Iannetta, former major league catcher for the Angels and other clubs, said the league and players should strive "to put the best product on the field and (deliver) the best fan experience we can have."

"The game is driven by fan interest," he added, "and if something is hurting from the fans' perspective, that's a detriment in their eyes, we have to make adjustments."

Regardless, batters basically ignored the rule by constantly stepping out of the box under many different scenarios as umpires truly never enforced the measure. However, those adjustments Iannetta spoke of led to additional rule changes designed to speed up play, such as a limit on mound visits. Before 2019, mound visits were reduced to five. Later, in 2020, Commissioner Rob Manfred imposed a three-batter minimum on relievers.

Regardless of these additional strategies, Dave Ziedelis, with his three decades in major and minor league baseball, is still concerned. "They have to figure out the pace of play. It's vital. It is not as easy as everyone thinks. It is complicated mainly because the MLBPA [players union] has to agree on any changes. It's a huge problem," said Ziedelis.

He added, "I talk to a lot of people inside and outside of the game. It is hard to stomach watching a whole major league game, even for the diehard baseball fan. I'm a Red Sox fan and a Yankees Red Sox game is over four hours long. That's crazy."

Major League Baseball's efforts to speed up play run up against the reality of a changing game and, according to Gabe Lacques (September 3, 2019) of *USA Today*, "look more and more like acts of futility."

The problem is that the game has seemingly come to a screeching halt as hitters are seeing more pitches than before. "They [hitters] are seeing an average of 3.92 pitchers per plate appearance, the highest mark in the 21 seasons the stat has been tracked," said Lacques. There has also been a record number of strikeouts, which is the recipe for a longer game. There are fewer contact pitchers and that is adding more time to games.

This led Lacques to ponder, "How much more MLB-driven legislation can solve the problem? While Commissioner Manfred imposed the three-batter minimum without the need to reach agreement with the MLBPA it's fair to wonder how many more competitive facelifts players will accept," especially considering the players don't seem to like it as they feel it is taking jobs away from players.

"If you ask most pitchers," major league pitcher Daniel Hudson said to *USA Today* (Lacques, September 3, 2019), "it's beating a dead horse a bit to say you want all this stuff to improve the game and get young people involved and make it more exciting and have more home runs and more offense—it doesn't correlate to fast games. It just doesn't."

"Some guys are going to have to adjust what they do," former Angels manager Mike Scioscia told the *Los Angeles Times* (2015). "Walking 15–20 feet out of the box between pitches serves no purpose, and that needs to be eliminated."

Baseball officials have fretted as the average game time has passed three hours, but Atlanta Braves president John Schuerholz, chairman of MLB's pace-of-play committee, said the primary goal of the new rules was to eliminate routines that put a drag on the game (Svrluga, 2015).

At the end of the day, there are games that are two and a half hours that are brutally boring while there can be games that are four hours in length that keep fans on the edge of their seats. As a result, as Turner suggests, pace of play should refer to the action within the game, and I agree. It raises the questions: Has the game become unwatchable? Has it changed for the worse? More on that later in this chapter.

Perhaps surprising to some baseball purists, the idea of a computerized strike zone, or robo umpire, may be inevitable. It was mandated in AAA in 2022. With MLB game telecasts now routinely including a strike zone projected on the screen, baseball fans have clamored for such reform after a heavily scrutinized 2019 postseason of officiating that saw fans and observers calling their own balls and strikes, often at odds with umpires' decisions (Bogage, 2019).

Thanks to those controversial ball and strike calls in the 2019 World Series, Rob Manfred announced that the technology would arrive in select minor league parks in 2020. However, the COVID-19 pandemic shelved those plans. The idea of such a system is to offer a strike zone that is totally consistent, not just from hitter to hitter, but from team to team, game to game, season to season.

In 2019, the independent Atlantic League, an eight-team minor league unaffiliated with MLB franchises, piloted the Automated Ball-Strike (ABS) system, the league's proprietary automated balls-and-strikes system developed by sports data firm TrackMan. MLB followed that initial testing by instituting the robo ump in the Arizona Fall League in September that same year.

Opponents of the digital strike zone need not worry too much. This is not the end of umpiring as we know it, says the *Washington Post*. The ABS still requires a home-plate umpire to administer the game. Regardless, what do umpires think of this? Surprisingly, the umpires' union struck a deal with MLB officials in late 2019 to cooperate and assist with the implementation of a digitally governed strike zone as part of a larger contract (Bogage, 2019).

The five-year agreement between umpires and MLB, part of a new labor deal first reported by the Associated Press, provides umpires significant increases in compensation and retirement benefits designed to let older umpires retire sooner. In exchange, the umpires will advise Commissioner Rob Manfred on the development and implementation of the ABS system.

Word is that the digital strike zone may roll out in the big leagues as soon as 2024 or 2025.

While calling balls and strikes has never been an easy job, it is interesting that the data suggests umpires still get a great number of ball and strike calls wrong. A 2019 study from Boston University that examined 11 years' worth of MLB ball/strike calls found umpires get approximately one in every five calls wrong. Umpires have blind spots in some areas of the strike zone, the study found. It appears that umpires have difficulty with the calls at the bottom left and bottom right portions of the strike zone—the most important parts of the zone—14.3 percent and 18.3 percent of the time, respectively (Bogage, 2019).

One might think the players would be ecstatic with this idea. Not so fast. "It's part of the game," Nationals outfielder Adam Eaton told Emma Baccellieri (2019) of *Sports Illustrated* of an umpire error after Game 5 of the 2019 World Series, which his team lost after several questionable calls. "It's what makes baseball great. Sometimes you're on the bad end of it [an umpire's call], and it's not all that fun, but that's baseball."

Not surprising, former general manager Wayne Krivsky isn't on board at all. "The umpires are being marginalized. The idea of robo umps, that's not baseball. Come on! I am totally against it. Sadly, now it appears that umpires are not bearing down on making every call because of replay," and he feels this will worsen if a computerized strike zone is instituted.

Pitch Clock

The most important solution to improving the game in terms of attendance and fan interest just might be implementing a pitch clock. Players, coaches, and managers past and present, along with front-office executives, seem to believe that this will make a difference. Major League Baseball is committed to the idea behind the clock with the goal of speeding up the game, and specifically, eliminating dead time.

A rule was being used in parts of the minor leagues in 2021 as an experiment initiated by Major League Baseball. According to Fox Sports (2018), it "mandates that pitchers get 'set' … the moment before they throw—within 20 seconds of receiving the ball. Failing to throw in time results in a ball being called; if a batter delays, a strike is [called].

"In attempting to shorten the length of games … the International League average dropped 16 minutes to 2:40 … the Pacific Coast League fell 13 minutes to 2:45 … the Eastern League dropped 12 minutes to 2:38, the Southern League 11 minutes to 2:41 and the Texas League six minutes to 2:45," Fox Sports reported.

The Arizona Fall League experimented with the pitch clock and game times decreased from an average of 3:10 to 2:46. Jed Hoyer, president of baseball operations for the Chicago Cubs, said, "I was just down there in the Fall League and it seems like it's going well.… I think we all want quicker games.... So if this is a means to an end, I think it's great" (Taylor, 2021).

Jay Jaffe added, "I think a pitch clock is certainly something that it seems like an easy solution and people who see it really do remark upon its effectiveness."

Thankfully, in September 2022, MLB announced that beginning the following season a pitch timer would be implemented. According to Major League Baseball, "In an effort to create a quicker pace of play, there will be a 30-second timer between batters. Between pitches, there will be a 15-second timer with the bases empty and a 20-second timer with runners on base."

Interestingly, there may be unintended consequences to speeding up the time between pitches. Erik Lief, the director of communications for the American Council on Science and Health, has over 25 years of experience in major media and journalism. His 2016 piece titled "Speedier Baseball Games Risks Pitchers' Arms, Study Says" noted "there's another precinct checking in to voice concern about the controversial proposal: medical science."

He added that researchers in Canada suggested that forcing pitchers to throw pitches over a shorter period of time will give rise to injuries such as arm muscle fatigue. Specifically, he cites that researchers from the Department of Kinesiology at McMaster University in Hamilton, Ontario, "have determined that placing pitchers on a 'pitch clock' would result in reduced arm rest, and a 7 percent increase in muscle fatigue."

So, who bears the responsibility to speed up the game? Craig Calcaterra said, "The real issue is how long these guys are taking between pitches. It's mostly a pitcher issue. I know hitters step out and everything like that, but it's mostly a pitcher issue with guys having high-90s velocity and insane scouting reports and charts on every batter. There's a lot that goes in between pitches."

George Will says the pitch clock is a viable option for speeding up the game and would not cause a great deal of disruption. He said, "I mean, by now 90 percent of existing major league pitchers have pitched under a pitch clock in the minor leagues. And if they can't adjust to it, fine. Go sell aluminum siding ... because you just can't play baseball this way. Most important thing they could do is enforce the rule, and it's news to a lot of people that there is a rule that you're supposed to stay in the batter's box. Right."

New York Mets manager Buck Showalter told me, "Make the players play faster. That will take care of a lot of the issues [the game is facing]. The pitch clock would definitely help move the game along, but how about a hit clock? These hitters should get into the box and be ready to hit. That is also something to consider."

"But if you have a pitch clock," added Will, "it'll force it because the pitcher's going to throw the ball. And if you're not in the batter's box, call it a strike. Now, I mean, Buck knows more about baseball than anyone, and he's thought long and hard about this. I know he has. So those are the first two things, the pitch clock and stay in the batter's box. Then maybe lower and widen the strike zone a little bit. That would go a long way. It's too late now to reconfigure the ballparks, but we should have built bigger ballparks [to increase the possibility of] triples."

Will continued, "A home run is about two and a half seconds of the flight of the ball and a jog around the infield. It's not exciting. I'm sorry. Mae West said too much of a good thing is wonderful, but she was talking sex, not home runs."

Showalter agrees. "I find the home run boring. The game is won or lost in 90-foot increments. The team that does that the best wins. We have lost that. Today we think 360 feet." In other words, the home run, which is 90 feet times four bases.

Jerry Reuss, who spent 22 years as a major league pitcher, feels differently about the negative impact of the pitch clock. "I think it might be better [for pitchers to be on a pitch clock]. I always worked quickly and didn't have arm issues, but I understand everyone is different."

In terms of which, or any, pace of play initiative has potential, Calcaterra suggests, "I think the only one that is certain to work is a pitch clock that is enforced. It doesn't have to be a really draconian one. I don't think you're going to get anyone who's been in baseball for a while to agree to something like that. I live in Columbus, Ohio. I go to Columbus Clippers games. When you're there in person, the first time they had that clock going, you noticed it. Then you stop noticing it by the second inning."

There is an insane amount of scouting reports and charts on every batter and therefore there's a lot that goes on in between pitches, but no one wants to sit and wait forever until the pitcher is finally ready to throw.

"You could theoretically go an hour between pitches and just come up with the most efficient pitch possible," said Calcaterra. "No one wants to see that. At some point you have to get the ball, throw the ball, and pitch to a guy in sequences and try to get somebody out over the course of an at bat, as opposed to making every single pitch perfect."

Instant Replay

Also contributing to the pace-of-play issue is MLB's instant replay. Instant replay was introduced by Major League Baseball in the summer 2008 and it has been a drag on the pace of play ever since. You'd be forgiven if instant replay reviews, and the minutes-long pauses of in-game action they demand, leave you a little drowsy or reaching for the remote.

MLB became the last of the four major North American sports leagues to use instant replay, mostly over the objections of baseball purists and former commissioner Bud Selig, who believed that replays would break the long-standing tradition of putting each game's fate in the hands of the umpires on the field. Others objected to replays lengthening an already long game.

Also, according to Baseball-Reference, after the 2011 season, Major League Baseball sought to extend the use of instant replay to additional game situations with the renewal of the collective bargaining agreement, namely:

- whether a ball hit down the foul line is fair or foul;
- whether a fly ball was caught or trapped; and
- whether fan interference occurred anywhere on the field.

In 2013, another expansion occurred. "Selig announced plans to expand review even further, by allowing each manager up to three challenges per game. After receiving agreement from the Players Association and the World Umpires Association, the new rule was formally accepted. Under these rules, each manager started a game with one challenge; if he is successful, he could challenge one other decision. From the 7th inning onward, the umpire crew can also decide on its own to submit a decision to video review. Almost all decisions were then reviewed (e.g., whether batted balls are foul or fair, tag and force plays, balls caught or trapped, etc.), but not decisions regarding balls and strikes, and obstruction or interference calls," said Baseball-Reference (2022).

MLB tweaked the rules again before the 2017 season, in order to reduce excessive delays associated with the procedure: managers would have 30 seconds from the completion of a play to initiate a challenge, and reviewers would then have two minutes to come to a decision (if clear evidence to overturn a call was not present after that delay, the original call would stand) (Baseball-Reference, 2022).

The league announced in 2020, when the MLB season was shortened due to COVID-19, that without fans in the stands additional cameras would be installed in ballparks. As a result, the number of isolated camera angles doubled from 12 to 24. Also, the league placed enhanced resolution 4K cameras to overlook fields.

"The cameras are generally used to look at a base runner's placement and other wide-angle things that may not be available during the broadcast," said Chris Marinak, MLB vice president of strategy technology and innovation. It's the first upgrade since the league rolled out its expanded instant replay technology system in 2014.

Marinak said the tech upgrades will help get footage to umpires faster to cut down on the time spent reviewing plays. It will also help the team to decide whether or not to challenge a call (Young, 2020), also with hopes of being a time saver.

Along with the new cameras, MLB transitioned its Statcast system to Hawk-Eye, giving the league better data analysis. Five pitch-tracking cameras were installed behind home plate with seven cameras tracking players across the field up to 100 frames per second (Schuster, 2020).

Not addressed were some of the other quirks caused by the rule: for example, the trend of baserunners being called out for breaking contact with the bag for a microsecond after having otherwise beaten the throw, which players have an issue with.

"It is being used for reasons it wasn't meant for—namely tag plays," Justin Turner of the Dodgers told me. The concern is the safety of the players.

"Guys now have to hang in there and it is putting us in harm's way. I'm knocked down all the time because I have to hang in there to make the tag. It used to be if a guy was out by a couple feet the umpire would call him out even if the tag wasn't completely on him. I can't tell you how many times I've been blown up. It's bad for runners too," said Turner.

Another problem of instant replay is the inconsistency in how umpires use the system. Turner said, "It is interpreted by different umpire crews every series. For example, is the runner out when the ball is inside the glove or is he out when it hits the back of the glove? The interpretation is loose. I can't tell you how many times I can't believe a call was not overturned or vice versa. Replay should be used for safe or out."

Krivsky, who initially drafted and signed Turner when he was an executive with the Baltimore Orioles, agrees. "Currently, video replay is the number one thing that is slowing down the game. The game is moving along nicely and then a replay where we sit for four to five minutes while New York tries to figure out if a runner was safe or out on a tag play. It's ticky-tack. It's ludicrous," bemoans Krivsky.

Trey Hillman told me that while he is happy with the idea of replay in general, he is not on board with its current model. "There are too many challenges," said Hillman, adding, "it is far too confusing. I would prefer some simplification. People who are a lot smarter than I can figure it out."

To that point, Hillman shared an anecdote that when a questionable play occurs, the coaching staff has but a few seconds to make the decision on whether to challenge the call or not. They often look at each other and ask, "Is that reviewable? It was last year. How about this year?"

Speaking of challenges, how many are actually overturned? According to Savant (n.d.), in 2019, 800 calls were upheld (53.26 percent) versus

702 that were overturned (46.74 percent). These numbers may suggest that umpires are missing a lot of calls and managers are successful in challenging only about half the time.

In the same 2019 season, the Philadelphia Phillies initiated the most challenges with 65 (4.44 percent of all challenges) while the New York Yankees had the fewest that year at 28 (1.91 percent). Tag plays dominated the type of call challenged in 2019 with 616 challenges (41.01 percent) followed by a close play at first, with 443 (29.49 percent).

Sadly, one of the unintended consequences of video replay challenges is fans are no longer treated to heated manager-umpire arguments. The days of former major league manager Lou Piniella kicking dirt on an umpire or hurling third base into the outfield are over. Instead, today's managers simply point to their ears to indicate they want to challenge a call. If they lose the challenge, the manager, by rule, is automatically ejected if they argue. The result is a game that some say has already become boring just got even more uninteresting.

As Joe Maddon told me, "I don't even argue anymore."

According to a 2022 Major League Baseball press release, umpires were equipped with microphones to inform crowds in the ballparks and the viewing audience at home of instant replay reviews. Umpiring crew chiefs now wear a microphone to announce when a play is being challenged and what is being challenged and reviewed. When a team issues a challenge, the umpire will proceed to either baseline and face the press box to make the announcement, prior to communicating with the replay official in New York.

After reviews are completed, the crew chief will return to the same spot to make a post-review announcement of the ruling and any changes to the placement of runners.

According to ESPN, Major League Baseball was going to begin informing fans about replays in this manner in 2020, but the pandemic delayed the rollout.

Product Quality

Strikeouts and lower batting averages have impacted the quality of the game. As I shared in chapter 2, strikeouts are on the increase. From 2010 to 2019, MLB saw 24.8 percent more strikeouts, and the 42,823 punchouts in 2019 were the most in a season—ever. The MLB batting average in 2019 was a dismal .245, which is the worst since 1972, when it was .244. Also, the number of base hits has plummeted. In 2006, major leaguers pounded out 45,073 hits while in 2019 there were just 42,039 hits, a decrease of 6.7

percent. The bottom line is the action on the field, in terms of offense, has dramatically declined.

Marlins coach Rob Flippo spends his time during games preparing the team's pitchers for battle. During the downtime throughout the game, he notices the "games are dragging. Fans today do not want to see an abundance of walks and strikeouts. It's not enjoyable. There are no stolen bases. The strategy is gone. The game has changed but not for the better in terms of engaging the fans into the game itself."

He suggests the game's tempo has changed, and since he focuses on pitching, that is the difference maker for him. "The tempo of the game is driven by the pitch sequence with a runner on second. There's paranoia that signs will be stolen. Illegal sign stealing has lengthened the game and in turn paranoia creeps in. We see the pitcher constantly stepping off the rubber and then there are delays. It's a waste of time," said Flippo. As he is a former Dodgers coach, it's hard not to understand why he is laying blame at the feet of both the Houston Astros and Boston Red Sox. As we learned in chapter 2, their sign-stealing scandals most likely impacted the Dodgers' chances of winning not one but two World Series titles.

"Regardless," said Flippo, "it's miserable at the park watching a pitcher go through sequence after sequence so the runner doesn't pick their sign."

"I always worked quickly but I realize that every pitcher is different. But I don't understand why pitchers don't work quickly," said 22-year major league pitcher Jerry Reuss. He added, "I prefer that games move along faster. Otherwise, [defensive] players are on their heels. With the slow play we currently have, I see fatigue throughout all aspects of the game from players, fans, and broadcasters. When I was broadcasting games, I needed a suitcase full of stories to fill the time."

Additionally, a major complaint to the modern game is the defensive shift and how it seemingly is leading to decreased batting averages. You'll recall that former major league pitcher Scott Karl spoke to this earlier.

Another lost art, according to Karl, is the lack of teams "manufacturing runs" by using speed and timely, strategic hitting, an offensive strategy that doesn't seem to exist any longer. "I struggle to watch the game. It is not what I like to see or the baseball I grew up loving [or played at the MLB level]. When I was young I loved watching the St. Louis Cardinals manufacture runs," said Karl.

Maddon would agree. He told me, "The game has become a socialist sport. There is no individuality per team. It used to be that the Earl Weaver–led Orioles were known for waiting for the three-run home run, and Gene Mauch [who managed in the majors from 1960 to 1987] was a tactician. Now everyone wants to be the same. It is now just a matrix, a math equation. The game is being changed on an executive level. Front offices are taking over the dugout with analytics."

Karl added, "When there's a runner on first, these days there are so few running teams that the pitcher doesn't have to have their attention diverted from the hitter to concentrate on the runner. I used to hate when guys like Hall of Famer Rickey Henderson would get on first because he demanded my attention." Where have you gone, Vince Coleman?

Paralyzed by Tradition

Why does a sports league change its rules? Typically, it's to make the sport more exciting, to generate fan interest and engagement, or to improve player safety. Take the NFL, for example. It constantly creates new rules or updates existing ones for those reasons. Seemingly, this occurs in the NFL every year. During the offseason, the NFL Rules Committee convenes with the aim to make the game better through rule changes or tweaks, which proves the league is innovative and unafraid to take risks. When a rule doesn't work, they own it. They acknowledge it. In recent years, the NFL has made significant rule changes, such as adding a two-point conversion and also increasing the distance for the extra-point kick after a touchdown. Both of these significant changes came about without much pushback or controversy at all.

Unlike Major League Baseball, the NFL has been able to keep the game in the forefront of sports fans' minds not only during its season but in the offseason as well. For instance, as a result of the NFL adding an extra game to the regular season and deepening its playoff pool, the Super Bowl is now played in mid–February. After the game, fans are still discussing the result for the better part of the month. March is dedicated to the NFL combine and free agency. Next, the NFL draft dominates sports talk in April. May is when team workouts are in full swing. Brilliant.

Conversely, when Major League Baseball considers rule changes, it is usually met with nothing short of anarchy—especially from those who consider themselves "traditionalists." I get that because at one time I considered myself one, but as time has moved on, so have I and now I embrace what I believe are rule changes and initiatives that make the game better.

So, what are the barriers Major League Baseball faces when it proposes rule changes? First, baseball is beholden to tradition, or more accurately, it's paralyzed by tradition, and as Dave Ziedelis, former Frederick Keys general manager, told me, "I don't know if Major League Baseball understands they have a problem."

I discussed this issue with George Will, and he said, "Well, first of all, if you want to get away from the three true outcomes, start by getting rid of the shifts, either a soft rule against it—that is, that there have to be two players on each side of the second base, two infielders—or a hard one, which they have to have their spikes in the dirt as the pitch is delivered. That would have the effect of decreasing the incentive to hit the ball over the shift. That is the launch angle. I think you could probably change the strike zone somewhat, which is to broaden it but lower it again.... Velocity has simply overwhelmed the game at this point. Time was baseball said, let's run up the pitch counts, get the starting pitcher out because such mediocrity ... is in middle relief. We'll get into their bullpen and make hay.

"Well, the problem is now the bullpens are stacked with guys who are six-five and throw 95. In fact, they throw 95 on their secondary pitches. So physically, baseball has changed, the ballplayers have changed. The NBA changed the configuration of its court because of Wilt Chamberlain. And now you've got six-foot-nine-inch point guards. And you have to tweak the rules. The NFL tweaks the rules to preserve quarterbacks and encourage offense every year. The NBA changes its concept of what is and is not a foul probably every year. So, baseball's going to have to modify itself," said Will.

Slow to Change

Ziedelis knows firsthand that "baseball is a traditionalist game and is slow to make changes. The NFL and NBA make changes every single year. Baseball's history and traditionalism are working against it. The first step to recovery is looking into the mirror and acknowledging there is a problem. Then you get to work to fix that problem."

Bill James, American baseball writer, historian, and statistician, added, "I think, really, that this is one reason that so many intelligent people drift away from baseball, that if you really care about it at all you have to realize, as soon as you acquire a taste for independent thought, that a great portion of the sport's traditional knowledge is ridiculous hokum" (Lewis, 2004).

On the other side of the issue stands the outspoken former general manager of the Reds, Wayne Krivsky, who said, "Leave the rules alone. It's a beautiful game. It's not broken. [Commissioner] Manfred is tinkering with the game. He's hurting it. Fans are confused by the rules. Baseball is not like other sports. It's a different animal. It's not the NBA and NFL where you can change rules every year."

If you're on the side of strategy, you'll disagree with the recent rule changes. If you're on the side of the pace of play and moving the game along, most likely you'll be on board. Mark Hyman, who has spent decades covering the game, says the rule changes and proposals are a difference only on the margins and that reducing commercials will make the biggest difference in game times—but that's the revenue stream for local television.

Trey Hillman added that rule changes have posed challenges for him as a coach. He said, "The rule changes have not been good. For example, the slide rule—the 'Buster Posey' rule." In 2011 after San Francisco Giants star catcher Buster Posey suffered a season-ending injury during a collision at home plate, a rule was enacted stating a runner attempting to score may not deviate from his direct pathway to the plate in order to initiate contact with the catcher (or other player covering home plate).

"I certainly do not want to see anyone getting hurt, but this rule is designed to protect the business part of the game because it will suffer if a star player gets hurt and is out for a while. Rule changes have forced me," said Hillman, a one-time Miami Marlins infield coach, "to adjust my teaching. For example, when there is a stolen base attempt at second [for a tag play], it used to be, get in [with the tag] and get out. No longer. It's now tag and hold," in the event the player slides off the bag. This poses additional risk to players, as Justin Turner mentioned earlier.

Joe Maddon added, "Those rule changes, which have taken away the excitement of the game, were the result of bad technique [when injuries had occurred]."

While the league rarely makes rule changes, they are not new to Major League Baseball. In the late 1960s, MLB lowered the height of the pitcher's mound and altered the strike zone because pitchers dominated and the league desired more offense. According to MLB, in December 1968, "a Major League Baseball rules panel got together and voted to lower the mound from 15 inches to 10, shrinking the strike zone to the top of the knees to the armpit (rather than shoulders and knees) and to be extra vigilant against doctored baseballs. In the end, it worked, with the offense jumping from an average of 6.84 runs per game to 8.14. The run-scoring environment in 1969 was much greater than it was in 1968, with teams averaging 0.65 more runs per game (going from 3.42 to 4.07, an increase of greater than 19 percent)."

Jerry Reuss, 22-year major league veteran, told me that rule changes are nothing new to baseball's history. He added, "In 1969, Major League Baseball, in its infinite wisdom, elected to go to divisions [coinciding with expansion of Kansas City, San Diego, Montreal, and Seattle] and also lowered the mound to generate offense. Later, in 1973 the American League went to the DH [designated hitter]."

Said On This Date in MLB (Instagram): "Long before 1973, National League President John Heydler proposed the idea of a designated hitter for pitchers to speed up the game. He proposed the idea at the National League Meetings, where he explained that fans are tired of seeing weak-hitting pitchers. He described his idea as the 'tenth regular'—in 1928! Ninety-four years later the National League finally got on board with Heydler's suggestion."

To Reuss's point, while rule changes in Major League Baseball over the past few decades have been seemingly scarce, he is right. Throughout the history of the game, there have been rule changes—some seemingly without controversy and others that sparked great debate and gnashing of teeth.

For instance, in 1903, at the American League meeting, Ban Johnson was reelected American League president and some rule changes were passed. Coaches were allowed at third base and first base at all times; until then, only one coach was permitted except if there were two or more runners on base. Additionally, the American League also instituted the "foul strike" rule, used by the National League since 1901, which stated a foul will be counted as a strike unless there are already two strikes (On This Date, 2022).

Also, in 1910, according to On This Date:

- Both the National and American Leagues banned syndicate baseball where the syndicate allowed owners to have financial ties to more than one team.
- The National League adopted a 154-game season, which the American League had already implemented.
- Umpires were required to announce team changes to spectators.
- Batting lineups were required to be delivered to the umpire at home plate prior to the first pitch.
- A hitter was ruled out if he crossed the plate from one batter's box to the other while the pitcher was set to pitch.
- A runner was ruled out if he passed another runner before the latter had been put out.

Also noted by On This Date, "In 1963 Major League Baseball's Rules committee increased the size of the strike zone from the top of the batter's shoulders to the bottom of the knees. The committee hopes the return to the 1950's strike zone will result in a decrease of runs scored."

Regarding Reuss's lowering-the-mound comment, On This Date added that MLB at the time said of the decision to lower it from 15 inches to 10, "The result will exceed the committee's expectations and after the 'Year of the Pitcher' in 1968, the strike zone will be tweaked again to give the hitters a break."

The definition of the strike zone has also undergone numerous changes throughout the history of Major League Baseball:

1950: under the armpits to top of knees
1963: top of shoulder to knees
1969: armpits to top of knees
1988: midpoint between the top of the shoulders and the top of the pants to the top of knees
1996: midpoint between the top of the shoulders and the hollow beneath the kneecap
2001: Umpires would begin to follow the rulebook, which stated the high end of the strike zone is midway between the belt and the shoulders and two inches off the plate would no longer be strikes.

Today's major league pitchers, who are under intense scrutiny when it comes to the potential for using a foreign substance on the baseball, would be shocked to learn, "In 1920 the American League voted to allow pitchers who used the spitball in 1920 to continue using it as long as they are in the league. The National League will do the same. There were 17 designated spitters in all. Eight in the National League and nine in the American League" (On This Date, 2022).

National League Designated Spitters	*American League Designated Spitters*
Bill Doak	A.W. Ayres
Phil Douglas	Slim Caldwell
Dana Fillingim	Stan Coveleski
Ray Fisher	Red Faber
Marvin Goodwin	Dutch Leonard
Burleigh Grimes	Jack Quinn
Clarence Mitchell	Allen Russell
Dick Rudolph	Urban Shocker
	Allen Sothoran

Recently, two excellent rule changes from the 2022 collective bargaining agreement with the Major League Baseball Players Association was the universal DH and expanding the playoffs.

After nearly five decades of traditionalists beating their chests that the designated hitter had to go, MLB implemented it into the National League, and guess what happened? The game survived and it actually improved the experience of watching games. As stated earlier, having pitchers hit may add an element of strategy, but as others have suggested, at what cost? Watching pitcher after pitcher look feeble striking out?

Secondly, the postseason expanded to 12 teams beginning with the 2022 season. Each league now has three division champions and three wild cards. The teams with the two best records in each league receive a first-round bye. The other four clubs play a best-of-three wild-card round. I suggest that his model does not water down the regular season and cheapen the postseason. More teams in the playoffs means more fan bases being excited and engaged in baseball all the way through the season.

Three-Batter Minimum

Pandemic or not, the three-batter minimum rule instituted in 2020 was going to be implemented. The rule requires pitchers to face at least three hitters or pitch to the end of a half inning before a pitching change can be made. On the surface, the rule seems straightforward and, as MLB hopes, shorter game times will result from fewer pitching changes. However, not everyone is on board.

As Justin Turner told me, "The three-batter rule is terrible. If a team wants to use one reliever for a single hitter, leave that up to the team."

From the standpoint of strategy, which is a hallmark of baseball, Krivsky said, "The three-batter rule takes away strategy and the manager's instinct. Not one manager, former or current, that I have spoken to likes the rule. None are for this."

At the 2019 MLB Winter Meetings, Maddon did not sugarcoat his disdain for it when he told CNBC, "I don't like it. I didn't like it from the beginning; I don't quite get it." Maddon said he's all for changes to increase the pace and shorten the length of a game. But as Krivsky pointed out, this new rule can change a team's strategy, which he called sacred. "Anything that deals with strategy," he said, "I'm not into it. Anything that deals with pace, I'm into it" (Young, 2019).

Conversely, Scott Karl said, "I love the rule. I have nothing against the relievers today, but pitching to one hitter is a joke. I understand [managers] are playing the odds and matchups but people are disinterested in constant pitching changes."

Also in favor of the rule is Jeff Montgomery, another former MLB pitcher, most notably with the Kansas City Royals. He said for pitchers, "It provides more challenges. If you're a lefty, prove that you can get righties out too. You have to get ahead, pitch backwards, and compete." He also talked about teams pinch-hitting to gain a better matchup. In his opinion, strategy is not compromised.

While the sample size from 2020 was small with each team playing only a 60-game schedule instead of the typical 162 games, the new rule might have had a small impact on game times. In 2020, the average game time was 3:06, a slight decrease from 2019, when it was 3:10. However, 2018 game times were 3:04. In short, it's too soon to tell if this new rule will have any real impact on game times, but it does seem to improve the pace, or flow, of the game when a manager isn't constantly making pitching changes.

Pandemic Rules

Brought on by the COVID-19 pandemic, rules changes were added, as MLB suggested, to increase the safety of players; these included seven-inning doubleheaders and beginning each half inning of an extra-inning game with a runner on second base.

Minor League Baseball had been using the runner-on-second rule for the past two seasons. The rule places at second base the player who is listed in the batting order ahead of the leadoff hitter in the extra inning. It is typically the player who made the last out in the previous inning. The pitcher is not charged with an earned run if that runner crosses home plate; it is scored as if that runner scored via error.

Also, in those minor leagues that implemented the rule, 73 percent of the games ended in the 10th inning. Prior to the rule's adoption, 43 percent of the games ended in the 10th inning.

More than two-thirds of baseball fans nationally (67 percent) think the proposed rule change by Major League Baseball to start extra innings with a runner on second base was a bad idea while 17 percent believe it was a good idea and 16 percent are unsure.

Thankfully, the seven-inning doubleheader was short-lived (2020 and 2021 seasons) but the "ghost runner" on second continued into the 2022 season as, despite an easing of pandemic restrictions after the 2021 season, the league and players agreed to keep the controversial rule.

Rule changes such as the seven-inning doubleheader and beginning each extra inning with a runner on second base made the game feel more like wiffleball at the local sandlot than Major League Baseball.

"It's not real baseball," Los Angeles Dodgers star pitcher Clayton Kershaw told reporters after the Dodgers beat the Arizona Diamondbacks 6–4 in 10 innings. "But it's fine for this year [2020], and I hope we never do it again" (Ribadeneyra, 2020).

His manager, Dave Roberts, feels differently. "I didn't know how it was going to play out and how it was going to be received, but as we've had some runs with it, I really like it," Roberts said. "I think it really shortens the game. It adds strategy for the fans, the managers, the players.

"I think it's playing out pretty well, and our guys have done a really good job in the situation. I like it permanently. [However], I don't like it for the postseason" (Ribadeneyra, 2020).

It's too early to judge it completely, but this rule honestly still feels more like a slow-pitch softball rule than one from MLB. Again, any changes may be fought by the players union. But if TV ratings and attendance keep slipping, this change may be inevitable.

Craig Calcaterra told me, "I don't know who liked that [rule]. I think the only people that liked that were baseball writers with deadlines."

He added, "I don't think that [extra-inning rule] is going to stay. I think they might change it to where it'll be okay, if we get to the 13th thing or something, then we'll put the man on second, just let's put an end to this."

Mound Visits

According to MLB, mound visits had no time limit prior to the 2016 season, when Major League Baseball began limiting visits by managers and coaches to 30 seconds. Also, the rule limiting each team to six mound visits per nine innings was instituted prior to the 2018 campaign and then changed to five per nine innings before the 2019 season.

Forbes reported that, excluding pitching changes, there have been an average of 3.78 mound visits per game, down dramatically from 2018, before the new rule. In 2017, the comparable figure was 7.41 mound visits per game, for an average decline of nearly four (3.63) visits per game.

In terms of moving the game along, from 2016 to 2020 the average length of a Major League Baseball game was only two minutes shorter. It appears this rule change hasn't made the impact many thought it would. But in time, it might.

Solutions

The issue of pace of play in Major League Baseball appears to be a real dilemma and one that Commissioner Rob Manfred has put on the top of his to-do list. Certainly, there are opinions on both sides, and while the league has tried some initiatives, here are a few solutions I propose—and best of all, they are easy and affordable to implement.

The approach here I believe is simple. Major League Baseball needs to keep being innovative and give these rule changes some time to see if they make a positive impact on the length, pace, and excitement of the game.

Fans may not all like all of the rule changes that Commissioner Manfred has experimented with, but he deserves credit for trying to be innovative. For example, piloting the pitch clock in the minor leagues was a smart strategy and hopefully, with the support of the players and coaches, its launch in 2023 will prove to be successful.

Rules like limiting the number of mound visits and the extra-inning rule give at least a sense that the game is moving along at a quicker pace. Also, a rule like a universal designated hitter is certainly an example of doing what is best for the game in terms of engaging fans, and a DH is far more exciting to watch than pitchers who can't hit their weight bat. Let's see some real hitters at the plate and bring some excitement to the game.

Pitch Clock

It's here and thankfully so. Commissioner Manfred pushed this forward. The experimentation phase in the minor leagues and Arizona Fall League has yielded positive results, and it is certainly worth trying at the major league level. However, MLB learned a cautionary tale years ago when it tried to implement a rule that the batter must have at least one foot in the batter's box at all times. While the intent was to speed up the game, umpires rarely enforced it and it crashed and burned. So, MLB, if you are serious about the pitch clock, it must be adhered to with accountability measures in place for it to succeed.

Shorten Commercial Breaks

We could actually stop there. Problem solved. In 2019, breaks were reduced from two minutes, five seconds to two minutes in local games, and from two minutes, 25 seconds to two minutes in national games. I suggest cutting another 20 seconds off for both local and national broadcasts. In an average nine-inning baseball game, there are 17 between-inning commercial breaks, and my suggestion of a one-minute, 40-second limit would decrease game lengths by more than five minutes. Before television and MLB marketing executives lose their minds, there is a way networks and teams can make up that time lost, and it is something we are seeing in MLB telecasts and in other sports like NASCAR and soccer. Imbed two 15-second commercials within the live broadcast when there's downtime, which there is plenty of in an MLB game. The Cubs, for example, are already doing this on their games being aired on Marquee. Airing commercials during the live broadcast could be more valuable to an advertiser knowing their audience is more engaged and not changing channels as they do during typical commercial breaks.

Be Better and Make Adjustments

Scott Karl said the pace-of-play issue is solvable. "The owners and the players need to work together to speed up the game," said Karl. "It begins with the desire of the players," reasons Karl. "Specifically, it's on the pitcher, catcher, and the hitter to speed up the game."

He suggests catchers should simply give the sign quickly and the pitcher get the sign and throw the ball. Today, there is far too much time between pitches. When he pitched, he wanted the batter to work at his tempo, not the other way around. As for the hitter, Karl says, get in the batter's box and be ready to go right away. "This also helps your fielders be on their toes and be prepared. I wanted my fielders ready. Not looking around the stands. Tempo keeps the fielders sharper. However, none of those three [positions] want to speed up the game. The players do not want to get up and go."

Improving Video Replay

There is a place for replay in the game and it is not going away so let's work to improve video replay. Currently, it's death. Is there a bigger buzzkill to a game than seeing the umpiring crew motion to their ears indicating they need to put on headphones and confirm a call with New York on a play that most likely has no business being reviewed? Fans ask: How many minutes will we have to endure this? More than we should, that's for certain.

Here are two simple solutions offered by Wayne Krivsky: "Two challenges—that's it. It eliminates the coach wasting time on the phone and it eliminates the video guy. Also, the manager has five seconds, not 20 or 30. Use your eyeballs. Managers would use it sparingly. They wouldn't use it in the first inning on a close play. They would save it for something important."

Alternative to Robo Umpires

He's back. Krivsky, as he stated earlier, cannot stand the idea of robo umpires. Instead, he suggests to "empower the umpires to pick up the pace. Get in the box or a strike will be called. It will only need it to happen once before they know not to do it again. They can have a positive influence on the pace of the game."

5

Generation Lost

*"The New Generation is playing
by different rules."*—Imagen

Is baseball cool? Of course it is! If you ask the average Major League Baseball fan, they provide that answer with a resounding yes! Then again, the average age of an MLB fan is 57 years old, which is the highest among the four major sports (Poindexter, 2021). This is astounding and a concerning date point and I contend it should be alarming for Major League Baseball because there is a cliff coming as the youngest generations are not engaged with the game. The impact, I am afraid to say, is that without those fans replacing the current generation, Major League Baseball will slip into obscurity.

While David Carter is just as concerned, he disagrees that baseball is cool. Carter told me, "Baseball isn't cool. Baseball *needs* a cool factor. Kids would rather hang out with friends than with their dad, sit in traffic, and watch a game that is over three hours long. They might as well tell their friends to make plans for the entire day because they won't be back."

Joe Maddon added, "Baseball is boring. It is not drawing kids to the game as fans as well as playing it. It is subtracting fun. The game is scripted and orchestrated [by front-office analytics departments]. They are fabricating fun. There is no charisma of the players or managers. I don't even argue anymore."

According to Nielsen Scarborough (2018), baseball is still most popular with older demographics, with 32 percent of people ages 50–69 saying they are "very" or "somewhat" interested in baseball. However, that number drops to 25 percent for those 21–34 and down to 23 percent for ages 18–20. Baseball is losing ground with younger fans compared with older age groups and other sports. The NFL, on the other hand, is gaining ground on baseball, especially in the youngest demographics. Nielsen reported that 37 percent of 18–20-year-olds are "very" or "somewhat" interested in football, 14 percent higher than baseball. Only about 24 percent of baseball fans are under age 35, compared with 45 percent of basketball fans.

"It's hard to captivate the young fanbase. If you told a fifth grader that there is no clock in baseball, he'd think that is crazy. When does the game end? Three and half hours later," reasons Carter.

Mac McArtor's (2020) study from the University of North Carolina, titled "America's Present Time: Reviving MLB Attendance by Marketing to Gen Z," suggested, despite the growth of Major League Baseball, "the league is losing favor with younger generations, namely Generation Z, and attendance rates are falling to historic lows with each new season. In order to sustain the financial growth of its league, MLB must better understand the attitudes and perceptions of Generation Z and thereby positively influence Generation Z attendance rates."

He continued: "MLB must offer a sufficient value exchange for attending games: a valuable experience at a sufficient price point. It is imperative that the MLB couples a new pricing strategy with an enhanced in-game experience that will make attending games worthwhile again. By delivering satisfactory value exchange at the forefront of this plan, the MLB can better address their attendance woes. Success will be determined by a rise in attendance, and the driving factor of this will be a new experience surrounding the sport that delights younger generations."

George Will, during my interview with him, addressed this generational issue. He said, "Well, there's a generational problem and a baseball problem. Generations have different appetites and expectations and those are working against baseball. That's half the problem. The other half of the problem is that baseball is boring. Didn't used to be. You talk to all kinds of former major league players, managers, coaches, they don't watch the games anymore. When the ball is put in play once every four minutes, when in 2020, in the most watched game of that truncated season in the last game, sixth and final game of the World Series, the ball was put in play once every six and a half minutes."

Also further hindering baseball's connection with the young generation is Major League Baseball's lack of effort to modernize and promote the game in a way that is relevant to the new breed of sports fan (Panacy, 2013).

But is reaching this generation mutually exclusive to Major League Baseball? Not according to Alex Silverman (2020) from the Morning Consult:

- 53 percent of Gen Zers identify as sports fans, compared with 63 percent of all adults and 69 percent of millennials.
- Gen Zers are half as likely as millennials to watch live sports regularly and twice as likely never to watch.

- Esports are more popular among Gen Z than MLB, NASCAR, and the NHL, with 35 percent identifying as fans.

Panacy (2013) added, "The millennial generation's coming-of-age coincided with massive growth in the North American sports industry. Between 2010 and 2018, the North American sports market grew more than 40 percent from $49.9 billion to $71.1 billion. With more access than ever to a wider range of competitions, the men and women born between 1981 and 1996 developed an insatiable appetite for live sports, lifting leagues, teams, networks and brands to unprecedented heights."

Interestingly, research indicates the next wave of consumers, Generation Z, is much less enthusiastic about sports. An analysis of recent Morning Consult poll results found that Gen Zers currently between ages 13 and 23 are less likely than the general population to identify as sports fans.

For example, according to the poll, only 21 percent of Generation Z considers themselves an avid sports fan, while 32 percent a casual fan and, surprisingly, 47 percent not a fan at all. This, and the following, should be concerning to Major League Baseball.

Gen Z Less Interested in Most Sports Properties Than General Public (*Morning Consult*)

Share of respondents who identify either as "avid" or "causal" fans of each sport

Sport	*All Adults*	*Generation Z*
NFL	59%	49%
NBA	45	47
Esports	19	35
College Football	41	33
MLB	**50**	**32**

In addition, says Silverman (2020), "Gen Zers were twice as likely as millennials to say they 'never' watch live sports. Keys to growing live viewership among young fans are accessibility and opportunities for engagement."

Also, not such good news here for Major League Baseball as Silverman adds, "Four of Gen Z's five favorite sports figures, based on an open-ended survey question, were either former or current NBA players. Seven months after his death, late Los Angeles Lakers legend Kobe Bryant (51 selections) topped current Lakers star LeBron James (46 selections) as the most popular athletic icon among young fans. The most popular non–NBA athlete was Argentinian soccer player Lionel Messi." It's crazy to think that former NBA players are more popular with this generation than current MLB stars.

Cameron Easley (2018), senior editor at Morning Consult, says, "The professional leagues for America's two pastimes, baseball and football, are at risk of losing their primacy in the sports world, with other leagues closing the gap among the youngest fans."

The Morning Consult's survey revealed that both Major League Baseball and the National Football League are feeling the impact of the success of the National Basketball Association and Major League Soccer, which have become more popular with Generation Z fans.

You'll recall in the introduction, the impetus for writing this book was the conversation I had with my son, Jacob, who at age 16 told me, "Dad, baseball is boring."

George Will agrees with Jacob. "Your son is right," Will told me. "Baseball is boring. People now live in a digital speed. They have their phones. They want things instantly. They get things instantly. And just as a generation, including your son, comes along that was raised on computers and video games and smartphones, baseball is coagulating. It'll either change or it won't."

Rick Schlesinger, president-business operations for the Milwaukee Brewers, said from a marketing perspective, this generation "is an incredibly challenging demographic to get to the ballpark right now. Our core audience, frankly, skews older and skews younger. So, we've got my age, we've got people with families, but the Gen Zs, getting them to the ballpark is something that we are still chasing. It's a work in progress."

SJ Insights added, "Part of the shift comes from cord-cutting, as fewer young people tune in for live broadcasts of games on major networks and opt instead to stream games online."

Shavonnah Schreiber, a marketing expert and managing director of SNR Creative in Houston, told me, "In terms of them [MLB] marketing to Generation Z, I don't see that much happening. I don't think the league has done much to attract anybody, actually. It doesn't appear that they do a good job of recruiting new fans or make an effort to sell their brand in the normal marketing sense to create demand for their product."

According to Marc Fisher (2015) of the *Washington Post*, a 2015 ESPN Sports Poll of young Americans' 30 favorite sports figures found no baseball players on the list. But what athletes are appealing to them the most today? Kids gravitate to the sport they see their idols play. If MLB players are not being marketed to them, then they are obviously not on the forefront of the minds of the youth, and that's a concern.

I asked Carter how MLB can engage the Generation Z fanbase. He replied, "I'm not sure they can get them [yikes!]. A problem seems to exist with young people when they hit about eighth grade where they veer from baseball. They seem to circle back when they are in their early 30s. That's a 15-year gap. During this time, other things are taking away from their attention being on baseball. They are doing other things—video games, hanging out with friends, playing other sports, and dating."

Carter also suggests that Major League Baseball is losing the technology arms race to other sports that are more innovative in their digital platforms.

Speaking of those platforms and the devices accessing them, small screens have not done MLB any favors as the younger generation seemingly lacks patience, which is required to follow baseball. Jon Swartz (2018) of *Barron's* says, "Baseball is a game that requires patience, especially when viewed remotely. Its leisurely pace has prompted the powers-that-be at Major League Baseball to impose several rules changes including the proposed institution of a clock between innings and a cap on mound visits, to speed things up."

But is the issue just the length of the game? Matthew Picus, who at 26 is the oldest of the Gen Z demographic and the youngest of millennials, considers himself a big baseball fan. His family are Dodgers season ticket holders and he says his friends think baseball is slow, boring, and time-consuming. He feels it is because they do not have the same appreciation and patience for the nuances of the game as he does.

Showalter also has a theory on the topic of Generation Z. With the apparent decline in interest from fans of that age group, Showalter told me, "It worries me about where the game is heading—especially generationally. They want constant action 24/7." He added, "What is entertaining to them? They want constant action and want to see the ball in play. Not dead time."

Back to our resident lefty, and my former radio partner on Honolulu Sharks broadcasts, Scott Karl, who won 54 games in the big leagues and is the father of two Generation Z daughters: "There is a deeper problem that exists here. The ability and need for younger kids to have immediate feedback is a concern. With electronics, their world is instant with feedback and information, but baseball is not instant and as far as other sports are concerned, it's slower."

To Karl's point, young people want an instant connection and they don't want to wait three to four hours for an outcome of a game.

Many defenders of the present state of the game would point to two issues to disprove that this is a concern. First, huge local television deals and ratings, which I covered in chapter 2, and also rising minor league attendance. CJ Kelly (2022) of HowTheyPlay suggests that proves the point further that this generational issue is a concern as the game is becoming more regional, and another significant concern, says Kelly, is that kids are not playing baseball anymore.

MLB's Fanbase Is Getting Gray

As stated earlier, one of the game's biggest problems relates to age. The average viewer on a local broadcast is 55, and the average age of the season ticket holder is only slightly younger. As stated earlier, the average Major League Baseball fan is 57 years old and only 29 percent of Major League Baseball fans are between the ages of 18 and 34.

Nielsen statistics indicate that the median age of Major League Soccer and National Basketball Association viewers in 2016 was 40 and 42, respectively, compared with a median age of 50 for the National Football League viewer and 57 for Major League Baseball (Easley, 2018).

Stephen L. Carter (2019) of Bloomberg suggests, "The baseball fan is, as advertisers like to say, aging up."

According to a 2017 study in *Sports Business Journal*, the average baseball television viewer is seven years older than the average pro football fan and 15 years older than the average pro basketball fan.

"The rising generation actually does like baseball, but it's hard to reach them because their heads are always on their screens," said Carter.

Dave Ziedelis offers, "The big problem … is this instant-gratification society we live in with mobile devices. MLB's demographic is growing older and will be a problem when the baby boomer generation drifts off into the sunset because they are not developing young fans."

The *Minneapolis Star Tribune*'s Chris Hine (2018) says Major League Baseball is losing interest with younger fans, even if the sport isn't in a state of crisis (yet). "There are computer screens, smartphone screens, tablet screens. Then there are so many applications within those screens—Netflix, Instagram, Twitter, Snapchat, Facebook—fighting for that time. Baseball's summer monopoly ended long ago. If it expects to thrive into the future, it must keep courting youth and convincing them the sport is great entertainment."

Minnesota Twins president Dave St. Peter told the *Star Tribune* that baseball must do more than improve the pace of play or cut down on strikeouts. "There's got to be more to it than that," said St. Peter. Surprisingly, he isn't afraid to say that he, the president of an MLB team, can't make it through a whole game without doing something else.

"And I don't apologize for that," St. Peter said to the *Star Tribune*. "I have my phone and I can see if something is going on, I can go back."

Hine says, "The challenge is getting fans, especially young people, to tune in at all."

Jeff Lantz, senior director of communication for Minor League Baseball, who also worked in the Baltimore Orioles' front office, has concerns about Major League Baseball's aging demographic. He's seen this before.

Lantz said to me, "I think the model that it seems like MLB is following, that they probably should try and avoid, is the NASCAR model. NASCAR, when 20 years ago and it was Dale Earnhardt and Richard Petty and Yarborough and ... a bunch of old white guys racing their cars around a track. It was being watched by a bunch of old white guys. And then ... Dale, Jr., came along, and Jeff Gordon and all these guys. Well, they were late 20s, early 30s, and they were drawing crowds of people that were old, white, and they didn't make any effort to go after the kids and get them interested in NASCAR. Well, now you watch NASCAR, the tracks are half-empty. That generation has moved on. If you're 65 or 70 now, you're not going to drive to Talladega and sit out in the sun all day and bake or go to Daytona. That generation has moved on and passed on or whatever. And now they're stuck with another aging crowd, but nobody behind them." A cautionary tale indeed.

So, Who Are These Kids?

While millennials are the largest group of consumers now, Generation Z is the future, and now is the time to begin thinking about how to engage them best. How will MLB serve them as consumers of Major League Baseball? Let's get to know them before answering that question.

Generation Z was between 1995 and the early 2010s. There are 74 million of them and they make up 25 percent of the population. They're interested in meaningful social change. Perhaps more than others before them, Generation Z has a chance to change the world for the better and they're taking it (Ita Group, 2022) and apparently embracing it as well.

Andy Reid, Super Bowl–winning coach of the Kansas City Chiefs, knows this generation intimately as his star quarterback, Patrick Mahomes, is a Gen Zer, and Reid clearly has admiration for Mahomes and his contemporaries. On NFL players protesting and demonstrating unity with the Black Lives Matter campaign, he said, "I am so fired up by our younger generation. We have this country and these kids know how great this country is. And they just want to make it better" (Ireland, 2020).

Those in my generation (Generation X) typically focus on Generation Z's heavy use of mobile devices and being distracted by technology, but I tend to agree with Reid. As I am a parent of two Generation Z kids, I think he is spot-on and I couldn't be more proud of their desire to serve society and truly make the world a better place. However, their heads are seemingly buried in their phones.

Schlesinger, also a Gen Z parent, said, "Generation Z is incredibly technologically savvy, sophisticated, and sort of wedded to their smartphone. And a lot of that does pose challenges for attracting them to become fans of baseball. From our perspective, it's not just about getting them to the ballpark, although that is a primary driver of our focus; it's about making them fans of the Brewers and of baseball in general."

Generation Z has seemingly had access to the internet since birth. Many of them grew up playing with their parents' mobile phones or tablets and received their first mobile phone at age 10. They have grown up in a hyperconnected world and the smartphone is their preferred method of communication. On average, they spend three hours a day on their mobile device.

As consumers, the members of this generation have seen the financial struggle of millennials and have adopted a more fiscally conservative approach, which could serve as a challenge to marketing initiatives.

"The one thing that we spend a lot of time on, both within the Brewers and also Major League Baseball on a centralized basis, is attracting the younger demographic," offers Schlesinger, "and that also includes the very young, so the 5–12-year-olds, but also the Gen Zs, who are somewhat of a unique demographic in the sense that they are mobile, they don't need parents to take them places, they have disposable income, they have discretionary spending capability, they are extremely sophisticated in terms of how they consume entertainment and how they use their leisure time."

Miami Marlins bullpen coordinator and coach Rob Flippo, who is the father of a Gen Z son, feels that younger people have short attention spans and that creates a challenge in trying to connect them to a game that requires patience. "They don't want to hang around for an extended period of time [to watch a three-plus-hour game]. They want something quick, then move on. Sadly, we are creating a society that is losing the ability to stay locked in," said Flippo.

Interestingly, in terms of Generation Z as members of the workforce, Jeremy Finch (2015) of Fast Company unearthed more in that area: "We found that while Gen Z like the idea of working for themselves, the majority are risk-averse, practical, and pragmatic. They're excellent team players. Sharing the bigger picture and being transparent about motives and outcomes are important. Gen Z won't blindly follow without justification, and that might be their biggest strength."

So, how does this transcend to Generation Z as customers and hooking them into being baseball fans for life?

Well, for starters, MLB and its teams must be purposeful about the content they push out. Generation Z is drawn to and buys into a strong mission and vision. So, what's the mission and vision they can get behind that is being voiced by MLB as it relates to societal issues? In short, they're a values-driven generation.

Another example, from *Adweek* (2017), notes that "studies have shown that Gen Z is interested in racial, gender and income equality, as well as environmental issues. Standing up for these values is becoming a differentiator for brands."

Generation Z members are markedly more socially conscious than their elders, influencing their fan affiliations. Gen Zers are three times more likely to believe that sports are a powerful vehicle for social progress (Lombardo, 2017).

As a result, Major League Baseball should focus its marketing and engagement strategies around these characteristics. More on this in the solutions section of this chapter.

Generation Z as Consumers of MLB Content

As it relates to sports, and especially being sports fans, each generation boasts certain characteristics. Gen Zers aren't watching less sports content, but their preferences, and how they engage with that content, differ significantly from prior generations (Imagen Insights, 2022).

Schlesinger of the Brewers would agree. He said, "Certainly, social media is a big part of our [the Brewers] marketing and branding. A lot of what we do on the social media front is designed to reach and communicate and connect to Gen Z because they are not going to be persuaded by traditional media. Frankly, they don't consume traditional media."

Ashley MacLennan's Fan Graphs piece titled "No, Millennials Aren't Killing Baseball" commented that the challenge is "how to sell a game to a demographic composed largely of people who can barely look up from their phones long enough to cross the street, let alone sit in a stadium for three straight hours … and [watch the] sometimes slow game of baseball unfold before them?"

"I cannot tell you the last time my teenagers listened to terrestrial radio or, frankly, watched, God forbid, broadcast television," added Schlesinger. "They're certainly into Netflix. And we have not completely figured it out but it's something we spend a lot of time trying to." To me, this seems like a social science project that is being played out in real time.

Kids are engaging and enjoying baseball via other entry points. The MLB app, videos, compressed games, and highlights are some of the ways Generation Z consumes big league baseball. According to Imagen, Gen Z's consumption of non-game video content is over three hours per week.

MLB suggests that 70–75 percent of followers on Instagram for @MLB and @MLBCut4 are between the ages of 13 and 34. Fans around the world, particularly across younger demographics, continue to consume the sport and their favorite players through MLB's popular and award-winning licensed video games in record fashion.

Mark Hyman, former longtime Orioles beat writer, agrees and suggests Generation Zers are consuming Major League Baseball differently and therefore fan interest with this generation is not down—they simply consume the game in a nontraditional manner and perhaps the data on how to measure their participation on social media is incomplete.

In *Sports Business Journal*, Vince Gennaro (2019) uncovered the differences between Gen Zers and baby boomers as consumers of sports. He suggests, "Boomers engage with their favorite sport primarily via watching games on broadcast and cable TV and attending live events. Conversely, Gen Z seldom watches full games, and it is rarely via broadcast or cable."

Compared with baby boomers, Gen Zers are more likely to consume sports by watching parts of games, listening to podcasts, playing fantasy sports, scouring highlights on social media, and searching websites that cover their favorite team (Gennaro, 2019).

"The launch of MLB.TV in 2002 and the At Bat mobile app in 2012 gave MLB the lead in putting games where young fans were spending their time—online," said Gennaro.

Interestingly, the Gen Z fan has a deeper devotion to individual athletes than teams. According to Gennaro, "When asked if they are bigger fans of specific athletes or teams and leagues, Gen Z favors athletes by a margin of 2-to-1 over baby boomers."

To Major League Baseball's credit, it has created various initiatives such as "We Play Loud" and "Let the Kids Play" to reach younger fans. Mac McArtor (2020) suggests these "branding campaigns effectively target younger generation fans; however, there is little evidence to suggest that MLB has instilled a marketing plan with the goal of driving attendance. In addition to expanding the branding campaign into next season, a successful marketing plan also must increase attendance levels."

McArtor dug deeper with focus groups composed of young people that revealed "Major League Baseball fans and non–MLB fans alike, consider games to be seldom action-packed and exciting, and entirely too long. However, MLB fans who participated in the focus groups insisted that cheering for a specific team or understanding the game well would make MLB more entertaining and interesting.

"[Also], a significant barrier is the time commitment. The majority of participants agreed that they did not want to be present in the stadium for an entire baseball game."

Three actionable insights emerged from his focus groups:

1. Creating a social experience around game attendance is a necessity, which connects to my earlier point about designing more social spaces in major league stadiums.
2. Incorporating philanthropy into ticket sales will further incentivize Gen Z sports fans to attend games. The key here is that the individuals buying tickets are incentivized by support for a cause.
3. Prioritizing affordability is essential.

Also, MacLennan (2017) commented on what she suggests is the most logical explanation for a lack of engagement among young viewers. "While apps and fun giveaways might help baseball reach a younger audience, they don't address the problem at a systemic level. There's one very specific reason Millennials don't buy the things they're blamed for killing, which is finances," said MacLennan.

MacLennan highlighted a study by advocacy group Young Invincibles that revealed that millennials are significantly not as financially savvy as their parents in terms of earning and saving. This leads to a challenge for Major League Baseball and its teams in creating interesting, engaging, and affordable product for the Generation Z fan base.

This suggests that Gen Z desires to interact with sports content beyond live games and has a strong preference for more personalized engagement with content, a shift from the traditional fan and league relationship (Business Wire, 2019).

Interestingly, Gennaro (2019) also said, "There are a few other notable trends among Gen Z when compared to earlier generations, all of which hold true for baseball." For example, "Gen Z is markedly more socially conscious than their elders, which influences their fan affiliations. Gen Zers are three times more likely to believe that sports is a powerful vehicle for social progress."

Business Wire's analysis of Imagen's research on the Gen Z sports fan said, "Being a sports fan is no longer just about the game itself.... Gen Z fans are more likely to comment, share and repost content than their older Gen X counterparts."

Some old-school media types may be threatened by these young content creators because it isn't the official voice of the team, but as long as they are not spewing hate or inaccuracies, let them have at it. Celebrate them. Encourage them. Recognize them. In short, Gen Z wants a voice and that voice equates to free marketing for Major League Baseball.

Solutions

The idea for this book began with a jaw-dropping revelation from my then 16-year-old son, Jacob, that he felt "baseball is boring." I couldn't believe what I was hearing, but it got me to consider that perhaps Generation Z was not interested in the game in its present state, and while that might be true, what we have learned in this chapter is perhaps they are engaged, just in a nontraditional manner—a manner that us old guys are just figuring out. Regardless, I believe there is hope that Major League Baseball and its teams can adjust their practices and bring Generation Z into the baseball-loving family. Here are some solutions to overcoming this challenge.

Online Presence

As Silverman stated, keys to growing live viewership among young fans are accessibility and opportunities for engagement, and one of those is to have an online presence, which is all but required for athletes looking to capture Gen Z fans.

Focus Group Feedback

McArtor (2020) offered three actionable insights that emerged from his focus groups, which should not be a heavy lift for Major League Baseball teams. Those are:

1. Creating a social experience around game attendance.
2. Incorporating philanthropy into ticket sales.
3. Prioritizing affordability.

Meeting Them Where They Are

No question Generation Z spends a tremendous time on social media, so why not bring the game and access to them? It's already happening, so let's give MLB some credit for its work in this area. As Commissioner Manfred said, "You have to be where they want to be."

MLB is on board with this concept and has deepened the relationship with both YouTube and Facebook to air live games free of charge. "Collaborating with Facebook will again drive the creation of new ways for us to deliver content to baseball fans that engage on the platform daily. Facebook provides a community-focused environment that will allow for fans to connect with their favorite teams via custom on-demand content and live game action driven by an original MLB Network social-first broadcast production," said Chris Tully, Major League Baseball executive vice president, global media.

To date, Major League Baseball is the only major sports league to stream games to Facebook, where the average MLB viewer is 36 years old—"literally decades younger than what we get with a broadcast audience," Commissioner Manfred said.

Keep it up, MLB. Expand the number of free games and perhaps look into Twitter or other platforms as well to air live games and post content.

Ticket Subscriptions

Here we go again—ticket subscriptions. This is the world we are all living in with seemingly everything connected to some type of subscription service. MLB realizes that its ticket challenges reflect broader competition for leisure spending, attention, and time, and the subscription service tackles those barriers.

The most popular new ticketing trend, though, is Major League Baseball's Ballpark Pass. This service, as you'll recall, mimics the video streaming model of Hulu and Netflix, for example. In 2019, the fastest-growing buyers of the Ballpark Pass were 22 years old and younger, and many were under 35.

In addition, the average age of the subscription buyer is 11 years younger than the buyers of traditional season tickets. Today's Gen Z fans may live near the stadium and want to attend more games at a reasonable price, making them the perfect candidates for a Ballpark Pass. I'm 53 (not young) and I would like to see my local teams—Angels, Dodgers, and Padres—get on board with the subscription option as well.

In-Venue Experience

Once teams have Gen Zers connected with their monthly subscription and inside the ballpark, they must then provide them with an experience that is engaging. Today's Gen Z sports fan wants a communal experience. Manfred said stadiums have focused on creating more social spaces for (younger) fans to congregate and experience the game atmosphere without being glued to their seats for nine innings (Hine, 2018).

In chapter 3 (Fan Experience), the Orioles' Greg Bader spoke of how Orioles Park at Camden Yards, arguably the best fan experience in all of baseball, is planning some changes designed to enhance the in-game experience for fans—especially Gen Z—that will include new spaces for socializing.

Also, the New York Yankees made a concerted effort to attract younger fans starting in 2017. They lowered some ticket prices, hired a new social media director, and created an open plaza behind the center field wall for standing and having an adult beverage with fellow fans (Bondi, 2017).

That type of open-air space is becoming far more common in MLB, and it should be. The St. Louis Cardinals added Budweiser Terrace before the 2018 season and Nationals Park, home of the Washington Nationals, also rebranded its space as Budweiser Terrace in 2016.

Oakland Athletics president Dave Kaval told *USA Today* (2019) that the organization found younger fans wanted "experiential things they can show on their Instagram, their Snapchat. Live sports are changing. Entertainment is changing."

"When we're thinking of deploying hundreds of millions of dollars for infrastructure, we need to stay with the times. Stadiums are iconic gathering places. You have to do it in the context of the way people are experiencing entertainment today," said Kaval.

Marketing to Generation Z

While Gen Z and millennial fans consume the most non-game content, they're also the most underserved audience. This should serve as a signal to Major League Baseball that this is a huge opportunity to engage with this generation by delivering the content they want (see Table 9)—archived videos, behind-the-scenes footage, funny clips, documentaries, stats, and player data (Business Wire, 2019).

For instance, said Ryan Rolf, CRO, Americas at Imagen (2019), "Providing authentic, high-quality video content that's easy to access is critical to keeping fans across all generations engaged. Sports fans, particularly Millennials and Gen Z, are craving a more personalized experience when interacting with their favorite sport, player or team."

Rolf also states, "Fans are taking the power into their own hands when it comes to content creation and it's up to the leagues, teams and players to keep up with this content consumption shift" (Business Wire, 2019).

Table 9: What MLB Content Does Generation Z Desire?

Desires more and is being underserved	Has plenty and still wants more
Archived/old games	Documentaries
Behind-the-scenes footage	Expert analysis
Mic'd up videos	Funny clips/bloopers
Player celebrations	Player interviews

Despite the assertion that attention spans have dwindled to goldfish proportions, Generation Z spends a lot of time on social media, and advertising on those platforms needs to be customized to fit the medium

(Kasasa, 2022). A warning to MLB marketing executives—it might not be as easy as uploading a highlight from last night's big win to grab their attention. Gen Z can sniff out canned or insincere messages in seconds.

Fast Company agrees and suggests that "Gen Z has a carefully tuned radar for being sold to and a limited amount of time and energy to spend assessing whether something's worth their time. Getting past these filters, and winning their attention, will mean providing them with engaging and immediately beneficial experiences." So why not consider employing some social-media-savvy Gen Zers in MLB teams' marketing departments?

As stated earlier, Generation Z is more socially conscious than previous generations. If MLB teams are engaged in social issues in their communities, celebrate it and market it. They will be more likely to support the club. An MLB team's commitment to the people and neighborhoods it serves is a major advantage in engaging the youngest generation. Look for ways to clarify your values and weave them into everything you do, which should include your marketing communications. Give Gen Z a reason to care about what you do and you'll find them more than willing to engage with you as a consumer.

Young people are drawn to sports whose athletes are active on social media and interact with fans. Major League Baseball, its teams, and players seem to be lacking in this area for a variety of reasons that I will get to in chapter 8. Regardless, the message to MLB is to do a better job marketing your players and encouraging them to connect with the Gen Z fan on social media.

I asked Rick Schlesinger how the Brewers uniquely and/or innovatively market to the Gen Z fan. He replied, "So social media is a huge driver of how we're communicating and getting our message to them. That message has to be sophisticated, it has to be tongue-in-cheek, it has to be subtle, and it can't necessarily do what you like to do with traditional media, which is make the ask.

"Because when we advertise and market on traditional media, we're making an ask in the sense of, 'Buy our tickets, come to the ballpark, watch our games on television.' We make an ask and social media, and for specifically for Gen Z, we cannot do those kinds of direct asks. It's going to be a turnoff, it's going to not be well-received."

Specifically, Schlesinger told me that the Brewers are trying to explain baseball analytics and highlight them on interactive media, during the television broadcast, and through other ways to communicate because those are things that younger fans are interested in and are going to respond to.

Shavonnah Schreiber suggests Major League Baseball should amplify its brand beginning with an education piece on the product (MLB), which she believes will attract new fans, and younger ones as well. Then she recommends that MLB focus on what the demand attributes are regarding baseball. Those attributes make a new fan want to learn more about the product and be a part of the sport.

"There's obviously a social media connection to this. Clicks take the potential new fan to places of inquiry. An idea would be to create a campaign focusing on coming out to the ballpark and how baseball brings communities together," said Schreiber.

Gennaro (2019) summed it up this way: "In order to maintain its popularity among Gen Z, MLB will need to stay ahead of the curve by using the latest technology to engage fans. This might mean creating a second (or third) screen broadcast, or using augmented reality to satisfy the analytical fan who wants deeper insights into in-game action. Smart stadiums wired with the latest technology and conveniences and leading-edge environmental practices will connect with young fans on their terms."

Regardless of the generation, fans of all ages regularly seek out and consume new content in ways we never imagined. It would behoove Major League Baseball to break free from its antiquated approach and become more innovative in connecting with fans of all generations.

6

Weakening Youth Participation

> *"The single biggest determinant of whether somebody is going to be a fan as an adult is what they play as a kid."*—Rob Manfred, MLB Commissioner

When Rob Manfred began his tenure as commissioner of Major League Baseball in 2015, he said his first 100 days on the job were to focus on youth baseball programs. This was Manfred's self-proclaimed number-one priority and thus far I give him and his team led by Tony Reagins, former Angels general manager and current executive vice president of baseball and softball development, high praise for their efforts to increase youth baseball participation.

Their efforts have been far-reaching into America's cities, and especially the inner city, but a problem still exists—today's youth are turning away from baseball in record numbers. There are many layers to this issue that I detail in this chapter, and yes, MLB has made inroads, but this is a huge issue that Major League Baseball's initiatives cannot solve alone.

Bill Bavasi says of MLB's efforts, "The idea is that if we can get more kids playing the game, then we make more fans."

Manfred added, "Baseball is a game firmly rooted in childhood experiences, and its vitality and growth rely heavily on giving young people from all backgrounds the opportunity to play and watch baseball."

To that point, children who attend their first baseball game before age five will go to 68 percent more games a year for the rest of their lives than those who wait until they are 14 or older.

It all starts when Dad plays catch with you in the backyard when you're a small child. If you're not playing baseball and softball as a kid, then chances are you won't appreciate it and love it as an adult. In short, kids need to be introduced to the game early on to be lifelong fans, but sadly kids are not playing baseball as much as they used to.

Where does the conversation about declining participation in baseball begin? If you ask Wayne Krivsky, it starts at the lowest levels. He suggests, "The grassroots of baseball is deteriorating." Let's find out how it is deteriorating, and what the solutions may be to overcome this problem.

Where Have the Kids Gone?

An HBO *Real Sports*/Marist Poll (2019) revealed that 15 percent of Americans consider baseball to be the most popular team sport for children to play, followed closely by basketball at 14 percent, with football (35 percent) and soccer (28 percent) surpassing baseball on the list. The results also stated that 40 percent believe the length of the game has something to do with why children don't gravitate toward baseball. It's true. Youth baseball games can be brutally long and boring. Kids today live in a world of instant gratification, and baseball with its slow pace is having a hard time attracting players. Soccer and lacrosse, on the other hand, offer an experience that includes shorter game times and nonstop action.

This is why a sport like lacrosse is dominating and more kids are gravitating toward it. When I was in high school, during the offseason many football players played baseball. They were typically good athletes, big and strong, and they were pretty good ballplayers. Today, high school football players are not playing baseball in the spring anymore and many have shifted to lacrosse. Why? The answer is because lacrosse coaches entice them by saying in their sport, you can put on pads and a helmet, grab a stick, and legally hit the other guy all while staying in shape. What's more appealing than that to a teenager?

The poll also showed that about one-third of respondents think baseball takes too much skill, and that factors into why some children do not play the game. Another third believes the lack of a nearby ball field is part of the reason children are not playing baseball, and yet another third of adults nationally believe some children don't play baseball because the sport is not fun.

However, 33 percent of Americans report baseball is the sport they would most like to play with their sons. So, there's hope and a desire, although again there is a bit of an age divide. Of Americans 45 and older, 40 percent are likely to pick baseball as the sport they would share with their child, compared with 25 percent of younger respondents.

During the 1990s, participation in youth baseball peaked, with about 4.5 million kids ages 6–12 playing the game. In 2015, that number was down to 2.4 million.

So, where are they? What happened?

6. Weakening Youth Participation

Specialization is one reason why participation in baseball dropped. The pressure for kids to specialize in one sport at a younger age is more prevalent than ever.

David Carter agrees. "Specialization is hurting baseball but other sports as well. [It used to be] kids could play soccer in the fall and baseball in the spring. The kids who now become focused on one sport are pressured into playing travel ball. It used to be that youth sports were a chance to have the kids have some fun while providing the parents an opportunity to connect and talk about neighborhood issues. The average kid is no longer playing," said Carter.

I asked Buck Showalter about today's kids specializing in one sport. He said, "If they only play baseball, that's a red flag. Those that play baseball year-round are more likely to have baseball-related injuries down the road—arm, shoulder. If I ask a kid, 'What do you do when you don't pitch?' and he says he doesn't play [any other sport], I put an X next to their name."

The goal shouldn't be to weed out the average players as they move, for example, from Little League to Senior League. It should be to cater to them. It does appear that many of those kids simply disappear after age 12. Where do they go? Soccer? Lacrosse? Quit sports altogether?

Another turnoff to playing youth baseball is an overemphasis on winning and rewarding the so-called best players with accolades like being named to an All-Star team when it is often "Daddy ball," where if you coach, your kid is in even if their skill level is not All-Star quality. The goal should be to keep all players, regardless of ability, engaged and playing baseball.

The data on participation in youth baseball might support the notion that baseball isn't popular. The baseball fields near my house lie empty on many spring and summer days (for that matter, year-round) in Southern California, where the weather is baseball-ready 12 months of the year. The sights and sounds of kids playing baseball in the park or in front of their homes that were so much a part of my childhood are missing. As a youngster, I was obsessed with playing baseball every day. We just don't see that anymore.

Dan Koosed, an associate scout for the New York Yankees and master hitting instructor out of Southern California, has over 30 years of coaching experience at the youth and collegiate level. He also works with MLB players across both leagues. Koosed believes that there are the same amount of kids playing baseball—it's just different. "When I played in the 1980s, if you didn't make the freshman baseball team your career was over, but not today. These days parents will put teams together themselves," said Koosed. So, perhaps they are playing, just in a nontraditional manner that makes it harder to track.

Major league coaches like Rob Flippo of the Miami Marlins consider themselves teachers, and Flippo believes the foundation of learning to play the game the right way while having fun in the process is missing from the youth game.

"From a kid's perspective, [youth coaches] are breeding the instincts out of players. We even see this at the big-league level when a player in the field pulls a card out of their pocket and goes to a [predetermined] dot. In youth baseball, before every pitch, the players look to the coaches for direction. That cannot be fun."

He's right, it's not. I managed my son's Little League teams for years and I agree with Flippo that with coaches controlling so many aspects of the game, the kids are not permitted to think for themselves and learn on their own at times. They are treated as pawns on a chessboard, and that's incredibly boring.

Vanderbilt University's baseball players were the first to wear electronic wristbands showing what pitch the coach was calling from the dugout in 2022, the first year it was legal in college baseball.

One of the crutches we see at the big-league level is the cards handed out to each defensive player telling them where to be positioned for each hitter. Major leaguers don't possess the instincts their predecessors had and took pride in.

Buck Showalter is no fan of such cards. "Don't get me started," he said, before adding, "For today's player, everything is programmed for them. I call it the teleprompter. What happens when the teleprompter breaks? They can't go off script. As the manager, my job is to be on top of and in charge of the 'what-ifs.'"

Flippo is quick to add that this isn't an indictment of youth coaches. However, let the kids play and figure it out without constant intervention by coaches whose main motivation is to win. Little League coaches are too concerned with winning and not promoting the fun of the game. They call every pitch and constantly position the players. Kids today do not talk about the game on the bench because the coaches control everything. They don't ask about what pitches they were thrown. They don't talk about how the pitcher went after them.

Scott Karl agrees with Flippo that kids need to learn the game while playing and not have youth coaches call every pitch or position them for every hitter.

"When I coached a 12U travel ball team, I would maybe call three pitches in a game," said Karl. "I knew that if I went through a series of signs to the catcher, then the catcher would have to go through the same series to the pitcher. It slows the game down and it would be boring.

"Same can apply at any level when the coach is calling every pitch and the pitcher does not have the authority to shake off the sign and as a result the pitcher is then relegated to make a pitch he's not sold on. That's not good," offered Karl.

Speaking of boring, Paul Langhorst (2016) of Engage Sports wrote the piece "Is Youth Baseball Too Boring for Today's Kids?" He said, "It's hard to imagine that baseball is an exciting sport for the average 9-year old.

"Baseball does have its exciting, action-packed moments, but overall baseball is one of the slowest, if not the slowest, team participation sports. Consider the following: On average, there is an 11% chance that a fielder will be involved in any given play. There are few set plays, except when attempting to pick off a base runner. Add it all up, and there is just a lot of standing around," said Langhorst.

Baseball also is the most humbling game, where a player's failure is public. In soccer, for example, 22 kids are running on a field and if a player makes an errant kick, it is often difficult to know who even kicked it—let alone if it was a poor kick. The game keeps moving and all is forgotten. Not the case in baseball. It's a truism that if you fail 70 percent of the time as a hitter, you may be destined for the Hall of Fame. But you cannot hide in baseball. As they say, the ball will find you. Make an error in the field or strike out at the plate and the whole world is there to witness it, or at least that's what it feels like. Kids do not want to be in the spotlight for the wrong reasons.

Kids these days are protected from failure. We have often heard of helicopter parents who constantly hover over their children and shelter them and intervene at every step of their life when even the smallest adversity comes their way, which is to their detriment. Let's face it, some parents do not have the stomach to be a Little League parent. When their kid makes an error, they can't rush the field and make it all better. For years, we have seen that everyone gets a trophy, which is certainly not the way the real world works. Kids are being set up for failure by coddling them too much.

Another issue is that top two-sport athletes are opting for a career other than baseball. Take, for example, these current NFL superstar quarterbacks who were once considered top MLB prospects and were even drafted by major league clubs: Russell Wilson, Patrick Mahomes, and, most recently, Kyler Murray. Murray was a first-round selection of the Oakland A's and also the number-one pick in the 2019 NFL draft. All three opted for what is considered a more dangerous career with shorter shelf life in the NFL, where the average career is a little more than three years. Perhaps they chose the NFL because they went straight to the league as opposed to bouncing around from small town to small town in baseball's minor leagues.

Bill Bavasi advocates for the best athletes to consider baseball first. "You're going to be a lot richer, you're going to be a lot healthier, and your head's going to be a lot more intact if you play baseball. It's just that there's no question that we need to give these kids that opportunity," he said.

Mark Hyman, author of *Until It Hurts: America's Obsession with Youth Sports and How it Harms Our Kids*, added, "We have devalued the other touch points of playing baseball—recreation ball or even Wiffle ball. Celebrate another way to play baseball. Now it has become only the most talented kids with parents who have money. It should be more egalitarian."

As Joe Maddon told me, "We are not drawing kids to play the game. With all of these travel ball teams, it is pay to play. The camaraderie and teamwork has been lost."

To Hyman's point, playing baseball is more than organized baseball, or at least it should be. Growing up I played Little League and high school baseball, which were organized ball, but I also spent thousands of hours playing Wiffle ball in the street with my friends, and that's truly where I developed a love for the game.

The goal for Major League Baseball is to grow its fanbase, and playing the game is far more than travel ball or Little League. I want children to enjoy the game, develop a passion for it, and become lifelong fans of baseball. MLB is doing more to create opportunities to play baseball informally in neighborhoods without the pressure and cost, which should lead to kids becoming fans.

However, youth baseball in its current state is not engaging to kids and it's killing their interest, mainly because most of the time they are standing around but also because of the rules at the youth level.

For example, pitching at that age is a problem. No matter how much coaching they receive, youth players have an incredibly difficult time throwing strikes. It is one of the most challenging skills to master in all of sports. I spent years providing pitching lessons to kids ages 8–18. In the bullpen they could throw strikes with ease, but then they took the mound in a game and it would sometimes fall apart. As a result, players, coaches, and spectators would endure ball four after ball four, which is excruciatingly boring.

However, one youth league in southern Ohio has a different approach. When there are three balls on the hitter, the coach comes in to pitch because he can throw strikes. It keeps the action going. That eliminates walks, which are boring, and the defense is not just standing there watching walk after walk.

Douglas Hartmann, a sociology professor at the University of Minnesota, told *The Morning Call*, "One of the challenges baseball has is how inactive it is as a youth participatory activity. Most of the parents don't care that much about any particular sport. They want the kid running around, getting exercise ... and does baseball really provide that?" (Hine, 2018).

Baseball Is Expensive to Play

Everyone I spoke to agreed that one cause of the decline of participation in youth baseball is cost. While Little League participation has fallen, travel baseball has grown—and travel ball costs are more substantial. Many children cannot afford to play and develop their skills. As a result, they either play another, more affordable sport like soccer or basketball or quit altogether.

An HBO *Real Sports*/Marist Poll (2015) asked why children weren't playing. One outcome was that finances are a factor. More than 6 in 10 Americans, 63 percent, say the cost of playing in top travel leagues is, at least, part of the reason. Additionally, 47 percent say the equipment is too expensive.

In terms of equipment costs, when I was a kid playing baseball in the 1970s and 1980s, the only equipment needed to play organized baseball was a glove and cleats. Many of us can recall our youth baseball coach who not only volunteered his time to coach an often unruly group of boys but also had to schlep the enormous equipment bags that contained the bats, helmets, catcher's gear, and balls to and from the field.

Times have changed. In addition to their gloves and cleats, youngsters today are required to have their own helmet, bat, and bag. Typically, equipment costs can range from $200 to $500 each season.

But the costs may not end there. For the better players, or for those whose parents think they are MLB material or worthy of a college scholarship, travel baseball averages out to around $3,700 per year. But families can also pay thousands more if they opt for extra training such as pitching or hitting lessons, and playing in out-of-state tournaments are additional costs.

Specifically, CJ Kelly (2022) of HowTheyPlay says the cost of playing baseball "is prohibitive.... The 'pay to play' system has become astronomical because parents use it to get into better schools and colleges. The kids have to show up at special camps ... [and] have to re-tryout for their travel team and high school every year. Some charge just to try out. The personal coaching business has exploded to disgusting proportions."

Sadly, the game is catering to the elite baseball player and leaving the casual player on the sideline. "Travel ball costs so much to play," said Wayne Krivsky. He added, "Whatever happened to free baseball?

American Legion? We played all summer for free when I was a kid. There are so many gimmicks out there and the parents don't know it's a money grab." In fact, today some travel ball coaches are being paid enough to make an income. That's crazy.

Justin Turner, then of the Dodgers, told me, "Playing youth baseball is too expensive for many families to afford with travel ball, showcases, plus equipment, and the travel itself, including hotels, is too much for families. Unfortunately, you have to promote yourself and play in travel tournaments and showcases. It can be $300 to $500 a month plus travel and the cost of the tournaments. It turns away families because they cannot afford it."

Those showcases that Turner speaks of are big business and can often cost players $1,000 to play in one tournament. Dan Koosed says it's not necessary. "It's a rip-off. Parents incorrectly believe it is the only way to be seen." Koosed, who has experience as a college coach, recommends kids to "just play. It doesn't matter where. If you are good enough, you'll be seen."

"The way that we feed amateur talent into the professional system is extremely broken right now," Jay Jaffe told me, "because of the costs of travel ball and the losses of scholarships. A lot of it does come down to the cost of equipment and things like that, and I know that baseball seems to be making noise about rededicating some effort into more urban grassroots efforts, but it's going to take a while for that to take hold and it has to be done right."

Of travel teams, Scott Karl says, "Travel teams create a financial divide." He should know—he has coached them. I experienced it as well as a coach and as a parent of a son who played. But in the past few years, it has truly gotten out of hand.

Jaffe added, "There's a lot of competition out there for kids' time and the limited resources that they do have. [For example], all you need for basketball is a basketball versus $100 for a bat and a couple hundred dollars for catching gear. The equipment costs are very real and the cost of being on a team, they're real too. It's something that baseball is trying to fix, but they're trying to fix it by taking over everything. I don't know that that's necessarily going to be the best way to do it. Major League Baseball has enough problems dealing with its control at the highest level."

Surprisingly, the analytics we have seen the past few years at the major league level has trickled down to youth baseball and has turned many away from the sport. Koosed suggests that there is too much focus on launch angle and exit velocity and says, "A lot of guys [coaches] don't know what they are doing with the information," which leads to the average player being marginalized.

Justin Turner also told me, "The technology has gone too far. We are going in the wrong direction. When I played we didn't have that [data and tools]. If we did, I may not have made it to the big leagues. We knew that we hit .320 because all we needed was a calculator. We have all these devices to study their swing without even hitting a baseball."

The costs associated with playing are not exclusive to the players and families—it is also expensive for coaches. Today's youth coaches typically spend their own money on additional equipment such as balls, L-screens, nets, and bags. Also, fields are tough to find and there is often a rental cost associated with using them. "Fields are costly because baseball is played on a diamond. Not like soccer, where just about any patch of grass will do," said Karl.

I believe MLB has an obligation to help make the youth game more affordable for all players, especially those in the inner city and lower socio-economic communities.

Decline in African American Participation

While growing up in the 1970s and 1980s, some of my favorite major league players were Don Baylor, Reggie Jackson, Dusty Baker, Dave Parker, and George Foster who all happened to be African American. Sadly, the number of African Americans playing baseball has decreased not only in the major leagues but in youth baseball as well. The contributions to Major League Baseball by African Americans cannot be understated. Since Jackie Robinson broke the color barrier in 1947 with the Brooklyn Dodgers, many of the most prolific and gifted athletes in the history of the game have been African American. Their decline in participation has deprived fans of enjoying their talents.

But why? What is happening here?

The late Hall of Famer Joe Morgan said, "There is a perception among African-American kids that they are not welcome here, that baseball is not for inner-city kids. It's not true, and I hate that the perception is out there."

The 2020 National League Rookie of the Year for the Milwaukee Brewers, Devin Williams, added, "Participation is always important.... I feel like you need someone who looks like you to show you it's possible. When you don't see anyone who looks like you, it doesn't feel like it's attainable, in a way."

Commissioner Rob Manfred said, "Baseball is a game firmly rooted in childhood experiences, and its vitality and growth rely heavily on giving young people from all backgrounds the opportunity to play and watch baseball" (MLB).

Shaun M. Anderson and Mathew M. Martin's (2019) piece titled, "The African American Community and Professional Baseball: Examining Major League Baseball's Corporate Social-Responsibility Efforts as a Relationship-Management Strategy," from the *International Journal of Sport Communication*, is an important contribution to the subject. The purpose of their study was to understand why African Americans are not interested or involved in Major League Baseball.

They suggest, "MLB continues to struggle in developing relationships and increasing involvement of African Americans."

The study yielded some themes regarding Major League Baseball's program managers' challenges: inconsistency in measuring success, lack of parental involvement, and lack of trust.

The game at the big-league level has seen a drastic decline in African American fandom and participation over the last 30 years, with only 7.8 percent of current players being African American. This is a significant drop from nearly 20 percent during the late 1980s.

The authors cite the work of Ogden and Hilt, who "found four factors that contributed to this lack of interest: a greater number of African American role models in basketball, perceptions of social mobility in basketball, authority figures describing basketball as more beneficial, and basketball's ability to allow players to express themselves and feel empowered."

Also, their study quoted Fortunato and Williams, who found that "professional baseball receives far less media exposure than professional football and basketball, which makes it less attractive for Black people to become more involved with the game."

Ogden and Rose, say Anderson and Martin, "found that mass-mediated factors such as advertisements of football and basketball players and the influence of hip-hop in these sports were some of the main reasons that the African American community is less involved with the game of baseball. They also explained that other sports are cheaper to play than baseball. Finally, factors such as peer pressure, perceived social mobility through other sports, and the lack of 'cool factor' in baseball were other reasons that African American involvement has declined."

Anderson and Martin also suggest, "Another factor affecting the decline of African American players is baseball's move to globalization. Much of baseball's globalization efforts have been concentrated in Latin America [which MLB has been recruiting in since the 1940s]."

Most likely the reason is economics. "MLB's recruitment system is intentionally designed to access baseball talent as young and as cheaply as possible," say Anderson and Martin.

They add, "U.S. recruiting in MLB is highly regulated, whereas recruitment in Latin American countries is not, and Latin players born outside the United States are not allowed to be drafted into MLB but are allowed to sign with any team requesting their services."

When it comes to recruiting younger players, "MLB maintains that players who are not eligible for the draft may be able to sign to a team by the age of 17 or by the age of 16 if their birthday is before the end of the season they signed (Hanlon). In addition, MLB teams engage in a 'boatload' mentality: For every $25,000 spent on four American-born players, recruitment efforts in Latin America can help teams gain 20 players at the cost of $5,000 per player," said Anderson and Martin.

Given this, Anderson and Martin (2019) offer that "it is understandable why MLB's 2017 total team roster consisted of 31.9% Latin American players as compared with 7.7% African American players."

"When we asked about the challenges in developing a relationship with African Americans in MLB communities, we discovered three themes," said Anderson and Martin. "The first was that RBI/UYA program managers lacked consistency in how they viewed the success of their programs. Next, they said that lack of family support was another challenge to the success of developing relationships with the African American community. Third, they told us that developing trust with youth was another hindrance."

Former Major League catcher Darrell Miller is the vice president youth and facility development for Major League Baseball. He works with youths from all backgrounds at the Major League Baseball Academy in Compton, California. He supports these athletes by trying to help further their playing careers either in professional baseball or at the collegiate level, and he sees several barriers for African Americans in both settings.

"The colleges don't recruit black players. I tell them that they are the 'Jackie Robinson, Jr.' However, there are a few programs, like Vanderbilt, that provide scholarships for underserved kids. Coaches need to be willing to take on black kids," said Miller.

He added that the reason black players are not being recruited is the lack of African American coaches at the college level. "MLB needs to follow the NFL's grad assistant program where they provide opportunities for former players to get their master's while being a grad assistant, which leads to coaching jobs.... The more black kids that do this, the more we see an increase in black coaches in college and pro football. Baseball needs this pipeline for their players. They also need a mentor so they are not alone," said Miller.

Professionally is another story, said Miller. "The best high school players can't hold the jock and compete with those that have three years' college playing experience. They don't have a chance and they are phasing out after two to three years, but they need time to develop. Also, some of these kids don't have the same opportunities as those prospects [in the Dominican Republic, Venezuela, etc.] that they have invested in. College is the key. That's where they can develop their skills. The best athletes are being ignored and are leaving the game. Some prospects in the Dominican have an advantage as they have been in MLB teams' academies since they were 17 years old."

"Baseball has an inherent problem there because if you're a hotshot baseball player in high school, you graduate and you go to Bluefield, West Virginia," said George Will. "If you're a hotshot running back, you go to Ohio State, and that's a very different kind of enterprise."

Former major league pitcher Jerry Reuss added, "Baseball loses athletes in the minors because of paltry wages."

"With regard to baseball," said Will, "I've been on several major league committees, one of which was on the blue-ribbon commission on baseball economics and all this. But one was called the commissioner's initiative of baseball in the 21st century. And among the data we got was data that demonstrated that the best predictor of being a baseball fan as an adult is having played as a child. So, you got to work on that. And I think with a particular attention to African Americans, the travel baseball phenomenon is expensive, and baseball, unlike basketball, requires parents.

"You can take a basketball and go down to a court, which is not hard to build, and play basketball. And baseball requires adults ... to hit the ball and give them infield practice and groom the field and all the rest. And 69 percent of African American children are born to unmarried mothers. Now, you can't talk about this in America because we've talked about everything else, except the elephant in the room during this last year of so-called racial reckoning. But ... a problem is an absence of fathers, which is different for baseball than it is for basketball. So that's a really intractable problem," said Will.

At fifteen percent, White Americans are more than twice as likely as African Americans (6 percent) to say baseball is the leading sport in which children participate. Also, baseball places third among whites in terms of popularity and fourth among African Americans.

Super-agent Leigh Steinberg said that in 1981, 18.7 percent of MLB players, and 22 percent of the All-Star game rosters, were African American. Recent All-Star rosters had less than 5 percent African American representation (Steinberg, 2018).

That same HBO *Real Sports*/Marist Poll in 2015 stated that more than one-third surveyed believe the decline in African American baseball players is a concern. This includes about one in eight who considers the decline to be a major issue. African Americans, at 49 percent, are more likely than whites (34 percent) to consider the composition of MLB players to be troublesome.

According to the HBO *Real Sports*/Marist Poll (2015), "These results help explain what we all suspect—that baseball lags behind other sporting pastimes for American youth, particularly for African-Americans," says Keith Strudler, director of the Marist College Center for Sports Communication.

6. Weakening Youth Participation

"What could be most problematic for baseball officials is that changing the nature of the game may not alter this trend, since the larger impediment is cost, something that will be more difficult to drastically change," said Strudler.

Stephen L. Carter (2019) addressed that concern. "The proportion of black players rose steadily in the Major Leagues until 1981, when it peaked at 18.7 percent. Since then, the figures have fallen.... In 2017, the figures dipped to 6.7 percent—exactly the same percentage as in 1956, the year Jackie Robinson retired."

Carter also pointed out that the decline in the number of black players can also be seen in the number of black fans. In a 2014 survey, the television audience for Major League Baseball was 9 percent black compared with 83 percent white.

I also believe that there should be a concern that African American youth may not gravitate to a sport in which they do not see themselves represented, whether it be as players, coaches, or managers.

To my point, Mark Hyman said, "Most MLB team stadiums are located downtown near neighborhoods that are predominately African American but only 2–3% of fans who attend games are African American. With only two African American managers and few in positions in management, perhaps African Americans would be more consumers if they saw themselves on the field or [in the front office]."

Steinberg (2018) added that one reason why African American players have disappeared in baseball appears to be the overall decline in youth playing the sport. In 2002, nine million kids between the ages of 7 and 17 played baseball, as reported in the *Wall Street Journal*. That figure had declined by 41 percent by 2013.

He also said, "With participation in decline, youth leagues and teams have been forced to shut down or merge, which restricts access for poorer youths, making the sport whiter and more affluent. The NBA dominates the inner city, and the alliance with shoe companies creates a real bond. Cost may be the most dominant factor in deterring the black youth from playing baseball. Some estimates have 45% of young black children living under the poverty line."

Another reason for the lack of African American players is the reduced number of rounds in the annual draft. As stated earlier, at one time it was 100 rounds and in 2020 teams drafted in only five rounds.

Bill Bavasi said the days of 100-round drafts are over and he also wonders what happened to the dual athletes like Bo Jackson, Deion Sanders, and Brian Jordan, who all excelled in Major League Baseball and the NFL. "We were drafting kids that were dual-sport athletes and drafting them just to at least communicate to them, 'Hey, we're watching you. We think you're a decent player.' We were drafting kids that weren't playing baseball their junior or senior year in high school because they had already switched to football only. Can't do that with a five- or even 20-round draft," said Bavasi.

He added, "The two-sport athlete is now going away in high school because if you play football, you play football. And then you have spring practice and all the rest. And if you play baseball, you're on travel teams. So, the two-sport athlete in high school is becoming a vanishing commodity. And that does not work to baseball's advantage."

The problem of reaching and providing opportunities to underserved communities is a real issue and one that MLB is taking seriously, but more needs to be done.

"Why can't we support teaching the game to all kids—but especially those in underprivileged communities?" wrote Ian Desmond (2020), an infielder for the Colorado Rockies.

"Why aren't accessible, affordable youth sports viewed as an essential opportunity to affect kids' development, as opposed to money-making propositions and recruiting chances? It's hard to wrap your head around it," said Desmond.

He added, "We've got a minority issue from the top down. One African American GM. Two African American managers. Less than 8% Black players. No Black majority team owners. Perhaps most disheartening of all is a puzzling lack of focus on understanding how to change those numbers. A lack of focus on making baseball accessible and possible for all kids, not just those who are privileged enough to afford it."

Jo Adell, a Los Angeles Angels outfielder and up-and-coming prospect, told The Undefeated, "It's important to know that by the time most black baseball players are being scouted professionally, many have been playing the sport for a decade. Just like white players."

MLB's Response

For the first time in a generation, Major League Baseball is addressing youth baseball participation with Play Ball and the Reviving Baseball in Inner Cities (RBI) initiatives. Both programs have proved successful and support Commissioner Manfred's charge of putting an emphasis on youth baseball programs. MLB has a vested interest in nurturing the game and has made strides in this area.

Leading this successful program is Tony Reagins, who joined Major League Baseball's Commissioner's Office in March 2015 to oversee the growth of youth and amateur levels of the sport, while also expanding the efforts on a more global level (MLB.com, 2020).

Reagins has also led the proliferation of the Breakthrough Series amateur development camps, and he oversees RBI, MLB Youth Academies, the Elite Development Invitational, and the Andre Dawson Classic. "All of these organizations are starting to be active in terms of Play Ball, which only helps our message and helps our brand as it relates to growth and engagement for young people around the country," Reagins said. "Our plan is to do the same activation around the world. Our ultimate goal is to engage young people wherever they are."

According to Major League Baseball, the MLB's youth movement has been working. Play Ball is an expansive program, but the premise is simple: invite kids to a baseball field; provide them with bats, balls, T-shirts, and instruction; and encourage them to just play ball.

"There is a direct correlation to being introduced to the game at a very young age and becoming a lifelong fan," Reagins said. "Not necessarily an avid fan, but a fan of the game. That's what we're trying to accomplish."

The program makes the game more accessible and affordable for kids. Koosed, who has served as vice president for the Angels' RBI program, adds, "It gives opportunities to kids to do something else. To play and learn the game."

One example of the RBI program in action is the Baltimore Orioles. Their program, sponsored by T. Rowe Price, is designed to promote interest in baseball and softball, increase the self-esteem of children, and encourage kids to stay in school and off the streets. The program is supported by the Orioles. In 2018, 600 Baltimore city youth participated in the Orioles' RBI program (Orioles.com, 2022).

Another example is the Miami Marlins' program, which offers free instructional and competitive summer baseball and fastpitch softball for youth ages 13–18. The Marlins supply uniforms, umpires, and equipment to more than 500 children annually. All participants enjoy a fun and competitive summer league in addition to clinics hosted by Marlins players and alumni. Participants can also take part in a career workshop series, an on-field recognition ceremony during RBI Night, and the opportunity to be selected for the RBI All-Star team that competes in the Southeast Regional Tournament. The Marlins also provide scholarships ranging from $2,500–$20,000 (Marlins.com, 2022).

Solutions

Create MLB Academies

Again, kudos to Commissioner Manfred and Tony Reagins for their efforts to deepen the league's outreach and support of promoting youth baseball. The Play Ball and RBI programs are accomplishing their goal of connecting kids to the game and reaching into the inner city. I suggest there is a way to deepen this outreach while having a profound impact on the game.

My suggestion is for each MLB team to create their own in-house academy that offers training and education. The baseball training side of the academy should be run under the baseball operations side of the organization while the education side should be overseen by a director who ensures the student-athletes are provided a rigorous and accredited academic program while participating in the academy. Numerous Major League Soccer teams offer this program, as do the academies of IMG, Chris Evert, and Nick Bollettieri.

My proposed MLB program looks like this. An MLB organization opens an academy for baseball (and softball) for high school-aged student-athletes. These kids are college-bound or considered a prospect for professional baseball.

The athletes are recruited to enroll. Students attend daily. The typical day consists of classroom instruction and baseball (and softball) training. Meals are included. Students may be housed at their own residence or with host families.

Once an athlete graduates from the academy with their high school diploma, they are either signed by the major league team or they are provided an opportunity to attend college and sharpen their skills. All college expenses would be paid for by MLB. The MLB team would retain that player's rights until it determines if they will be signed as a prospect or not. Clearly, the Major League Baseball Players Association would have to sign off on this idea, as a change to the draft might be needed as well.

Searching for talent could rest on the expertise of a team's scouting departments. With the reduction of rounds in the draft, many scouts feel marginalized, and having them go into the inner city to find these prospects would give them purpose.

The end game would be to provide prospects, especially those in the inner city, with an opportunity to play professional baseball or earn a college degree. It's a win all the way around.

Teach the Game

I strongly support Rob Flippo's solution of going back to teaching kids the game the right way and actually letting them play and figure things out without intervention by their coaches. Kids don't want to be told how to do every little thing. That's boring. As Flippo told me, "Reinforce the positives and let them experience the process. Don't control everything." Make the experience fun for all. MLB should create a marketing campaign to support that message.

Increase the Number of African American Players

Earlier, Anderson and Martin (2019) provided us an in-depth study and analysis of this issue and offered a few solutions based on the premise that Major League Baseball has a responsibility to various stakeholders, including those in African American communities.

They suggest that MLB should "consult with the communities in which they operate to determine the efficacy and relevance of their community initiatives, and future work should evaluate each RBI/UYA program to establish a uniform model of CSR outreach, as well as examining ways to increase African American parental involvement in MLB programs."

Moreover, added Anderson and Martin, "Future research should examine additional consumption behaviours catalyzed by youth sport programmes in order to identify which elements (e.g., identification, trust, commitment, loyalty) have the most impact towards building long-term relationships."

Consistent Experience

The experience of playing baseball can be inconsistent for players. By consistent, I mean that kids should play with others of similar ability to make the game fun and competitive. Baseball is a humbling game at every level and if kids are thrown into leagues and teams based on age alone, they risk feeling inferior if they don't measure up. In turn, they are more likely to quit the game, and then baseball suffers. Specifically, we must ensure that youngsters are provided an experience that is positive and focused on learning the game while having fun. We often see that as a mission statement of youth leagues, but it's rarely put into practice.

Messaging

This game is fun! Those of us who have played at any level, organized or casual, would agree. Therefore, I encourage Major League Baseball to create a marketing campaign showing kids playing the game for fun, from Wiffle ball to competitive levels. This game is truly for all of us. That should be celebrated and shared.

Youth Sports Benefits the Community

Finally, all of these solutions for increasing and improving youth participation in baseball positively impact the community as a whole. Youth sports unite communities in a number of ways, including:

- Boosting health. Youth sports can have many different positive effects.
- Youth crime reduction. Many factors play a role in youth crime rates, and youth sports can help with some of the key elements.
- Creating future role models. Sports can be a great platform for learning many life skills and lessons.
- Building community (Perfect Mind, 2017).

7

Major League Baseball's Brand

"It's like watching Mike Trout now. Every night he does something special. That's how [Michael] Jordan was."—Albert Pujols

Major League Baseball may not want to admit it, but it needs to do a better job marketing its product to improve the fan experience, and as you'll see, there is a lot of work to do in this area.

In this chapter I will highlight the research, experience, and knowledge of those experts who know the marketing side of baseball, from executives to players, and apply all of that to what MLB should do in terms of creating its brand to deepen its footprint. As a result, fan interest should increase.

David Carter has serious concerns about Major League Baseball's approach to marketing. "They have an aging fanbase. Revenues are leveling off. In regard to being high tech, baseball is slowest to adapt. They need to reinvent the game as a family sport, and of all the major sports leagues, baseball does not seem to have the moorings to remedy that," said Carter.

Earlier, I highlighted a research paper by Emily Cosler (2020) titled "An Analysis of the Decline in MLB Stadium Attendance and the Marketing Techniques That Can Be Utilized to Reverse It." She made numerous recommendations and, after looking at correlation tests, found that teams with winning records, high offensive stats, and strong social media presence had the greatest success in filling their stadiums. Cosler's research, conducted as an undergraduate honors project in Texas Christian University's Marketing Department, validated the work of others in this book that suggested teams can build momentum off offensive plays. The more a team produces offense, the greater the likelihood of increased attendance.

Cosler also points to in-game ideas to boost fan interest, such as fireworks after home runs, grand scoreboard/video board effects for big plays, and celebrations after each victory. Another example, says Cosler, is how "the Chicago Cubs play the song 'Go Cubs Go' after each win. It encourages fans to show up to games and stay for the entire duration."

Also, earlier in this book, I referenced an article from the *International Journal of Applied Sports Sciences*, "Applying the Concept of Sport Affordability to Professional Sporting Events: The Case of the Major League Baseball Games," by Sangkwon Lee and Chi-Ok Oh (2016).

Their study touches on the issues I have brought forward throughout this book: attendance and fan interest. They focused on the concept that "sport affordability is also closely tied to marketing strategies of sport franchises and organizations. Professional sport franchises are trying to attract their primary target market consumers, mostly in the middle class. However, when the franchises select their target market, they do not pay much attention to whether these consumers can afford to attend sporting events."

Lee and Oh added that "the relationship between a team's offensive performance and team financials is fully mediated by attendance. The findings imply future sales growth may need to come from marketing strategies and promotional efforts beyond a team's surrounding geographical area, and possibly through the adoption of new technology to reach their target market."

What Is Brand Equity? Why Is It Important?

In their *Journal of Marketing Analytics* piece titled "Exploring the Components of Brand Equity amid Declining Ticket Sales in Major League Baseball," Adam C. Merkle, Catherine Hessick, Britton R. Leggett, Larry Goehrig, and Kenneth O'Connor (2020) say, "Brand Equity is the value of a brand, or can be summarized as the perceived value by consumers over other products. The equity of your brand is important because, if your brand has positive brand equity, you can charge more for your products and services than the generic products or other competitors."

For example, most of us have probably enjoyed a beverage or two at Starbucks, and for some reason, we hardly shy away from paying five dollars for a cup of coffee. Perhaps it is Starbucks' brand equity, which, according to Starbucks, is built on selling the finest-quality coffee and related products, and by providing customers with a unique "Starbucks Experience," which is derived from supreme customer service and clean, well-maintained stores that reflect the culture of the communities they serve.

As for Major League Baseball, Merkle et al. add, "The brand equity model consists of two major categories of MLB marketing assets, their relationships with stakeholder value measured by attendance and local TV viewership, and firm value represented by team financials."

Merkle et al. asked the same question I have: Where have all the fans gone? They suggest, "Despite the efforts of sales and marketing professionals, ticket sales and game attendance numbers fell for the fourth consecutive year, leading sports pundits and long-term baseball loyalists to wonder if we are entering an early stage decline of the sport."

Some have also suggested that Major League Baseball's attendance decrease may result from a culmination of factors, including ticket prices, the poor performances of teams, and a robust secondary ticket market.

"We examine[d] marketing assets for MLB teams, their relationship with stakeholders, and the relative influence of those marketing assets, game attendance, and local TV viewership on team financial performance," wrote Merkle et al. "These relationships may have key implications for the sales and marketing efforts of MLB teams. For example, if declining ticket sales are more than offset by other sources of rising revenue, then sales and marketing teams need not be concerned with small ticket sales decreases. However, if declining ticket sales have a large impact on team revenue or are the result of an eroding fan base, more effort should be placed on driving game attendance. A marketing analytics approach may be helpful in taking the first step to explore these relationships."

Their study found that "non-seasonal marketing assets are more influential in every relationship … [and] evidence that alternative marketing assets (MA), such as Twitter, are associated with changes in multiple relationships within the brand equity model. One change involves the weakening of the relationship between non-seasonal MA and attendance, effectively resulting in a lower rate of increases in game attendance for those teams with higher numbers of Twitter followers."

They said MA may include "measures of long-term winning records such as division and pennant championships, along with World Series victories and the amount of Hall of Fame players. Thus, we can infer that a focus on consistent long-term success is more valuable to team brand equity than short-term strategies aimed toward winning now."

They suggested that those non-seasonal elements include the value of a well-known brand to the bottom line. For example, "Given the longevity of MLB teams, such as the Chicago Cubs, New York Yankees, and Boston Red Sox, brand equity plays a vital role as an intangible asset in the organization," as those teams typically do not struggle with attendance and revenue. In short, Merkle et al. hypothesize that non-seasonal marketing assets are positively related to attendance.

As for in-seasonal marketing assets, "We suggest that seasonal offensive output represents a distinct in-season marketing asset that is positively related to other elements of MLB brand equity ... [and] are positively related to attendance."

Major League Baseball's social media footprint has increased. However, the authors' findings asserted that, surprisingly, "devoted fans express their devotion over social media, but not necessarily with their wallets in the form of ticket purchases. Perhaps, instead, they choose to watch on the television ... [and] based on prior research ... increased levels of social media usage and larger followings on Twitter could be associated with lower likelihoods for game attendance by fans."

It seems shocking that as a team's social media followers grow, attendance seems to decrease. But why? According to Merkle et al., "The first reason is that Twitter posters fulfill their fan motivations on social media, which would otherwise require a trip to the ballpark. The second reason is that teams with very large followings may also face significant geographic barriers in attending a game and instead root for their team on Twitter and perhaps watch the game on television."

Also contributing to the topic of brand equity are Ali Hasaan, Rui Biscaia, and Stephen Ross (2021). Their study, "Understanding Athlete Brand Life Cycle," in *Sport in Society*, noted that "athlete capital ... may serve as inspiration in contemporary societies, and their popularity often turns them from local heroes into international stars (Kerr and Gladden) ... [and] athletes' activities off the field have become an important complement to their performance on the field promoting both ... as a brand and his/her sport (Cortsen)."

Their argument is that an athlete's brand, which includes their on-field and off-field life, is a powerful marketing tool. They provide two examples of athletes who have been successful in creating marketing brands that extend well beyond their playing careers—soccer star David Beckham and the NBA's Michael Jordan.

I suggest the personal brands of MLB players can (and mostly likely do) positively impact the popularity, interest, and attendance of baseball.

Branding, or lack thereof in Major League Baseball, is the crux of the issue. Branding applies to every aspect of business, including employees and executives who seek to establish and maintain their own brand names (Carter and Rovell, 2003). That raises the question, what is MLB's brand? If you are a fan of Major League Baseball and cannot answer that question immediately, then it is clear that MLB's branding needs to improve.

According to Carter and Rovell, establishing, building, and extending a brand requires the organization to have ongoing, hands-on management and leadership at every turn. They also suggest that successful branding needs a visionary leader at the helm. The question I ask is, does Major League Baseball have that leader or leadership steering its seemingly antiquated marketing efforts?

MLB should strive to have a powerful brand, but it must realize that it does not happen overnight. Instead, it evolves over time through a combination of timely and insightful decision-making (Carter and Rovell). It also doesn't hurt to implement the successful strategies and best practices of other sports leagues, like the National Basketball Association.

Lessons Learned from the NBA

The NBA was once a distant competitor to the NFL and MLB. That all changed when former NBA commissioner David Stern took over and built the NBA into a sought-after media property. Fox Business credited Stern as the architect who "built the NBA from struggling league to lucrative global juggernaut during a three-decade tenure as commissioner."

"Stern inherited a league in 1984 that earned roughly $100 million in annual revenue and little to show for its business beyond its on-court product. When he stepped down in 2014, the NBA was earning more than $5.5 billion per year, with a profitable international footprint, massive media rights deals, larger player contracts and several new franchises," reported Barrabi (2020) of Fox Business.

"Under Stern," said Sprung (2019) of *Forbes*, "the NBA established itself as the preeminent U.S. sports league in international markets. He fostered close ties with the Chinese market, building a base of tens of millions of fans in Asia and a business said to be worth $4 billion."

Case in point: the NBA airs games in more than 200 countries and territories and broadcasts in more than 40 languages.

What did Stern do and how did he do it? Pay attention, Major League Baseball. Take notes.

Carter and Rovell (2003) believe that Stern served as the NBA's visionary leader throughout the league's evolution. Stern understood the inherent value in brand building and had a vision for what the league could be, and he demonstrated outstanding skills as a consensus builder.

In the mid–1980s, Stern leveraged the NBA's emerging talent at that time, most notably Magic Johnson, Larry Bird, and, years later, Michael Jordan. Carter says they served as the league's brand messengers. This is one area that MLB is lacking—capitalizing on its stars as ambassadors. Major League Baseball's stars of today, such as Mike Trout, Mookie Betts, and Gerrit Cole, are the league's greatest products but are not carrying the MLB brand nationally or globally.

For more than a decade, Michael Jordan was the NBA and the NBA was Michael Jordan. Jordan demonstrated that great brands could transcend the actual product being marketed and attract a larger customer base in the process. He became interchangeable with the league. Stern knew that the more he allowed Jordan the limelight, the better both he and the league looked (Carter and Rovell, 2003), which is, as you will learn, not part of MLB's marketing philosophy.

The NBA also undertook creative marketing and management initiatives that made consumers recognize and remember the NBA, such as made-for-television events like the Slam Dunk Contest and allocating money and resources to grassroots, public-service-oriented programs, especially those with a "stay-in-school" theme. "Stern believed it was never too early to begin cultivating the next generation of fans," said Carter and Rovell.

The NBA is known for being a player-centered league and it markets its stars and the game nationally and internationally, which has proved to be a successful recipe in building its brand. However, "Major League Baseball is still about marketing their bellwether teams, the Yankees, Dodgers, and Red Sox. The NBA has grown the game internationally. While Major League Baseball has a diverse representation of players from numerous parts of the globe, they have not marketed internationally. The NBA features its players, NFL features the shield, MLB features its teams," said Carter and Rovell.

They are dead-on. The next time you see ESPN promote its Sunday night game, invariably you'll notice it highlights the teams and not the players. MLB's lack of marketing its stars is not doing the game any favors, and George Will added about the seemingly constant promotion of those bellwether teams: "I think baseball has to get over the fact that it thinks Boston-Yankees games are infinitely important and infinitely interesting. They're not."

MLB's Lack of Marketing Star Players

Others have noticed how little Major League Baseball is doing to promote its current and future stars. Cosler (2020) suggests the promotion "of current players and top prospects with high offensive power can be another tool utilized by MLB teams."

Specifically, she says, "Homerun replays posted to Twitter, a prospect spotlight series on YouTube, or high energy hype videos all gain traction among fans…. Promotional videos and infographics allow teams to boost a player even more than their resume may merit."

Love (2019) of the *New York Times* added that an area of concern for MLB is "the meager national profiles of its stars.... Baseball's best players rarely get airtime in markets outside their own. Baseball struggles to promote its ... stars on the same level as other sports do."

Not only are the stars of those sports more popular compared with Major League Baseball players, but those stars also bring fans into the stadium. Brad R. Humphreys and Candon Johnson (2020) published a study in the *Journal of Sports Economics* titled "The Effect of Superstars on Game Attendance: Evidence from the NBA." Their study investigated the effect of superstar players on attendance at National Basketball Association games from 1981-1982 through 2013–2014.

While theirs is a study of NBA attendance, their findings are transferable to Major League Baseball. Not to simplify their comprehensive study into a phrase, but here it is: star power matters. How many times have you as a baseball fan been motivated to attend a game that has stars and in turn you're excited to see them?

"Economic models predict that 'superstar' players generate externalities that increase attendance and other revenue sources beyond their individual contributions to team success," Humphreys and Johnson assert.

"The results show higher home and away attendance associated with some superstar players. Michael Jordan generated the largest superstar attendance externality, generating an additional 4,837/4,236 fans at home/away games."

In their research, Humphreys and Johnson found evidence of "specialization of superstar effects." They suggest, "Larry Bird and Magic Johnson appear to be ... deriving superstar status from performance while Julius Erving, Michael Jordan, Shaquille O'Neal, and LeBron James appear to be ... superstars deriving superstar status from popularity. These results indicate that the findings ... can be generalized to other settings."

If star players increase a team's attendance, as the authors suggest, one would have to speculate that the opposite would be true as well. Case in point is the Pittsburgh Pirates. Within a two-day span in January 2018, the Pirates traded away star players pitcher Gerrit Cole and outfielder Andrew McCutchen. The result at the turnstiles at PNC Park was a pretty significant attendance drop. The daily average went from an average in 2017 of 23,796 per game to only 18,786 in 2018, an alarming decrease of 20.7 percent. In terms of total attendance, the Pirates saw a whopping decrease of 454,131 fans from 1,919,447 in 2017 to only 1,465,316 in 2018, a 23.6 percent drop (Baseball-Reference, 2022).

It's astonishing to see the influence two star players, or the lack thereof, has on a team's attendance. What might be more surprising is that the organization chose to make those moves. Obviously, the cost of Cole's and McCutchen's salaries and future earnings had they remained Pirates might be more than the loss of revenue at the gate, but the message it sent to the fanbase, the appearance of not investing in the team's stars, might cause more of a financial hit.

Love (2019) cited YouGov's ratings of active sports personalities in 2019, which noted 91 percent of Americans have heard of the NBA's LeBron James and 88 percent have heard of Tom Brady of the NFL, but only 43 percent have heard of Mike Trout of the Los Angeles Angels, baseball's best player. Sadly, that is partly due to how few of Trout's games are shown outside Southern California. For example, only 2 percent of his games in 2018 were broadcast nationally.

However, "Part of the problem with Mike Trout," said George Will, "is that he has no personality. Let's face it. But then there's [Fernando] Tatis [of the San Diego Padres] and there are a lot of other guys out there who could be marketed."

When comparing the marketing of Major League Baseball stars with other major sports, the problem, says Will, is "the structure of the game. I don't know how many snaps Aaron Rodgers [the longtime quarterback of the NFL's Green Bay Packers who was traded to the New Your Jets in 2023] takes in a 60-minute game, but it's a lot. Mike Trout comes to bat four times. Another problem that baseball has is that now going through a lineup a third time is considered high risk. You're not going to have Seaver against Carlton and Koufax against Marichal, the great pitching matchups. That was destination television, but not anymore because they're going to be gone in the fifth or sixth inning."

Dave St. Peter, president of the Minnesota Twins, told Hine (2018) of the *Minneapolis Star Tribune*, "I admire what the NBA does as it relates to the marketing of their stars. I think we have room for improvement not just as an organization but as an industry."

Room for improvement is an understatement. Of the top 100 most recognizable sports figures on the planet, zero is the number of baseball players on that list.

Justin Turner of the Los Angeles Dodgers does not skirt the issue. He told me, "Baseball is behind in marketing their own players. Look at [NBA superstar] LeBron [James]. He's in a number of commercials and has his own shoe deal. MLB players do not have recognition. For example, think about [Hall of Famer] Ken Griffey, Jr., and what he meant to baseball. He was an icon. He was the first to get a shoe deal. Michael Jordan, of course, has his own shoes and they are most coveted. Even today, players in both the NBA and in baseball wear a Jordan-brand shoe, but why didn't the same trajectory for Jordan's shoes happen for Griffey?"

One reason might be that MLB is focused more on team-based

marketing, which, as Turner suggests, creates a barrier. "If I want to have a sponsorship deal with let's say Budweiser, they would have to go through my agent and then get permission from the Dodgers to use their logo," said Turner.

Turner then said that the sponsor has to pay the team for usage of that logo, which rarely happens. Often you will see commercials where the MLB player is wearing a plain blue hat and plain jersey. That is not marketing the player, and the average person wouldn't be able to connect him to a team.

Turner added, "It is about the team first over the player. That's not the way it is in the NBA." True. As you read prior, NBA commissioner David Stern encouraged and supported Michael Jordan to get notoriety because he knew the league would benefit from it.

"It is up to each player to create their own brand," said Turner. "Teams are not doing the players any favors. They are preventing the players from becoming a bigger brand. The bigger brand is the team."

Social Media and Digital Platforms

As stated earlier in the chapter, Major League Baseball has made some strides as a league building its social media footprint. Noah Garden, MLB's chief revenue officer, says that MLB has invested more into digital platforms like the MLB At Bat mobile application and Ballpark Pass. Downloads for the MLB At Bat app increased 18 percent in 2019 and reached over two billion users.

However, MLB has a long way to go in a number of areas. Specifically, as Two Circles Marketing suggests, MLB should be using its data to "effectively guide compelling digital content tailored for the right audiences, consistently resulting in growth across all business lines." That's not being done.

Those business lines include reaching the Generation Z demographic. Gen Z is so sophisticated that they can read through obvious measures to try to reach them directly. The approach, according to Brewers president Rick Schlesinger, is to do it indirectly. "We have to do it subtly," said Schlesinger. "We have to make our players relatable to them. We have to be funny, and we have to be edgy. We're also trying to impress upon that generation that baseball is not your grandfather's game anymore, the sophistication of our statistical analysis and how baseball analytics has transformed the game on the field. We're trying very hard to communicate to the younger fans that [the in-game] technology and analytics are sophisticated, intellectual and frankly, how interesting baseball is."

Easley (2018) of Morning Consult said social media has also elevated the profiles of basketball and soccer athletes who spend most of the game on the field of play and—unlike football or baseball stars—aren't partially concealed by helmets or time in the dugout.

In terms of an online presence, Cosler's (2020) research yielded numerous recommendations. "The first recommendation is to harness social media followers into purchasing tickets to games. This may be done through 'insider' ticket promotions, ticket giveaways to loyal fans, or stronger advertising of game day promotions. People like being a part of an exclusive group. Although following a team on social media is not inherently an exclusive group, teams can create this aura by providing perks not available to the general public. Real-life examples from teams include hiding tickets/merchandise around the city for fans to find, hour-long coupons for tickets only advertised on social media, and game day giveaways to those who follow and tag the team on a social media post."

The NBA is also in the forefront of extending its brand via social media. The NBA and its member teams are often recognized in the sports business community as innovators in fan engagement. The league and teams have embraced the use of social media channels to keep fans interested through behind-the-scenes access, game highlights, stats, and glimpses of players' lifestyles off the court (HBO *Real Sports*/Neilsen, 2015), which aligns directly to the research on how Generation Z wants its team and league to communicate with them.

Surprisingly, MLB players suggest they are on their own when it comes to their social media platforms. "We have to rely on ourselves for social media, but our reach can only go so far. The team may provide us a photo or highlight, but that's it," Justin Turner told me.

That is truly unbelievable and disconcerting to hear. Turner is exposing the ugly truth that for some reason Major League Baseball does not see the value of promoting its star players. For instance, stars such as former Most Valuable Players Giancarlo Stanton and Jose Altuve have only a combined 572,500 followers on Twitter, while James Harden, an NBA MVP, has 6.8 million Twitter followers, and nobody in baseball comes close to LeBron James's 46.8 million Twitter followers.

Many of us grew up following the MLB stars of generations past who were not just baseball players but were also icons, and today MLB is missing out on the opportunity to have the same connection between its stars and the nation.

Marc Ebersberger, 77, grew up in Maryland watching the Baltimore Orioles. I asked him about today's game and how it compares with the game of the 1950s and 1960s. "There are no heroes in baseball today. Where are they? When I was growing up, there was Mickey Mantle and Ted Williams. My goodness. Lou Gehrig made a nation cry."

Williams once said of Joe DiMaggio, "Joe DiMaggio was the greatest all-around player I ever saw. His career cannot be summed up in numbers and awards. It might sound corny, but he had a profound and lasting impact on the country."

Again, MLB should be sharing the stories of today's stars and the game's heroes of old with current and potential fans.

MLB's Business Model

Baseball is big business and half of MLB teams are worth $1.5 billion or more. *Forbes*, for example, has calculated that the average baseball team was worth $1.8 billion in 2019, up 8 percent from the previous year, and the average team annual revenue is $330 million. With numbers that enormous, perhaps MLB is complacent and therefore does not see a reason to change. It appears that Major League Baseball believes it must be doing something right on the business side. Right? Not so fast, says David Carter.

"MLB's business model is built upon slow-to-adjust with the backdrop of an unwillingness to overcome its tradition and history," said Carter. "That history and tradition [dominates] and therefore [the league is] slow to change perhaps because MLB has a richer tradition and history than other sports. If you ask a 25-year-old about, for example, an advertisement on the uniform sleeve or a pitch clock, they would be okay with that. Ask a 55-year-old, not so much."

MLB is more regional and less central, which supports Carter's theory of MLB being slow to adjust—and which, Carter says, is the opposite of the NFL. One team executive told me, "MLB makes an effort, but not a great one, in my opinion. Not because they can't and not because they're not talented in [MLB offices] New York, they are. But I think they believe that each team has its own belief in their own region in how to promote the league. The Mariners approach it way differently than the Yankees do, and the Yankees approach it way differently than the Cubs do. That's how they feel."

But why is Major League Baseball so focused on being decentralized? Shavonnah Schreiber is managing director of SNR Creative, a Houston, Texas-based marketing company that specializes in sports. Schreiber has expertise in building and leading marketing teams to create and execute global marketing programs and campaigns. SNR Creative's sports management arm offers marketing and branding services for athletes, sports clubs, and sports apparel companies.

Schreiber's experience includes working with leagues and teams within the National Football League, the NBA, Major League Soccer, National Collegiate Athletic Association, Canadian Football League, and others. Her experience working with Major League Baseball compared with other leagues has led her to conclude that MLB's marketing side of the house tends to be more insular and not as welcoming.

"MLB's persona is that they are a bit standoffish," Schreiber said. "They appear to be saying, 'We're baseball and if you like us and you've been a part of what we do, great, and if not, that's fine.' It appears that they are not looking to attract new fans or sell their brand. No matter what the data and stats show, they seem resolved to run their program their way. They rarely look outward for support and any conversations about improvement just aren't that welcoming compared to the NFL, for example."

That's unfortunate because as we have seen with the NBA's success, there are lessons to be learned and best practices to be emulated from many professional sports leagues.

A House Divided Will Not Stand

Interestingly, when interviewing those in the game about the barriers MLB is facing, was the recurring notion that within a Major League Baseball organization are two sides of the house—the baseball operations side and the business side—where friction sometimes exists.

Dave Ziedelis has witnessed this firsthand with his time as an MLB executive. "In the organization you have the baseball side and the business side. The baseball side rules every single major league organization. They have the upper hand and there are a lot of people on the baseball side that do not respect the marketing side. They think everyone is there for them and granted, yes, the superstar players are important, but that's the way it is. They are not always compatible."

Often, this appears to be a philosophical dilemma as to which side of the organization is more important, which leads to a power struggle. The baseball side of the house feels that the fans are interested in only the players. After all, aren't the players the ones fans are paying to see? Conversely, the business side contends that their keen marketing strategies are what support the bottom line and bring fans to the yard, especially for a team that is struggling in the standings. When these two sides do not see eye to eye, the lack of respect from one to other leads to dysfunction. However, one example where the baseball and business sides not only coexist but also work with great synergy is, once again, the Milwaukee Brewers.

Milwaukee is considered by many to be a small market in Major League Baseball. The population of the Milwaukee metropolitan area is a little over 1.5 million people, putting the Brewers second from the bottom (ahead of the Cincinnati Reds) in terms of market size. It is believed that a small-market team is likely to struggle to compete financially against teams from larger markets such as New York, Los Angeles, or Milwaukee's neighbor to the south, Chicago, and may also be outbid in the competition for acquiring top talent.

Rick Schlesinger says one aspect of their success is the willingness to partner with other MLB teams. "There's a very healthy exchange of best practices among the teams. We are competitors on the field, collaborators off the field, and we are good about sharing data with the other teams. Unlike baseball operations where they don't want to share anything with their comrades, we have working groups with other teams and we're not competing with them on the business side. Anything that the White Sox or Cubs or Twins or Dodgers are doing that can attract Gen Z, for example, we're going to learn about it and see if it has applicability to us. That's also been very helpful to help mold some of the strategies we're developing."

In-house, the Brewers have built an organization where both the baseball operations and business sides work harmoniously. How? "For certain clubs there is much more of a church-and-state mentality between baseball operations and business operations," admitted Schlesinger. "There's a lot more synergy in comradery and cooperation in our organization. I think it helps, frankly, that David Stearns, our general manager, is very savvy. He understands the importance of revenue generation for us because that obviously goes right into player payroll and player development expenses. He's very cognizant of the importance of generating attendance, generating revenue because he knows that's going to translate directly into his areas of operation and being in Milwaukee, we're never going to be among the league leaders in major baseball payroll."

Baseball's Gender Bias

Major League Baseball should be commended as it has made strides in promoting women to positions on and off the field formerly held by men only. To name a few:

- Kim Ng was hired as the general manager of the Miami Marlins.
- Rachel Balkovec was named manager of the Yankees' Low-A Tampa affiliate.
- Kelsie Whitmore was the first woman to join an MLB partner

league team when she signed with the Staten Island FerryHawks of the Atlantic League in 2022 as a utility player.
- Sara Goodrum was hired as the Houston Astros' director of player development.
- And Alyssa Nakken was Major League Baseball's first woman coach in 2020 with the San Francisco Giants.

While this is exciting and well-deserved, it is also decades late and there still seems to be an obvious disregard for women who are fans of Major League Baseball and an apparent gender bias, which is another marketing issue facing Major League Baseball.

Women love baseball, so why doesn't the game love them back? asked Jeva Lange (2018) of *The Week*. According to Lange, a 2010 survey showed that "45 percent of fans were women.... The number is likely even higher now. They deserve to have the sport love them back."

"Sometimes it really feels like Major League Baseball believes its female fans consist solely of baseball knowledge-impaired, wine-drinking moms dressed in pink," observed author Stacey May Fowles (2017) in her book *Baseball Life Advice: Loving the Game That Saved Me*.

Mary Craig (2017) of SB Nation added, "It has recently been made obvious (though not obvious enough) that Major League Baseball has an issue with marketing to female fans, either ignoring their existence completely or reducing them to caricatures of women who are interested in only the superficial nature of promotions."

Just take a look at recent giveaways targeting women, such as cosmetic bags and leopard print tote bags (Lange, 2018), which are truly condescending.

"Baseball is and always has been a male-run, male-dominated sport and there is no incentive to change this," said Nancy Doublin (2010) of Bleacher Report. "Anytime women attempt to make inroads into male-dominated areas, there is resistance. Not only from men, but from society as a whole. There is not enough attention paid to the lack of women in baseball, and not enough pressure brought to bear on the powers that be in MLB, to make this change."

Erica Hunzinger (2019) of National Public Radio suggests Major League Baseball is staring down a gender problem. "Despite initiatives meant to bring more women into its dugouts, executive offices and broadcast booths, everyone—including women in high-powered positions—believe things won't change quickly enough," said Hunzinger.

Major League Baseball is still an old-fashioned boys' club. The number of women employed in MLB front offices is low. The Orioles hired Eve Rosenbaum for the newly created position of director of baseball development. Rosenbaum is the highest-ranking woman in the Orioles' baseball operations department. The New York Yankees' Jean Afterman is one of only three women who've risen to the assistant general manager level.

"The sports media does not get a pass in its perpetuation of the boys club of baseball, either," says Lange (2018). "Coverage of women fans in MLB ballparks is often sexist."

"Look, I think there's no sugar-coating this. There's a lot to do," said Renee Tirado, Major League Baseball's chief diversity and inclusion officer, reported Hunzinger (2019). In 2018, MLB earned a gender grade of C on the yearly report card issued by the Institute for Diversity and Ethics in Sports. Essentially, that means 30 percent of employees in pro baseball are women.

Solutions

The solutions offered in this section demand resources. They are potentially expensive, time-consuming, and not easy to implement, said Carter. However, in order to create a strong marketing campaign and brand identity, they should not be considered optional.

Build the MLB Brand

Major League Baseball is faced with the challenge of asserting its brand on a hugely fragmented market, which is indeed one of the greatest challenges of 21st-century businesses (Samuelson, 2019).

Where should MLB begin? Major League Baseball needs to create a brand that is not easy to forget. It should be seen everywhere you look, from jerseys to billboards and more, especially on social media. Its brand should build external visibility by focusing on the league's social media visibility, content, and engagement, and by syndicating content on as many other sites as it can (Samuelson, 2019).

MLB needs to continue to increase its social media footprint with a steady diet of videos, articles, and blog posts showcasing its content with the added element of driving fans to the ballpark.

These strategies have proved to be a major driver in getting visitors to consume products. Major League Baseball must infiltrate Facebook, Instagram, Twitter, etc., with more MLB and team content. A specific example is that some MLB teams now have their own YouTube channel. Every team should have one and the league should promote its.

Part of building the brand should include Major League Baseball supporting and encouraging its players to have a robust social media presence and celebrating their individuality. For example, Cy Young–winning former pitcher for the Cincinnati Reds Trevor Bauer is one of the game's most interesting, controversial, and entertaining players. You may not always like what he has to say, but he is engaging. Baseball needs more of that. He's polarizing and somewhat of a villain. Villains drive interest and are good for the game.

Merkle et al. (2020) suggest, "Promotions that develop a nostalgic habit of coming to the ballpark many times in a season for new customers may be more beneficial than sponsoring the traditional one-off bat-days or hat-days. Ballpark development partnerships focused on excellent fan experiences regardless of the actual results of any one game, such as the new park in Atlanta, are another potential path to increase long-term brand equity."

Hasaan et al. (2021) add that professional athletes should "build and promote their personal brands [and] … to become a successful brand … being known among potential customers (i.e., fans), as brand awareness is critical in the development of a sport brand."

As a result, Major League Baseball needs to support players in creating and marketing their brand, which in turn will help grow the game and their organization's bottom line as well.

How About Some Fun?

Goldman (2019) interviewed a fan who said, "if baseball wants to appeal more to younger fans, do like the NBA: Make videos and clips of action more available."

He added, "Baseball is too buttoned up and needs to let the players have fun."

"When a player does a bat flip and people freak out," Grewal said, "traditionalists freak out. You know, it's 2019. They're pro athletes. Let them entertain."

Former Major League manager Trey Hillman agrees. He said, "We [MLB] are in the entertainment business and we should act like it."

I ask, where have all the characters of the game gone? To name a few whom I grew up with, Jerry Reuss, Jay Johnstone, Bert Blyleven, and Rex Hudler were not only fantastic players but they brought personality and fun to the game as well.

Show Consideration for Women

Major League Baseball should create a marketing campaign designed to celebrate its female fans and bring more women into the game as fans and employees without being condescending. There are steps that Major League Baseball as a league could take toward showing that it values the women who love the game. First, hire more women. The league is making progress here, but more should be done. The old-school thinking that baseball is a game for men only is antiquated and simply wrong.

Another step: "Keep the pandering pink out of logos when advertising 'Ladies Night' at the ballpark," said Lange (2018). Also, she says, "Harsher policies to deal with players accused of domestic abuse" are necessary as well. Sadly, we have seen MLB players convicted of domestic abuse face only minimal consequences from the league.

Social Consciousness

"Any brand that is not yet somewhat involved in social causes is a fading brand," Robert Patin, CEO at Patin & Associates, told Samuelson (2019). Clearly, social consciousness has never been as relevant to businesses as it is today. Major League Baseball and its players have been in conversation about how to incorporate social justice elements into the sport, according to league and player sources, and it is about time.

Major League Baseball, its teams, and players have the power and influence to lead the conversation about creating change, if they are able to connect with the youngest generations. Being connected to social issues is what the younger generation expects and respects even in sports.

Be a Community Partner

Along the lines of social consciousness, Shavonnah Schreiber suggests Major League Baseball should work on bringing communities together. She said, "Community outreach is important. It does matter who your stars are, and what they do for the community. Their contributions to the community are amplified and this increases the brand of that particular team and the league as well."

The Brewers' Rick Schlesinger added, "David [Stearns, the team's general manager] understands the challenges we face in Milwaukee and he understands and communicates to the players and the coaches that we need to be out in the community. The fans of Milwaukee sort of view the Brewers as a home, it's a team owned by the community. So, there's frankly a different responsibility I think that the players understand is required. When we asked the players to do things, they were very supportive. I think it starts from the top with the GM, the coaches, and [Manager] Craig Counsell making it clear to the community, making clear to the players that there are levels of expectation but there are rewards for that level of expectation and the rewards are big crowds and huge fan support."

8

Labor Negotiation Strife

> *"I have always been a firm believer that the game has never belonged to the owners. It has never belonged to the ballplayers. It belongs to the guy who puts his money up on the window and says, 'How much does it cost to sit in the bleachers?' That is who owns baseball. And it has got to stay that way."*—Johnny Vander Meer

When it comes to labor negotiations, says Jeff Passan (June 5, 2020) of ESPN, baseball is its own greatest enemy and the relationship between the league and union has been one of distrust.

Carter and Rovell (2003) agree. They note that there have been work stoppages in other sports leagues before, but baseball has provided numerous textbook examples of how not to handle employee relations. There is a decades-long history of acrimony between Major League Baseball owners and their players, and recent examples show only a greater divide. The impact of this animosity may be minimal for hardcore fans, as they have endured work stoppages and have not abandoned the game. However, the impact may be long-term and devastating to casual fans.

The clear animosity between the two sides often turns quite public, which we saw during the 2022 lockout—the first work stoppage in 26 years.

Although every major sports league has incurred highly publicized labor strife, Major League Baseball is in a class by itself and nothing has changed over the years as MLB continues to embarrass itself when it comes to labor negotiations. In fact, in baseball, there had been a work stoppage at every renegotiation of a collective bargaining agreement from 1972 until 2002, when it came to the 11th hour. Then a lockout began in December 2021. That's a pretty spotty track record—at best.

"Part of the problem is just that there is so much animosity between the owners and the players union, that all of these issues are secondary to the economic fights. And until … these two sides can find some common ground there, it's going to be very tough to implement changes and to address the concerns that people have over the quality of play and non-competitive teams," Jay Jaffe of FanGraphs told me.

Fans of small-market teams like the Pittsburgh Pirates should be outraged that their teams are not spending the competitive balance funds they inherit. They should pressure their owners to spend and strive to be competitive. However, fans typically do not get outraged. They simply tune out and/or spend their discretionary income elsewhere. This is why I advocate for a spending floor versus the competitive balance tax, which was designed to curb runaway spending from teams like the Yankees and Dodgers. How well has that worked out? The spirit of the competitive balance tax is to spend on players to be, as it's called, competitive.

Outfielder Joc Pederson (2022) called out owners of the Cleveland Guardians, Pittsburgh Pirates, and Baltimore Orioles: "[You have] embarrassed your fan base ... be better. If you can't, sell ur [sic] team to somebody that wants to show the fan base and baseball they're at least trying to compete. Sorry unacceptable."

The arrogance of both owners and players that fans will forgive and forget and the game will come through labor strife time and again is nothing short of shortsighted. While the end result of the 99-day lockout in the winter of 2021–2022 was a settlement that gave both the players association and owners many of the things they had desired in the negotiations, how they arrived there was embarrassing for them and the game.

No one should fault either side for desiring to get what they believe they deserve or are entitled to in a contract negotiation. However, the public manner in which they "work together" reminds me of the work stoppages I have lived through as a fan in 1981 and again in 1994. The lost summer of 1981, when MLB players went on strike and I was a 14-year-old baseball fanatic, is without question the worst summer I can recall. The strike began on June 12 that year and forced the cancellation of 38 percent of the season. Day after lonely day without baseball that summer was dreadful. Thankfully, play resumed and the season finished.

The 1994 strike was far more devastating. On August 12, 1994, the players went out on strike, rather than acquiesce to the owners' demand for a salary cap. The strike ended the next April. The season was a total loss, including no postseason and no World Series for the first time since 1904. While diehard fans were upset, most came back to the game they loved. However, countless others swore off Major League Baseball for good. They felt betrayed, alienated, or simply disgusted. Sadly, many of those fans have Generation Z children who never grew up in baseball-loving homes and the consequence is that they are not drawn to the game. Many are not fans today. In short, the fallout has been generational.

On the impact of the 1994 strike, Carter and Rovell (2003) said,

"Disillusioned fans, believing that both sides in the dispute were consumed by greed and unconcerned about them, switched allegiances to other sports during—and perhaps well after—the work stoppage."

A concern with negotiations looming in 2022 was that current owners and players didn't understand the damage that can be done by a work stoppage. Most players who were born after the strikes in 1981 and 1994 or were too young to remember are doomed to repeat the cycle.

When players and owners wrestle over gaining the sympathy of fans by airing their grievances publicly they are wasting their time and energy because, in truth, fans don't care. Fans just want to see the game on the field without interruption. The message to owners and players is to keep it between yourselves.

Jerry Reuss played during the 1972 strike and served as a player representative for the Cardinals. According to Reuss, "St. Louis Cardinals owner Auggie Busch bad-mouthed the players and that ended up in the fans being upset, and on opening day there was only 7,800 in attendance at Busch Stadium. Things won't truly change until Congress takes away the antitrust exemption from baseball and everything under that umbrella."

To Reuss's point: "MLB has been operating with an antitrust exemption since 1922, after the Supreme Court decided the league could suppress wages and make other business decisions impacting teams not normally allowed under anti-monopoly rules," said Olafimihan Oshin of *The Hill*.

Self-Inflicted Wounds

The poor interaction between players and owners was also evident during the COVID-19 pandemic in the spring and summer of 2020. While millions of Americans were filing for unemployment benefits at a rate not seen since the Great Depression, the owners and players acted like spoiled children as they haggled over what the abbreviated season would consist of. It was simply embarrassing behavior.

Baseball had a chance to be a major part of the USA's recovery from the 2020 COVID-19 pandemic, but it failed. Instead, we were reduced to listening to owners and players squabbling like a couple of people arguing over a sale item during Black Friday. Even though Commissioner Rob Manfred works for the 30 owners, he was front and center on these negotiations.

Scott Karl, who served as an MLBPA player representative during his time in the majors, saw a similar disconnect between the players and owners. "Both sides do not have the viewpoint of the bigger picture and the collective good [of the game]. The greater good is not considered. It's foolish and frustrating," said Karl.

For the 2020 season, there was a need from both sides to show unity and put the game first. As notable sportswriter Jayson Stark, from The Athletic, added, "At times like this, neither side should be trying to win or lose, no matter how ugly their relationship or their history. These are the times to shove all of that aside and solve those common problems—because the solutions benefit everyone."

Unfortunately, it wasn't to be as MLB's owners and players did everything but focus on solutions. There is so much anger and distrust between the MLBPA and MLB, said ESPN. "It's not good. They all look bad. The process to reach an agreement to play during the summer of 2020 in the midst of a pandemic … [was] embarrassing for all…. No sympathy or empathy for either side." Thankfully, both sides eventually came together and the result was an exciting 2020 Major League Baseball season that included a terrific World Series between the eventual champion Los Angeles Dodgers and the Tampa Bay Rays.

Lacking a Partnership

MLB's owners and players have a history of working against one another as opposed to in a partnership, agrees major league manager Buck Showalter. He told me, "The commissioner and Major League Baseball are aware of the issues facing the game and a lot is being done behind the scenes, more than most know. The issue is that no matter what MLB proposes, the Major League Baseball Players Association approves everything. Get the players and owners together. Right now, the two sides can't agree on what's best and there's no cooperation."

Showalter added, "The players acknowledge we have a problem but it [the solutions] might hurt them in the pocketbook."

This presents an interesting dilemma and one that former major league pitcher Jerry Reuss has seen before. "I was the player representative for 10 years," said Reuss. "The key [in labor negotiations] is it's not about what you want, it's about what you can live with. Also, you can't negotiate through the media. It does not help the cause. Let the negotiators do their job."

Currently, one barrier to creating a partnership between owners and players is there is no revenue sharing in MLB like other sports. Revenue sharing is a mechanism to pool and redistribute certain revenues among competing franchises in a league, in order to lessen economic inequalities among teams (Baseball-Reference, 2022).

However, revenue sharing can be quite controversial as the measures will typically prevent the more successful franchises, such as the Yankees and Dodgers, which are often in that position because they occupy larger or more lucrative markets, from maximizing the competitive edge they could gain from the revenues they can extract from their position. But a consequence of not having this type of system is that a sports league will typically polarize between a few rich and successful franchises and all others that struggle year after year (Baseball-Reference, 2022).

Revenue sharing was taboo for years in Major League Baseball, apart from the national television contracts that were not particularly lucrative once split among all the existing franchises. That damaging experience led to the adoption of some of the measures listed above. However, baseball is still well behind the National Football League or Major League Soccer in terms of revenue sharing (Baseball-Reference, 2022).

Are Owners Really Not Making Money?

Major League Baseball has enjoyed steady financial growth in the recent past, which is largely attributed to media and sponsorship deals.

McArtor suggests, "Even as MLB's total revenue is growing, attendance continues to fall. Although the MLB lost $93.7 million in ticket revenue and an additional $50 million in concessions sales, its total revenue increased because of TV and streaming (Mathewson). For example, a streaming-media rights deal with the sports streaming service DAZN and a $5.1 billion deal with FOX slated for 2022 will accelerate the financial growth of the league (Brown, 2019). MLB has undoubtedly benefited from lucrative streaming deals, yet the growth of the league will not be sustainable if no one is in the seats."

Earlier, I proved that the owners are actually enjoying a strong bottom line in large part to Commissioner Manfred's business deals. Regardless of the owners' rhetoric about how they are losing money, that doesn't add up.

George Will also pointed out they are making money—a lot of it. He said business partnerships are up and the owners should actually be ecstatic and thankful to the commissioner because, obviously, they are in this to make money.

How financially fragile are franchises? St. Louis Cardinals owner Bill DeWitt, Jr., told a local radio show, as reported by Buffa, "The industry isn't very profitable, to be quite honest."

"Those statements are at odds with the record revenue of $10.7 billion the league made in 2019, according to Forbes. Contrary to DeWitt's claims, it sounds like there's room in there for a healthy profit. Let's face it, today's owners are shrewd business people who are not in the business

8. Labor Negotiation Strife 175

of buying into industries that aren't very profitable," said Passan (June 15, 2020) of ESPN.

Seemingly, owners today don't have the same love for the game as when family-owned teams dominated the game decades prior. Many owners today consider it a business venture, toy, or tax write-off.

"While the owners are indeed wealthy, they aren't necessarily liquid the way you or I might think a billionaire is," said David Carter. Nearly three-quarters of the game's primary owners have a net worth north of 10 figures, and all but one of them (Miami) have seen their franchise values appreciate since their purchases, often extraordinarily.

Over the past decade, the value of the average MLB franchise has increased by approximately 300 percent, to $1.85 billion. The annual contract of the average MLB player has increased by about 40 percent, to $4.4 million. As the Associated Press reported, salaries have stagnated over five years from 2015 to 2020.

Max Scherzer, then of the Washington Nationals, would say owners are making money and went as far as asking the owners to open their books in May 2020 during the COVID pandemic.

Today's MLB owners are quite different from the ones I grew up with in the 1970s and 1980s. Not many teams today are family-run like decades ago. Craig Calcaterra told me, "I would even say that even to the extent it still is a family business with a couple of the franchises, when it becomes a second or third generation family business, it's a very different thing."

He added, "It's still a family business, but these guys didn't have a passion for baseball. It was just there. Then it was just handed to them. There's a pretty strong suspicion that what the Angelos boys have been doing in Baltimore for the last couple years has been trying to position the team for making a lot of money on a sale one day. The same thing has been said about the Illich boys in Detroit."

"Owners are better today," George Will told me. "We don't have the Yawkeys and the Marge Schotts and Phil Wrigley who didn't really like baseball. I'm all for getting the hobbyists out of there. Get the hedge funds in. I don't care, get people who are rational, but rationality is a science of incentives. And we have to change the incentives in baseball."

"[Former New York Yankees owner] George Steinbrenner obviously had other businesses," said Calcaterra. "He had his ship building, he had all that kind of stuff, but he had a passion for baseball. He wanted to win because it was vanity and ego and everything else. That's why [former Atlanta Braves owner] Ted Turner got into it too. That level of, if my team wins, I am better than you was obnoxious in a lot of ways, don't get me wrong. It led to all kinds of toxic, horrible crap that we all love to talk about, but it also did something for the game and it did something for fans. There's no way whatsoever that Mark Walter, a billionaire who owns the Dodgers, is interested in seeing the Dodgers win it all as Walter O'Malley might have been."

So, if that is the mindset of today's owner, is their team simply a commodity? How invested are they truly into the game of baseball? Are they personally connected to it? It certainly doesn't appear so. What is evident is that today's owners are more vested in the commodity notion than the love of the game.

What Do the Players Stand to Lose?

A challenge to a successful negotiation moving forward will be that teams' values have grown at a far quicker rate than players' incomes. This is sure to be a sticking point. The concern is that the potential for labor strife will continue to loom over the game as future negotiations move forward.

Fay Vincent, who was MLB commissioner during the 1994 work stoppage, said, "The owners [were] politically clueless and [were] on the wrong side of the COVID dispute … [and] baseball's timeless principles still apply and that is: the players are the talent, they're the game's oxygen. No matter what they earn, they're still getting ripped off" (Klapish, 2020).

Vincent also said to Klapish (2020) that the idea that the players have prospered more than the owners is pure fiction.

"The Yankees are worth $10 billion," said Vincent. "If the Steinbrenners sold the team … the players wouldn't get a nickel. For all the owners: after tax dollars and capital gains [tax], they've held on to every bit of equity. So tell me who is the winner and who is the loser?" asked Vincent.

The issues for the players run deep. Buster Olney (2020) of ESPN said that the problems have been ongoing since the 2016 talks. "The inequities they predicted would cost the players many hundreds of millions of dollars: the shockingly low competitive balance tax thresholds, which have been treated as a soft salary cap by big-market teams such as the Dodgers and Yankees; the failure to address the problem of tanking; [and] the failure to address service-time manipulation."

Barry Svrluga (2021) of the *Washington Post* suggests there's money to go around for everyone. "Ask Corey Seager, owner of a new 10-year, $325 million contract with the Texas Rangers. Ask Max Scherzer, who will earn more than $43 million annually for three years from the New York Mets. It's hard for either side to cry poor if they're giving and accepting those types of deals."

Former New York Yankees shortstop Derek Jeter, now part owner and chief executive officer of the Miami Marlins, commented on the 2020 negotiations: "It was pretty sad to see the back and forth being played out publicly in a time like now. I think some things should have been done behind the scenes. It was disappointing, it was embarrassing at times, the back and forth." Jeter continued, "There is no trust [between the owners and players] is the best way to put it. We owe it to our fans to be better than we've been for the last three months [during the summer of 2020]" (Bradburn, 2020).

In my interview with Calcaterra, we discussed the checkered past of player/owner negotiations in Major League Baseball, and while it's been nothing short of an embarrassing history, he is optimistic that things this time around have the chance to be better.

Calcaterra suggested, "There are more professional adults at the table now than there were 25–30 years ago. It's two sides of the same coin. We like the family ownership of baseball teams. We like these guys, used car salesmen and shipbuilders, to come in and want to run baseball teams. Those are the kind of guys that get really, really animated and personal and angry in the course of labor negotiations. Whereas you get a bunch of businessmen who have seen it and done it all running baseball teams, it could be a drag for how baseball runs, but they also understand that sometimes you gotta have contentious labor negotiations and it's not the end of the world.

"I know some people at the Major League Baseball Players Association," said Calcaterra, "and I think there's been a pretty big change in their philosophy when it comes to public negotiation over the last few years. Their chief negotiator now is a fellow named Bruce Meyer, who is a longtime litigator. He used to work for the NHL Players Association under Donald Fehr, but he was also a litigator in private practice for years and years.

"He [Meyer] said in interviews that he doesn't see a big upside to negotiating through the press or running to a friendly reporter and saying, 'Hey, those guys are being bad and we're being good and righteous.' It happens. You know it happens. There are a lot of people in those rooms and you can't make everybody be quiet, but there are a lot of things that go on in these negotiations now that 10 years ago would've been headline news and now just never get reported."

However, Calcaterra agreed with me that the negotiations during the 2020 COVID-shortened season were very, very contentious. He recalled, "There were maybe one or two stories that came out about the highest points of contention. There are a lot of stories, but one or two incidents within the negotiations that were reported generally, but overall it was a lot uglier than people realize. The reason why that wasn't all out in the public the way it might have been back in the days of Donald Fehr and Bud Selig was because people are generally keeping it closer to the vest now."

He added, "That doesn't mean that the labor negotiations are going to go better. I mean, it could still be ugly." Sadly, he was correct.

In short, owners, you are billionaires, and players, you are millionaires, and fans do not care about how you divide the billions Major League Baseball earns. Stop whining and waging a public war on social media trying to gain support. It has never worked and never will. The bottom line, you're all winners.

No surprise that players also stand to lose out on money as well. Jaffe suggests, "The biggest issue is ensuring a fair pay structure for players because players produce most of their value when they're in their twenties, before they reach free agency.... For the first three years they're being paid some function of the minimum salary, and by the time they get to 30, they're likely to be just replaced by younger players who are less expensive, and teams have gotten wise to the folly of paying huge contracts to 32-year-old free agents as if there's no way that they're going to age and just baseball has to get players paid sooner."

I followed up with Jaffe by asking why would fans care about that issue. He replied, "It has to do with the quality of athletes that choose baseball if they have the choice between baseball and basketball or football. I mean look, the collection of talent that we've got in the game is amazing, yet you're still losing quality, talented athletes to other sports too. That's one issue.... I think a lot of fans resent free agency because they think it's making their ticket more expensive. They think it's taking away the good players from them. I think if you've got players getting paid at a younger age, getting paid fair market value at a younger age, they're more likely to stick around. I think you're less likely to have transient players.

"So much of the friction that happens between players and ownership is over free agency. Are you going to pay me what I'm worth when I can accept full market value for my services? And if you can't, I'm gone. I'm leaving the Twins, I'm leaving the Padres, I'm leaving the Pirates. And there's just this festering, this resentment that's built in. And you've got fan bases that feel like they're feeder systems for the Yankees and the Mets and the big-money teams," said Jaffe.

When I asked George Will if he was optimistic that things will change for the better, sadly, he replied, "No, not right now. I mean baseball's experimented in the various minor leagues and the independent leagues with some of these changes of pitch clock and all the rest. And that's good, but we're now in the middle of a collective bargaining agreement where they've decided not to talk about these things. They're going to talk about economics. Well, baseball's economic model, noted, has to be improved, but they're arguing about how to carve a pie like this big. And in a few years, it's going to be that big. It's going to shrink because people are just not going to go."

He added, "What makes baseball's problems today intractable and interesting is that everyone is behaving reasonably on the basis of abundant, accurate information. That's the problem. So, you have to change the incentives within this system."

Solutions

Act Like Grown-Ups

Numerous solutions are offered in this book, and one that is critically important and wouldn't cost owners or players a cent during labor negotiations is to act like grown-ups and the professionals you claim to be. No one is winning here. The fans and general public are sick of the way both sides treat one another and behave when it comes to labor negotiations, and I would assume both sides are tired of it as well. The public bickering and shot-taking casts a shadow on the game. Enough already. At least do this one for the sake of the game.

Reuss added, "The game is a whole lot different but it has evolved. I liked it better when I played because I was playing. It is up to the players and owners to improve it. They owe it to the fans."

In the event both sides need some best practices on how to conduct a civil negotiation, Table 10 provides recommendations from LinkedIn and SmallBusiness.com (2022).

Table 10: Strategies and Best Practices for Successful Negotiations

LinkedIn	*SmallBusiness.com*
Shut up and listen	Active listening skills
Do not take it personally	Keep emotions in check
Be willing to walk away	Clear and effective communication
Do your homework	Collaboration and teamwork

The bright spot is that there is hope. During the 2020 COVID-19–shortened season, with the virus canceling game after game, MLB and the MLBPA finally came together and agreed to get the season underway with some unique rule changes that I cover in chapter 9. They pivoted and worked together. Use that success, albeit small, as a springboard to future negotiations.

Learn from the Past

Tom Glavine, a Hall of Fame pitcher and former player representative, told Steve Hummer (2020) of the *Atlanta Journal-Constitution* that, looking back on the 1994 strike year, "The accessibility thing was a miscalculation on my part. I just felt like if I did an interview on the radio or TV, or if I had five or 10 minutes, I could make somebody understand what was going on and come to our side. That just wasn't going to happen." Glavine would seemingly be recommending that owners and players today not bother having a Twitter war; you're not going to win in the court of public opinion.

I've clearly made the point that baseball is on a downward spiral in terms of fan interest. Why jeopardize greater damage by waging a battle over social media? Do the dirty work in private. Behind closed doors. The war between the two sides on social media is a no-win. As Scott Karl told me, the two sides need to find a way to build and grow their sport together even though long-term solutions seem miles away.

Revenue Sharing

Earlier I spoke of a salary cap, and while that is an insurmountable mountain to climb, at least consider revenue sharing or a spending floor versus the competitive balance tax. Having this in place would ensure that the owners and players would be working together for a common purpose and not fighting over the same slice of the pie. David Carter agrees: "A variation of it is possible. MLB now calls it a luxury tax, but they can create some type of mechanism to create more of a level playing field."

9

Save Situation

> *"Baseball was born here, and I personally want baseball to be the most popular sport in the United States so if I can contribute in any way to help that, I'm more than open to it."*—Shohei Ohtani, Los Angeles Angels MVP Pitcher, Outfielder, Designated Hitter (Riley, GQ)

Baseball swept me off my feet at an early age. It became part of my soul and it has never left. That may sound silly to some, but many of you know exactly what I am referring to. It is the reason I have been here, researching and writing for hundreds of hours—to provide solutions to issues facing Major League Baseball. It has been a labor of love. I love baseball, and like most things we love, we want what is best for it. But I am worried about the future of Major League Baseball. Clearly, I'm not alone.

Many of those I spoke to feel that the issues the game is facing are of major concern. Those have been addressed in this book along with viable and achievable solutions. However, if Major League Baseball doesn't address these concerns, the cliff that is approaching is destined to reduce baseball to a niche sport. The plea to MLB from those of us who love the game is to simply acknowledge there are problems that need to be addressed. Be proactive, not reactive. Sooner than later.

Baseball is not dead like some proclaim, but it might be on life support. If baseball was a patient and went into its doctor for a physical, what would the doctor say about its health and what would the doctor prescribe? That question is at the heart of this book. Treatments or solutions are presented, some of which are my ideas but most are from experts such as current and former players, managers, and executives. The solutions we suggest will not be easy to implement. They will take a change in mindset. They will buck tradition. They will involve risk. They will disrupt the status quo. They will require courage. But if we are serious about improving the game and increasing fan interest, I believe these solutions will lead to a rally in the bottom of the ninth for the game we love.

This is a call for MLB and its teams to be innovative, especially on the heels of COVID-19. The pandemic clearly wreaked havoc on America's economy and is predicted to negatively impact it for years to come. As a result, it is even more incumbent upon the league to be more creative to attract fans to ballparks and generate fan interest as a whole. There has never been greater competition for the consumer's dollar than there is today. The public has a right to know why they should invest it in baseball.

I am optimistic that baseball can and will take notice—otherwise, why would I have taken on this project? Some are not as optimistic as I am. CJ Kelly of HowTheyPlay said, "The ... executives, union reps, and journalists, share this responsibility. They've turned a blind eye to the changes going on around them because of their greed."

Former major league pitcher Jerry Reuss is optimistic. He told me, "Throughout the history of baseball, it has always had problems but it has always found new solutions and looked to more on the horizon. The game has always found a way to get from here to there. The game has evolved [over time] and will continue to do so."

Others, like former pitcher Scott Karl, believe in the collective power of both sides needing to come together to solve issues. "Until they [owners and players] come together, nothing will be done. Not one individual has the platform to bring about change. No one is going to do anything about it until the fans do not come, television contracts decrease, and the pain is felt—and that pain is a decrease, a significant one, in revenue. Maybe then they will move on this."

MLB executive and former general manager Bill Bavasi suggests, "I think right now everybody feels like they're surviving because the revenues are up, but I do know that, eventually, that decline has to catch up to you and damage your revenue at some point."

It does come down to the bottom line and revenue. Major League Baseball is a multibillion-dollar entity and until that is in jeopardy, things may not change. However, I am optimistic that the solutions offered here will be implemented for the good of the game.

Everyone I interviewed for this project was asked the same question to begin our conversation: "What solutions could you suggest to Major League Baseball to overcome declining attendance and fan interest?" Their first response was typically, "That's a great question and I am not sure." In the end, each concluded the interview with the same request—to let them know what I found out. They care and my hope is that you do as well. Here is a recap of those solutions and best practices.

Solutions: A Recap

Understanding Constraints

The study by Davis and Miller (2021) revealed that constraints, or barriers, have an influence on attendance at Major League Baseball games and noted, "The pace-of-play initiatives may make the games' flow more appealing in the long run, but with no conception of the constraints being placed on fans in their everyday lives."

The researchers concluded, "The implications of this study indicate that fans may be willing to negotiate work or personal elements for more excitement at the MLB game. Decreased attendance of major league baseball games because of constraints may threaten the potential sustainability of the sport. This study underscores that MLB should try to understand the elements of constraints that will assist a fan's negotiation to attend a game" (Davis and Miller, 2021).

Build the MLB Brand

MLB needs to increase its social media footprint with a steady diet of videos, articles, and blog posts showcasing its content. Major League Baseball needs to infiltrate Facebook, Instagram, Twitter (or "X"), etc., with MLB and team content. Also, every team should have a YouTube channel and the league should promote its channel. Finally, part of building the brand should include Major League Baseball supporting and encouraging its players to have a social media presence and celebrate their individuality.

Increase Social Media Presence

Major League Baseball should increase its digital footprint. The suggestion here is to keep pressing, deepen the offerings, and invest more into their digital platform, especially to engage the young Generation Z fans. Teams should be creating a digital voice to connect with their fan base. It is important for teams to keep in mind that the fan experience away from the ballpark is just as important as the one inside.

Ticket Subscriptions

There is no reason every Major League Baseball team should not be offering a subscription-based ticket option to their fans. There's no team too big not to get on board. One million Ballpark Pass tix sold should be reason enough. As I discussed throughout the book, you can now binge-watch your favorite team live and in person—if they offer a ticket subscription service, that is. Offering this option definitely provides an innovative experience for fans. This is the world we are all living in with seemingly everything connected to some type of subscription service. MLB realizes that its ticket challenges reflect broader competition for leisure spending, attention, and time, and the subscription service tackles those barriers.

Social Consciousness

Clearly, social consciousness has never been as relevant to businesses as it is in today's increasingly changing society. Major League Baseball and its players have been in conversation about how to incorporate social justice elements into the sport.

Be a Community Partner

Along the lines of social consciousness, community outreach is critical. The stars of the sport need to be more active in their community. Their contributions to the community are amplified, which will increase the brand.

Improve Video Replay

Here are two simple solutions offered by former MLB executive Wayne Krivsky: "Two challenges—that's it. It eliminates the coach wasting time on the phone and it eliminates the video guy. The manager has five seconds, not 20 or 30. Use your eyeballs. Managers would use it sparingly. They wouldn't use it in the first inning on a close play. They would save it for something important."

Follow the Brewers' Lead

The Brewers clearly have the secret sauce. A small-market team that is crushing it at the box office year after year. Learn from them. They are a collaborative organization and willing to share.

Minor League Lessons

In recent years we learned that MLB teams have started to include some of the fun promotions that have been the hallmark in Minor League Baseball for decades. Wholesome, family fun is starting to creep into major league stadiums. Teams should embrace this and go deeper. Let loose and focus on the families.

World Series Game Times

Major League Baseball should recognize the obviousness that the World Series is the game's moment to shine. Unfortunately, half the nation is in bed asleep during World Series games or tuned out because their team isn't in it. Consider the idea of moving the games earlier. Move the weekend games to a daytime start like the NFL does with most of its playoff games. As for the weekday games, at least move them one hour earlier to 7:00 p.m. Eastern Time.

Salary Cap/Spending Floor Proposal

Major League Baseball is the last holdout of the major sports leagues to implement a salary cap or spending floor. The suggestion is to strongly consider it as it could improve fan interest because it prevents "one team from gaining an unfair advantage over the rest of the competition because they can afford more star players. Enable smaller franchises to remain competitive and grow their fan base" (University of Kansas).

In-Venue Experience

Once teams have Gen Zers connected with their monthly subscription and in the ballpark, teams must then provide them with an experience that is engaging. Today's Gen Z sports fan wants a communal experience.

Just as teams like the Orioles have successfully implemented, creating more social spaces for fans with views of the game and the surrounding city helps generate excitement.

However, with games dragging on sometimes well past three hours, it is a tough ask to expect fans to come to a game that starts after 7:00 p.m. and ends after 10:00 p.m.—especially on a weeknight. Follow the lead of numerous teams and start games no later than 6:40 p.m.

The Korea Baseball Organization was front and center at the beginning of the 2020 baseball season. MLB could certainly replicate some of its best practices as they relate to fan engagement. For example, MLB teams should consider having real cheer squads leading the fans in cheering and singing. Sounds like a blast.

Sports Betting

Sports betting has become legal and, with MLB's support, clearly acceptable in American culture. Teams should embrace sports betting and, better yet, increase their marketing revenues by creating a partnership with a sports betting entity.

Shorten Commercial Breaks

We could actually stop there. Problem solved. In 2019, breaks were reduced from 2:05 to 2:00 in local games, and from 2:25 to 2:00 in national games. I suggest cutting another 20 seconds off to 1:40 between all breaks local and national (add commercials during the live action).

Be Better and Make Adjustments

Scott Karl says the pace-of-play issue is solvable. "The owners and the players need to work together to speed up the game," said Karl. "It begins with the desire of the players. Specifically, it's on the pitcher, catcher, and the hitter to speed up the game." He suggests catchers should simply give the sign quickly and the pitcher get the sign and throw the ball.

Alternative to Robo Umpires

Krivsky, who cannot stand the idea of robo umpires, suggests to "empower the umpires to pick up the pace. Get in the box or a strike will be called. It will only need to happen once before they know not to do it again. They can have a positive influence on the pace of the game."

Meeting Them Where They Are

No question Generation Z spends a tremendous amount of time on social media, so why not bring the game to them? It's already happening, so let's give MLB some credit for their work in this area, and Commissioner Manfred agrees. He said, "You have to be where they want to be." This will require innovation and a willingness to change.

Marketing to Generation Z

While Gen Z and millennial fans consume the most non-game content, they're also the most underserved audience. This should serve as a signal to Major League Baseball that this is a huge opportunity to engage with this generation by delivering the content they want: archived videos, behind-the-scenes footage, funny clips, documentaries, stats, and player data (Business Wire, 2019).

Create MLB Academies

Kudos to MLB on its efforts as a league to deepen outreach and support for promoting youth baseball. The Play Ball and RBI programs are great and reach into the inner city. I suggest there is a way to deepen this outreach while having a profound impact on the game. My idea is for each MLB team to create its own in-house academy that offers training and education.

Teach Kids the Game

Teach the kids to play baseball the right way and actually let them figure the game out without constant intervention by coaches. Kids don't want to be told how to do every little thing. That's boring. As Marlins coach Rob Flippo said, "Reinforce the positives and let them experience the process. Don't control everything." Make the experience fun for all.

Consistent Youth Experience

Kids should play within the same ability level to make the game fun and competitive. Baseball is a humbling game at every level and if kids are thrown into leagues and teams based on age alone, they risk feeling inferior if they don't measure up. Specifically, we must ensure that youngsters are provided an experience that is positive and focused on learning the game while having fun.

Messaging

This game is fun! Those of us who have played at any level, organized or casual, would agree so. Therefore, I encourage Major League Baseball to create a marketing campaign showcasing kids playing the game for fun from Wiffle ball to a competition level. This game is truly for all of us. That should be celebrated and shared.

Show More Consideration for Women

MLB needs to respectfully focus on bringing more women into the game as fans and employees without being condescending. Major League Baseball as an organization could take steps toward showing that it values the women who love the game. First, hire more women. Another step should be to stop pandering to them—treat them as equals. Also, imposing harsher measures on those who violate the domestic abuse policy is needed. Send the message that this type of behavior has no place in the game.

Deepen Amateur Draft

While the commissioner works for Major League Baseball team owners and part of his responsibilities is to support their financial interests, it is painful to see once again that dollars override what is best for the long-term health of the game. In short, the draft should have at least 40 rounds.

Rule Changes

The solution here is simple—keep being innovative and give the recent rule changes some time to see if they are making a positive impact on the length, pace, and excitement of the game. Implement the pitch clock and game times will shrink.

Rules like limiting the number of mound visits and the extra-inning rule have a feel to them that the game is moving along at a quicker pace.

Act Like Grown-Ups

No one is winning the public labor negotiations battle. The fans and general public are sick of the way both sides treat one another and behave. Fans are over the bickering, and shot-taking casts a shadow on the game. Enough already.

Learn from the Past

Baseball is on a downward spiral in terms of fan interest. Why jeopardize greater damage by waging a battle over social media? Do the dirty work in private. Behind closed doors. The war between the two sides on social media is a no-win.

Revenue Sharing

Consider revenue sharing or something similar. Having this in place would ensure that the owners and players are working together for a common purpose and not fighting over the same slice of the pie.

Have I achieved my goal in writing this book, which is simply to make the greatest game on the planet better and sustainable for generations to enjoy? I believe I have succeeded in presenting not just the issues Major League Baseball is facing but, more important, I have also shared solutions and best practices. Now it's up to others who have the influence and same desire that I have to see Major League Baseball succeed and thrive for another 175 years.

There you have it, MLB—your marching orders. Now get to it. Your future depends on it.

Bibliography

Adweek. 2017. "Engaging Generation Z: Marketing to a New Brand of Consumer." https://www.adweek.com/performance-marketing/josh-perlstein-response-media-guest-post-generation-z/.

Allentuck, Danielle, and Kevin Draper. 2019. "Baseball Saw a Million More Empty Seats. Does It Matter?" *New York Times*, September 19. https://www.nytimes.com/2019/09/29/sports/baseball/mlb-attendance.html.

American Negotiation Institute and Kwame Christian. "Mindsets and Strategies for Negotiation Success." LinkedIn. https://www.linkedin.com/learning/mindsets-and-strategies-for-negotiation-success.

Anderson, Shaun M., and Matthew M. Martin. 2019. "The African American Community and Professional Baseball: Examining Major League Baseball's Corporate Social-Responsibility Efforts as a Relationship-Management Strategy." *International Journal of Sport Communication* 12.3: 397–418.

Ask Sports. 2014. "When Did World Series Games Start Being Played at Night?" October 20. https://account.kansas.com/paywall/subscriber-only?resume=3075191&intcid=ab_archive.

Associated Press via ESPN.com. 2022. "Major League Baseball stops testing its players for steroids after nearly 20 years, report says." February 7. https://www.espn.com/mlb/story/_/id/33238595/major-league-baseball-stops-testing-players-steroids-nearly-20-years-report-says.

Associated Press via *Tampa Bay Times*. 2020. "Rockies' Ian Desmond to sit out season for family, help youth baseball in Sarasota." June 30. https://www.tampabay.com/sports/rays/2020/06/30/rockies-ian-desmond-to-sit-out-season-for-family-help-youth-baseball-in-sarasota/.

Atlanta Journal-Constitution. 2020. "Baseball players' reactions to Astros sign-stealing scandal." February 18. https://www.ajc.com/sports/baseball/baseball-players-reactions-astros-sign-stealing-scandal/SpZErZLP2wLVr3jsfgkKBI/.

Baccellieri, Emma. 2019. "Is MLB Ready for Robo-Umps and an Automated Strike Zone?" *Sports Illustrated*, November 19. https://www.si.com/mlb/2019/11/19/robot-umpires-automated-strike-zone.

Bader, Greg. Personal interview (2020). Baltimore Orioles senior vice president, administration & experience.

Baer, Bill. 2019. "MLB execs go to bat in favor of shrinking minor leagues." NBC Sports, December 15. https://mlb.nbcsports.com/2019/12/15/mlb-execs-go-to-bat-in-favor-of-shrinking-minor-leagues/.

Ballparksofbaseball.com. 2022.

Baltimore Orioles. 2022. "Orioles RBI & Junior RBI Programs." Orioles.com. https://www.mlb.com/orioles/community/rbi.

Baltimore Orioles. 2022. "Oriole Park A-to-Z Guide." Orioles.com. https://www.mlb.com/orioles/ballpark/information/guide.

Baltimore Orioles. 2022. "O's at Home." Orioles.com. https://www.mlb.com/orioles/fans/orioles-at-home.

Bibliography

Barrabi, Thomas. 2020. "David Stern built NBA into $5B global powerhouse." Fox Business. January 2. https://www.foxbusiness.com/sports/david-stern-nba-commissioner-business-legacy.

Baseball Almanac. Milwaukee Brewers Attendance. https://www.baseball-almanac.com/teams/brewatte.shtml.

Baseball Almanac. New York Yankees Attendance. https://www.baseball-almanac.com/teams/yankatte.shtml.

Baseball Pilgrimages. 2022. https://www.baseballpilgrimages.com/national/pittsburgh.html.

Baseball Savant. N.d. https://baseballsavant.mlb.com/leaderboard/statcast?type=batter&year=2021&position=&team=&min=q.

Baseball-Reference. "Instant Replay." https://www.baseball-reference.com/bullpen/Instant_replay.

Baseball-Reference. "Major League Baseball Attendance." https://www.baseball-reference.com/leagues/majors/misc.shtml.

Baseball-Reference. "Major League Baseball Strikeouts—by year." https://www.baseball-reference.com.

Baseball-Reference. "2019 Major League Baseball World Series." https://www.baseball-reference.com/postseason/2019_WS.shtml.

Bavasi, Bill. Personal interview (2020). Former Major League Baseball general manager and senior director of baseball and softball development with Major League Baseball (retired).

Blanchette, John. 2020. "Spokane Indians owner Bobby Brett prepares for inevitable changes." *Spokesman-Review*, April 7. https://www.spokesman.com/stories/2020/apr/07/john-blanchette-spokane-indians-owner-bobby-brett-/.

Bogage, Jacob. 2019. "Robo umps will help bring baseball into 21st century more ways than one." *Washington Post*, December 24. https://www.washingtonpost.com/sports/2019/12/24/robo-umps-will-help-bring-baseball-into-st-century-more-ways-than-one/.

Bondi, Filip. 2017. "With a new breed of fans, even the Yankees must adapt." *New York Times*, April 4. https://www.nytimes.com/2017/04/04/sports/baseball/yankees-falling-ticket-sales-price-changes.html.

Bradburn, Michael. 2020. "Jeter: 'There is no trust' between players, owners." The Score, July 1. https://www.thescore.com/mlb/news/1981366/amp.

Brown, Maury. 2019. "From Terrible Teams To Rising Costs: Why MLB Attendance Is Down Over 7% Since 2015." *Forbes*, October 4. https://www.forbes.com/sites/maurybrown/2019/10/04/from-terrible-teams-to-rising-costs-and-more-why-mlb-attendance-has-been-down-over-7-since-2015/?sh=b1680d031a8d.

Brown, Maury. 2019. "MLB Sees Record Revenues Of $10.3 Billion For 2018." *Forbes*. January 7. https://www.forbes.com/sites/maurybrown/2019/01/07/mlb-sees-record-revenues-of-10-3-billion-for-2018/?sh=74ab61405bea.

Buffa, Dan. 2020. "Opinion | Bill DeWitt Jr.'s 'baseball isn't profitable' comment isn't a good look, or near true." 5 On Your Side KSDK, June 11. https://www.ksdk.com/article/sports/mlb/stl-cardinals/opinion-bill-dewitt-jrs-baseball-isnt-profitable-comment-isnt-a-good-look-or-near-true/63-7ca2653c-e185-4648-bbec-689f07cbe917.

Bumbaca, Chris. 2019. "Report: As many as 42 minor league baseball teams could be eliminated in new MLB proposal." *USA Today*, October 19. https://www.usatoday.com/story/sports/mlb/minors/2019/10/19/minor-league-baseball-many-teams-could-be-eliminated-mlb-proposal/4035666002/.

Burns, Ken. 1994. *Baseball: A Film by Ken Burns*. PBS.

Business Wire. 2019. "New Research Reveals Millennial and Gen Z Sports Fans Changing the Game for Leagues, Teams and Players." November 4. https://www.businesswire.com/news/home/20191104005245/en/New-Research-Reveals-Millennial-and-GenZ-Sports-Fans-Changing-the-Game-for-Leagues-Teams-and-Players.

Calcaterra, Craig. 2020. "2020 MLB Draft will only be five rounds." NBC Sports, May 8. https://mlb.nbcsports.com/2020/05/08/2020-mlb-draft-will-only-be-five-rounds/.

Calcaterra, Craig. Personal interview (2022). Baseball writer of *Cup of Coffee* and author of *Rethinking Fandom: How to Beat the Sports-Industrial Complex at Its Own Game*.
Carter, David. Personal interview (2020). Professor, University of Southern California. Author.
Carter, D.M., and D. Rovell. 2003. *On the Ball: What You Can Learn about Business from America's Sports Leaders*. FT Press.
Carter, Stephen L. 2019. "Baseball Fans Are Too Old, Too White and Too Few." October 31. https://www.bloomberg.com/opinion/articles/2019-10-31/baseball-s-diversity-problem-fans-are-older-whiter-and-fewer.
Castillo, Jorge. 2020. "Rob Manfred acknowledges Astros banged trash can in sign-stealing scheme in 2017 playoffs." *Los Angeles Times*, February 18. https://www.latimes.com/sports/dodgers/story/2020-02-18/rob-manfred-astros-sign-stealing-continued-through-2017-playoffs.
Castrovince, Anthony. 2022. "Umpires to wear microphones, announce replay reviews to fans." April 1. https://www.mlb.com/news/umpires-to-announce-replay-reviews-to-fans.
CBS News/*New York Times* poll. n.d. https://www.cbsnews.com/2100-500160_162-3982412.html/.
Champion, Walter. 2020. "The Commissioner Goes Too Far: The Best Interests of Baseball Clause and the Astros' 'High Tech' Sign-Stealing Scandal." *Marquette Sports Law Review*, 31, 215.
Cisyk, Jeffery, and Pascal Courty. 2017. "Do fans care about compliance to doping regulations in sports? The impact of PED suspension in baseball." *Journal of Sports Economics*, 18(4), 323–350.
Cisyk, Jeffrey. 2020. "Impacts of performance-enhancing drug suspensions on the demand for Major League Baseball." *Journal of Sports Economics*, 21(4), 391-419.
Cooper, JJ. Baseball America. 2020. "Which MiLB Teams Are On The List To Be Eliminated? It's Impossible To Say." April 22. https://www.baseballamerica.com/stories/which-milb-teams-are-on-the-list-to-be-eliminated-its-impossible-to-say/.
Cosler, Emily. 2020. "An Analysis of the Decline in MLB Stadium Attendance and the Marketing Techniques That Can Be Utilized to Reverse It." Undergraduate Honors paper, Texas Christian University.
Craig, Mary. 2017. "Craig: Baseball's tumultuous relationship with the female fan." SB Nation, June 23. https://www.beyondtheboxscore.com/2017/6/23/15851676/mlb-promotions-advertising-sexism-female-fans-history.
Davis, Mark A., and John Miller. 2019. "A fan's choice: An application of the theory of consumer choice to Major League Baseball." *Applied Research in Coaching and Athletics Annual* 34: 146–175.
Davis, Mark A., and John Miller. 2021. "Major League Baseball's War on Time: An Analysis of Game Times' Impact on Attendance Using the Theory of Leisure Constraints." *Journal of Sport Behavior* 44(2): 166–182.
Doublin, Nancy. 2010. "Baseball Isn't For Girls: How Title IX and a Sexist Culture Keep Women Out Of MLB." Bleacher Report, September 9. https://bleacherreport.com/articles/456060-how-title-ix-and-a-sexist-culture-keep-women-out-of-mlb.
Drea, David. 2019. "Bringing Business Back to the Ballpark." Honors thesis, Ursinus College.
Dusenbury, Wells. 2019. "Fox Sports Florida acquired by Sinclair—How does that impact Marlins' TV deal negotiations?" *South Florida Sun-Sentinel,* May 6. https://www.sun-sentinel.com/sports/miami-marlins/fl-sp-marlins-braves-separate-sun-20190505-story.html.
Easley, Cameron. 2018. "Past Time for the Pastimes? NFL and MLB Lose Ground With Gen Z." Morning Consult, October 15. https://morningconsult.com/2018/10/15/past-time-for-the-pastimes-nfl-and-mlb-lose-ground-with-gen-z/.
Ebersberger, Marc. Personal interview (2020). Casual Major League Baseball fan.
Eddings, Jay. Personal Conversation (2022). Major League Baseball pro scout, Texas Rangers.

Edwards, Craig. 2019. "April Attendance Was a Mixed Bag for Baseball." FanGraphs, May 2. https://blogs.fangraphs.com/april-attendance-was-a-mixed-bag-for-baseball/.

ESPN.com. 2021. "Agent Scott Boras: Tanking, MLB's 'competitive cancer,' led to Atlanta Braves' World Series title." November 10. https://www.espn.com/mlb/story/_/id/32600372/agent-scott-boras-tanking-mlb-competitive-cancer-led-atlanta-braves-world-series-title.

ESPN.com. 2012. "The Steroids Era." December 5. https://www.espn.com/mlb/topics/_/page/the-steroids-era.

Estes, Gentry. 2019. "Morning Coffee: Can Major League Baseball fix its attendance woes?" *Courier Journal*, May 13. https://www.courier-journal.com/story/sports/mlb/2019/05/13/mlb-attendance-woes-can-they-be-fixed/1185468001/.

Field, Carson. 2020. "Minor League Baseball Contraction Proposal Worries Some MLB Players, Managers." *Baseball America*, March 27. https://www.baseballamerica.com/stories/minor-league-baseball-contraction-proposal-worries-some-mlb-players-managers/.

Finch, Jeremy. 2015. "What Is Generation Z, And What Does It Want?" Fast Company, May 4. https://www.fastcompany.com/3045317/what-is-generation-z-and-what-does-it-want.

Fisher, Eric. 2017. "MLB clubs move to start games earlier." *New York Business Journal*, November 29. https://www.bizjournals.com/newyork/news/2017/11/29/mlb-clubs-move-to-start-games-earlier.html.

Fisher, Marc. 2015. "Baseball is struggling to hook kids—and risks losing fans to other sports." *Washington Post*, April 5. https://www.washingtonpost.com/sports/nationals/baseballs-trouble-with-the-youth-curve—and-what-that-means-for-the-game/2015/04/05/2da36dca-d7e8-11e4-8103-fa84725dbf9d_story.html.

Flippo, Rob. Personal interview (2020). Major League Baseball coach. Miami Marlins.

Fowles, Stacey May. 2017. *Baseball Life Advice: Loving the Game That Saved Me*. McClelland & Stewart.

Fox Sports. 2018. "Extra innings throughout the minors to start with a runner on second." March 14. https://www.foxsports.com/stories/other/extra-innings-throughout-the-minors-to-start-with-a-runner-on-second.

Gennaro, Vince. 2019. "MLB stays ahead of the curve with Generation Z." *Sports Business Journal*, July 7. https://www.sportsbusinessjournal.com/Journal/Issues/2019/07/08/Opinion/Gennaro.

Goldman, Tom. 2019. "America's Favorite Pastime Is Back—And Some Wish It Would Just Hurry Up!" NPR, March 27. https://www.npr.org/2019/03/27/707007648/americas-favorite-pastime-is-back-and-some-wish-it-would-just-hurry-up.

Gonzales, Alden. 2022. "Tampa Bay Rays say split-season plan with Montreal rejected by MLB." ESPN, January 20. https://www.espn.com/mlb/story/_/id/33109350/tampa-bay-rays-say-split-season-plan-montreal-rejected-mlb.

Hasaan, Ali, Rui Biscaia, and Stephen Ross. 2021. "Understanding Athlete Brand Life Cycle." *Sport in Society* 24(2): 181–205.

HBO *Real Sports*/Marist poll. 2015. "More Than One-Third Believes Decline in African American Baseball Players is a Concern … Race Factors into Perceptions of Baseball." https://maristpoll.marist.edu/wp-content/misc/usapolls/us140922/Sports/Complete%20April%202015%20Marist%20Poll%20Baseball%20Release%20and%20Tables.pdf.

HBO *Real Sports*/Marist poll. 2019. "Do You Follow Professional Baseball?" Marist Poll National Results & Analysis, Baseball in America. July. https://maristpoll.marist.edu/polls/marist-poll-national-results-analysis-baseball-in-america-july-2019/.

Heller, Dave. Personal interview (2020). President and CEO of Main Street Baseball.

Hillman, Trey. Personal interview (2020). Former Major League, Japanese League, and Korean Baseball manager.

Hine, Chris. 2018. "Major League Baseball fans turning gray while millennials tuning out." *Minneapolis Star Tribune*, July 21. https://chippewa.com/major-league-baseball-fans-turning-gray-while-millennials-tuning-out/article_586fcef8-fcc0-5b80-9eed-335b0d5f55be.html.

Hine, Chris. 2020. "The sports fan experience might never be the same." *Minneapolis*

Star Tribune, May 12. https://www.startribune.com/sports-fan-experience-may-never-be-the-same-after-pandemic/570388841/.

Hummer, Steve. 2020. "Braves great Tom Glavine knows who you'll blame if baseball stays out." *Atlanta Journal-Constitution,* May 19. https://www.ajc.com/blog/further-review/braves-great-tom-glavine-knows-who-you-blame-baseball-stays-out/dZ2gzK6Ux9NoVlRNrDwjeP/.

Humphreys, Brad R., and Candon Johnson. 2020. "The effect of superstars on game attendance: evidence from the NBA." *Journal of Sports Economics* 21.2: 152–175.

Humphreys, Brad, and Thomas Miceli. 2020. "Outcome uncertainty, fan travel, and aggregate attendance." *Economic Inquiry* 58.1: 462–473.

Hunzinger, Erica. 2019. "Major League Baseball Is Trying To Bring More Women Into Front Offices And Fields." NPR. April 8. https://www.npr.org/2019/04/08/711169787/major-league-baseball-is-trying-to-bring-more-women-into-game-related-roles.

Hyman, Mark. Personal conversation (2021). Veteran journalist, professor, author, and lawyer.

Imagen Insights. 2022. "Gen Z Reports." https://imageninsights.com/.

Ireland, Kyle. 2020. "Andy Reid Says Black Lives Matter 'Absolutely They Matter, Man. I Think It's A Beautiful Thing.'" KSL Sports, July 10. https://kslsports.com/435899/andy-reid-says-black-lives-matter-absolutely-they-matter-man-i-think-its-a-beautiful-thing/#:~:text=I'm%20so%20happy%2C%20I,is%20make%20this%20country%20better.%E2%80%9D.

Ita Group. 2022. "3 Things Employers Should Know About Generation Z and Technology." https://www.itagroup.com/insights/three-things-employers-should-know-generation-z-technology.

Jaffe, Jay. Personal interview (2022). Baseball author. Contributing baseball writer for *Sports Illustrated* (SI.com) and the founder of the Futility Infielder website.

Kasasa. 2021. "Gen Z is here. Get to know them better." September 20. https://www.kasasa.com/exchange/get-to-know-gen-z.

Kelly, CJ. 2022. "Strike Three: Baseball Is Dead." HowTheyPlay, April 6. https://howtheyplay.com/team-sports/Baseball-A-Changing-Landscape.

Klapish, Bob. 2020. "Former MLB commissioner warns owners: players union 'cannot be broken … it looks like it's 1994 all over again.'" *NJ Advance Media,* June 7. https://www.nj.com/yankees/2020/06/former-mlb-commissioner-warns-owners-players-union-cannot-be-broken-it-looks-like-its-1994-all-over-again.html.

Koosed, Dan. Personal interview (2021). Associate scout for the New York Yankees and master hitting instructor.

Krivsky, Wayne. Personal interview (2020). Former Major League Baseball general manager, Cincinnati Reds (retired).

Lacques, Gabe. 2019. "Baseball's future: Declining attendance—and shrinking stadiums to match." *USA Today,* August 8. https://www.usatoday.com/story/sports/mlb/2019/08/08/mlb-attendance-stadiums-future/1941614001/.

Lacques, Gabe. 2019. "MLB's efforts to speed up play run into reality of modern game: 'It's not going to happen.'" *USA Today,* September 3. https://www.usatoday.com/story/sports/mlb/2019/09/03/baseball-pace-of-play-rules-home-runs-strikeouts/2195267001/.

Lange, Jeva. 2018. "Women love baseball. Why doesn't baseball love them back?" *The Week,* September 9. https://theweek.com/articles/793920/women-love-baseball-why-doesnt-baseball-love-back.

Langhorst, Ben. 2014. "What Do Your Fans Want? Attendance Correlations with Performance, Ticket Prices, and Payroll Factors." Society for American Baseball Research, Spring. https://sabr.org/journal/article/what-do-your-fans-want-attendance-correlations-with-performance-ticket-prices-and-payroll-factors/.

Langhorst, Paul. 2016. "Is Youth Baseball Too Boring for Today's Kids?" Engage Sports, February 22. http://engagesports.com/blog/post/1486/is-youth-baseball-too-boring-for-today-s-kids.

Lantz, Jeff. Personal interview (2020). Senior director of communications for Minor League Baseball.

Lee, Sangkwon, and Chi-Ok Oh Chi-Ok. 2016. "Applying the Concept of Sport Affordability to Professional Sporting Events: The Case of the Major League Baseball Games." *International Journal of Applied Sports Sciences*, 28(1).

Leitch, Will. 2018. "Nobody's Going to Sports in Person Anymore and No One Seems to Care." *New York Times: Intelligencer,* July 11. https://nymag.com/intelligencer/2018/07/nobodys-going-to-sports-in-person-and-no-one-seems-to-care.html.

Lewis, Michael. 2004. *Moneyball: The Art of Winning an Unfair Game.* WW Norton & Company.

Lief, Eric. 2016. "Speedier Baseball Games Risks Pitchers' Arms, Study Says." American Council on Health and Sciences, May 24. https://www.acsh.org/news/2016/05/24/speedier-baseball-games-risks-pitchers-arms-study-says.

Lombardo, John. 2019. "How subscription ticketing is redefining MLB ticket sales." *New York Business Journal,* June 20. https://www.bizjournals.com/newyork/news/2019/06/20/how-subscription-ticketing-is-redefining-mlb.html.

Lombardo, John, and David Broughton. 2017. "Going gray: Sports TV viewers skew older." *Sports Business Journal,* June 5. https://www.sportsbusinessjournal.com/Journal/Issues/2017/06/05/Research-and-Ratings/Viewership-trends.aspx.

Lopez-Gonzalez, Hibai, and Mark D. Griffiths. 2018. "Understanding the convergence of markets in online sports betting." *International Review for the Sociology of Sport* 53.7: 807–823.

Los Angeles Times. 2015. "New baseball rules should speed up games." February 20. https://www.latimes.com/sports/sportsnow/la-sp-sn-mlb-pace-changes-20150220-story.html.

Love, Juliette. 2019. "How Popular Is Baseball, Really?" *New York Times,* October 22. https://www.nytimes.com/interactive/2019/10/22/sports/baseball/baseball-popularity-world-series.html.

MacLennan, Ashley. 2017. "No, Millennials Aren't Killing Baseball." Fan Graphs, August 25. https://blogs.fangraphs.com/no-millennials-arent-killing-baseball/.

Maddon, Joe. Personal interview (2022). Major League Baseball manager.

Mathewson, T.J. 2019. "TV is biggest driver in global sport league revenue." Global Sport Matters, March 7. https://globalsportmatters.com/business/2019/03/07/tv-is-biggest-driver-in-global-sport-league-revenue/.

McArtor, Mac. 2020. *America's Present Time: Reviving MLB Attendance by Marketing to Gen Z.* https://cdr.lib.unc.edu/concern/honors_theses/5x21tn20x

McCullough, Andy. 2022. "The 2017 Astros' title doesn't have an asterisk. For Brian Cashman, the Yankees' World Series drought does." The Athletic, March 21. https://theathletic.com/3220682/2022/03/31/the-2017-astros-title-doesnt-have-an-asterisk-for-brian-cashman-the-yankees-world-series-drought-does/.

Merkle, Adam, Catherine Hessick, Britton Leggett, Larry Goehrig, and Kenneth O'Connor. 2020. "Exploring the Components of Brand Equity amid Declining Ticket Sales in Major League Baseball." *Journal of Marketing Analytics*, 8(3), 149–164.

Miami Marlins. 2022. "Miami Marlins Scholars." Marlins.com. https://www.mlb.com/marlins/community/foundation/empowerment.

Miller, Darrell. Personal interview (2021). Vice president youth and facility development for Major League Baseball.

MLB.com. 2015. "Commissioner Rob Manfred's letter to fans." January 15. https://www.mlb.com/news/new-mlb-commissioner-rob-manfreds-letter-to-fans/c-107424384.

MLB.com. "Competitive Balance Tax." https://www.mlb.com/glossary/transactions/competitive-balance-tax.

MLB.com. 2020. "Tony Reagins named Chief Baseball Development Officer." August 20. https://www.mlb.com/press-release/press-release-tony-reagins-named-chief-baseball-development-officer.

MLB.com. 2019. "2019 MLB season generates increases in consumption and youth participation." September 30. https://www.mlb.com/press-release/press-release-2019-mlb-season-generates-increases-in-consumption-and-youth-parti.

Montgomery, Jeff. 2020. Kansas City baseball telecast.

Moran, Eddie. 2019. "Another Year Of Declining Attendance: How Worried Should MLB

Be?" Front Office Sports, October 7. https://frontofficesports.com/mlb-attendance-2019-2/.

NBA Communications. 2019. "NBA and William Hill announce sports betting partnership." October 2. https://pr.nba.com/nba-and-william-hill-sports-betting-partnership/.

Nielsen. 2018. "America's Pastime: Popular with Fans and Sponsors." July. https://www.nielsen.com/insights/2018/americas-pastime-popular-with-fans-and-sponsors/.

Norman, Jim. 2018. "Football Still Americans' Favorite Sport to Watch." Gallup, January 4. https://news.gallup.com/poll/224864/football-americans-favorite-sport-watch.aspx.

Olney, Buster. 2020. "How Major League Baseball can save itself beyond 2021." ESPN, June 7. https://www.espn.com/mlb/story/_/id/29275541/olney-how-major-league-baseball-save-2021.

O'Malley, Nick. 2020. "Astros (and Red Sox) sign-stealing scandal, explained: How did they cheat? Why is Alex Cora MLB's main culprit?" *MassLive*, January 14. https://www.masslive.com/redsox/2020/01/mlb-sign-stealing-scandal-explained-what-did-astros-red-sox-do-to-cheat-why-is-alex-cora-the-main-culprit.html.

On This Date in MLB. 2022. https://www.instagram.com/onthisdateinmlb/?hl=en.

Oshin, Olafimihan. 2022. "Sanders calls for end to MLB antitrust exemption." *The Hill*, March 10. https://thehill.com/regulation/business/597767-sanders-calls-for-end-to-mlb-antitrust-exemption/.

Palm, Mike. Personal interview (2020). Vice president of operations for The Circa, The D, and Golden Gate Casinos.

Panacy, Peter. 2013. "MLB: How Major League Baseball is Losing its Appeal in the Modern Era." Bleacher Report, March 1. https://bleacherreport.com/articles/1566029-mlb-how-major-league-baseball-is-losing-its-appeal-in-the-modern-era.

Passan, Jeff. 2020. "Inside MLB's financials fight—and the numbers to solve it." ESPN, June 5. https://www.espn.com/mlb/story/_/id/29269242/inside-mlb-financials-fight-numbers-solve-it.

Passan, Jeff. 2020."Will there be baseball this year or not? Jeff Passan breaks down MLB's ugly labor fight." ESPN, June 15. https://www.espn.com/mlb/story/_/id/29313238/will-there-baseball-year-not-jeff-passan-breaks-mlb-ugly-labor-fight.

Passan, Jeff, and Kiley McDaniel. 2020. "What the MLB deal with players means for 2020 season and beyond." ESPN, March 28. https://www.espn.com/mlb/story/_/id/28964249/what-mlb-deal-players-means-2020-season-beyond.

Paulsen. 2020. "MLB Division Series viewership down substantially." Sports Media Watch. https://www.sportsmediawatch.com/2020/10/mlb-division-series-ratings-down-big-tbs-fs1/.

Pederson, Joc. 2022. Twitter, March 22. https://twitter.com/yungjoc650/status/1506497016116834304?lang=en.

PerfectMind blog. 2017. "The Many Benefits of Youth Sports in your Community." October 3. https://blog.perfectmind.com/the-many-benefits-of-youth-sports-in-your-community.

Petco Park Insider. "Gallagher Square is the Park at the Park." https://www.petcoparkinsider.com/gallagher-square#:~:text=Gallagher%20Square%20is%20the%20Park%20At%20The%20Park&text=It%20contains%20a%20mini%20little.

Picus, Matthew. Personal interview (2020). Los Angeles Dodgers fan and millennial.

Poindexter, Owen. 2021. "MLB Looks to Grow Its Younger Fanbase." Front Office Sports, March 31. https://frontofficesports.com/mlb-looks-to-grow-its-younger-fanbase/.

Rafael, Thomas. 2019. "Baseball Hall Of Famer Rich 'Goose' Gossage: I Can't Watch These Games Anymore. It's Not Baseball. It's Unwatchable." Too Athletic, August 21. https://tooathletic.com/baseball-hall-of-famer-rich-goose-gossage-i-cant-watch-these-games-anymore-its-not-baseball-its-unwatchable/.

Reuss, Jerry. Personal interview (2021). Former Major League Baseball pitcher (retired).

Ribadeneyra, Nico. 2020. "Dodger's Clayton Kershaw Slams MLB's New Extra-Inning Rule." US Sports, September 15. https://usports.org/dodgers-clayton-kershaw-slams-mlbs-new-extra-inning-rule/.

Riley, Daniel. 2022. "How Shohei Ohtani Made Baseball Fun Again." *Gentleman's Quarterly (GQ)*, January 12. https://www.gq.com/story/shohei-ohtani-february-cover-profile.

Ring, Sheryl. 2019. "MLB needs a salary floor." SB Nation, November 4. https://www.beyondtheboxscore.com/2019/11/4/20927613/mlb-needs-a-salary-floor-athletics-rays-pirates-puig-calhoun-betances-stanton-yelich-osuna.

Roach, John. Personal interview (2020). Professor, University of Southern California.

Rymer, Zachary D. 2020. "Power Ranking Wrigley, Fenway and All 30 MLB Ballparks Ahead of 2020 Season." Bleacher Report, July 6. https://bleacherreport.com/articles/2898278.

Samuelson, Chidike. Entrepreneur. 2019. "5 Brand Marketing Tips Every Brand Can Learn From the NBA." June 12. https://www.entrepreneur.com/author/chidike-samuelson.

Schaerlaeckens, Leander. 2020. "Take notes, MLB. The KBO has some pointers for making baseball more fan-friendly." Yahoo Sports, May 7. https://www.yahoo.com/lifestyle/take-note-mlb-the-kbo-has-some-pointers-for-making-baseball-more-fan-friendly-153534796.html.

Schlesinger, Rick. Personal interview (2020). Milwaukee Brewers president-business operations.

Schmidt, Mike. 2021. "Hall of Famer: 'Frisk the Pitcher' policy an excuse for poor hitting by MLB players." Associated Press, June 26. https://www.usatoday.com/story/sports/mlb/2021/06/26/mike-schmidt-column-poor-hitting-frisking-pitchers/5359465001/.

Schreiber, Shavonnah. Personal interview (2020). Marketing expert and managing director of SNR Creative.

Schuster, Blake. 2020. "MLB Increases Number of Camera Angles for Video Reviews Ahead of 2020 Season." Bleacher Report, July 20. https://bleacherreport.com/articles/2900982-mlb-increases-number-of-camera-angles-for-video-reviews-ahead-of-2020-season.

September 28, 2020. https://morningconsult.com/2020/09/28/gen-z-poll-sports-fandom/.

Sheinin, Dave. 2018. "These World Series games are ... moving ... at ... a ... glacial ... pace." *Washington Post*, October 25. https://www.washingtonpost.com/sports/these-world-series-games-are—moving—at—a—glacial—pace/2018/10/25/45341b2a-d883-11e8-aeb7-ddcad4a0a54e_story.html.

Sherman, Joel. 2020. "The purist argument doesn't make sense in MLB playoff-expansion debate." *New York Post*, February 11. https://nypost.com/2020/02/11/the-purist-argument-doesnt-make-sense-in-mlb-playoff-expansion-debate/.

Showalter, Buck. Personal interview (2021). Major League Baseball manager.

Silverman, Alex. "The Sports Industry's Gen Z Problem." Morning Consult.

Small Business.com. https://smallbusiness.com/.

Spangler, Todd. 2019. "Facebook Cuts MLB Live-Streaming Schedule to Just Six Games for 2019." Yahoo! Finance, March 29. https://finance.yahoo.com/news/facebook-cuts-mlb-live-streaming-170446281.html.

Spotrac. 2022. "Best Winning Percentage and Top Average Attendance 2017–2021." https://www.spotrac.com/.

Spotrac. 2022. "MLB Luxury Tax Tracker." https://www.spotrac.com/.

Sprencel, Theodore. N.d. "Why Baseball is Losing its Popularity." Suite 101. https://suite101.com/article/why-baseball-is-losing-popularity-a205456.

Sprung, Sholmo. 2019. "Inside The NBA's Push To Make Basketball The World's Most Popular Sport." *Forbes*, March 4. https://www.forbes.com/sites/shlomosprung/2019/03/04/nba-china-ceo-derek-chang-takes-us-inside-nbas-push-to-make-basketball-worlds-most-popular-sport/?sh=761fba9c51b0.

SSRS/Luker on Trends. "SSRS/Luker on Trends Sports Poll." https://ssrs.com/ssrs-luker-on-trends-sports-poll/.

Stark, Jayson. 2020. "Stark: If you think Major League Baseball is ugly now ..." The Athletic, June 17. https://theathletic.com/1877320/2020/06/17/stark-if-you-think-major-league-baseball-is-ugly-now/.

Statista. "Average regular season home attendance of the Tampa Bay Rays from 2009 to 2021." https://www.statista.com/statistics/246830/average-per-game-attendance-of-the-tampa-bay-rays/.

Statista. "Major League Baseball: total attendance at regular season games from 2006

to 2021." https://www.statista.com/statistics/193421/regular-season-attendance-in-the-mlb-since-2006/.
Steinberg, Leigh. 2018. "Baseball Has A Serious Injury Problem." *Forbes,* July 24. https://www.forbes.com/sites/leighsteinberg/2018/07/24/baseball-the-most-dangerous-sport-in-america/?sh=6d47eb604656.
Stephen, Eric. 2020. "Jo Adell: 'Why are we 'raw and toolsy' and considered 'high-risk'?" SB Nation, Halos Heaven, June 20. https://www.halosheaven.com/2020/6/20/21295013/jo-adell-racial-bias-scouting-reports-angels.
Stephen, Eric. 2019. "MLB's plan to eliminate 42 minor league baseball teams, explained." SB Nation, November 21. https://www.sbnation.com/mlb/2019/11/21/20973264/mlb-minor-league-realignment-proposal-teams-near-me.
Stitzel, Brandli, Ryan Mattson, and Rex Pjesky. 2021. "The trashy side of baseball: An econometric analysis of the Houston Astros cheating scandal." *Economics Bulletin,* 41(2), 507–522.
Stutman, Gabe. 2016. "If MLB Really Wants Shorter Games, It Needs to Figure Out Instant Replay." Vice.com, July 11. https://www.vice.com/en/article/yp8wa5/if-mlb-really-wants-shorter-games-it-needs-to-figure-out-instant-replay.
Svrluga, Barry. 2021. "Baseball's lockout is about economics. What needs to be fixed is the sport." *Washington Post,* December 2. https://www.washingtonpost.com/sports/2021/12/02/mlb-lockout-economics-fix-sport/.
Svrluga, Barry. 2015. "No clock in baseball? MLB's new pace of play guidelines get results." *Washington Post,* May 1. https://www.washingtonpost.com/news/sports/wp/2015/05/01/no-clock-in-baseball-mlbs-new-pace-of-play-guidelines-get-results/.
Swartz, Jon. 2018. "Watching Baseball on Facebook Requires Patience." *Barron's,* May 10. https://www.barrons.com/articles/watching-baseball-on-facebook-requires-patience-1525982295.
Taylor, Brett. 2021. "Everyone loves the pitch clock." Bleacher Nation, November 11. https://www.bleachernation.com/cubs/2021/11/11/everyone-loves-the-pitch-clock/.
Team Marketing Report. "Fan Cost Index (FCI) (2015–2021)." https://teammarketing.com/fci/2022-mlb-fan-cost-index/.
TickPicblog. "Top 5 Most Expensive Average MLB Ticket Prices 2021." https://www.tickpick.com/blog/how-much-are-mlb-tickets/.
Tierney, Jim. 2019. "Why the Oakland A's New Loyalty Program Will be a Hit—Featuring Chris Giles." Clarus Commerce blog. https://www.claruscommerce.com/blog/why-the-oakland-as-new-loyalty-program-will-be-a-hit/.
Tracy, Jeff. 2020. "Baseball's shrinking minor leagues." Axios, September 9. https://www.axios.com/2020/09/09/minor-league-baseball-contraction-affiliate-status.
Trade Group. 2022. "What is experiential marketing?" https://www.tradegroup.com/what-is-experiential-marketing/.
Traveling Mom Blog. 2022. "Why Minor League Baseball Rocks." March 14. https://www.travelingmom.com/why-minor-league-baseball-rocks/.
Turner, Justin. Personal interview (2020). Major League Baseball player, Los Angeles Dodgers.
Two Circles Marketing. 2022. https://twocircles.com.
Vander Meer, Johnny. https://www.azquotes.com/quote/700326.
Vintage Bubble Gum. 2022. https://www.instagram.com/vintage_bubble_gum/?hl=en.
Wagner, James. 2018. "M.L.B. Extends TV Deal With Fox Sports Through 2028." *New York Times,* November 15. https://www.nytimes.com/2018/11/15/sports/mlb-fox-tv-deal.html.
Walker, Ben. 2005. "Lack of black players noticeable at Series." *Pittsburgh Post-Gazette,* October 25. https://www.post-gazette.com/sports/pirates/2005/10/26/Lack-of-black-players-noticeable-at-Series/stories/200510260185.
Warneke, Kevin, John Shorey, and David C Ogden. 2013. "Prospects, Promotions and Playoff Races: Do They Bring Fans to Minor League Games?" Society for American Baseball Research, Fall. https://sabr.org/journal/article/prospects-promotions-and-playoff-races-do-they-bring-fans-to-minor-league-games/.
Waters, Matthew. 2020. "First MLB Team Signs Sportsbook Deal, as Detroit Tigers Pair

Up With PointsBet." Legal Sports Report, July 2. https://www.legalsportsreport.com/42369/detroit-tigers-sports-betting-deal/.
Weinrib, Ben. 2019. "Report: MLB has a radical proposal that would eliminate 40 minor league teams." Yahoo Sports, October 18. https://www.yahoo.com/now/mlb-radical-proposal-eliminate-40-minor-league-teams-211937863.html.
Will, George. Personal interview (2022). American political commentator and author of *Men at Work: The Craft of Baseball* (1990).
Williams, Devin. Major League Baseball player, Milwaukee Brewers. Twitter. https://twitter.com/dtrainn_23.
Yellon, Al. 2019. "What would a MLB salary cap look like?" Bleedcubbieblue.com, January 30. https://www.bleedcubbieblue.com/2019/1/30/18203489/mlb-salary-cap.
Yoo, Jeeho. Personal interview (2020). Sportswriter, Yonhap News Agency.
Young, Jabari. 2020. "Apple, Google and Sony will be critical to MLB season shortened by coronavirus." CNBC, July 21. https://www.cnbc.com/2020/07/21/apple-google-sony-critical-mlb-ready-covid-19-2020-regular-season.html.
Young, Jabari. 2019. "Major League Baseball managers don't like proposed pitching rule for 2020 season." CNBC, December 12. https://www.cnbc.com/2019/12/10/major-league-baseball-managers-dont-like-new-pitching-rule-for-2020.html.
Ziedelis, Dave. Personal Interview (2020). Former general manager of the Frederick Keys.

Index

academies 145–146, 149–150, 186–187
accountability 10, 55, 57–58, 61, 76, 117
administration 83–84, 97, 125
adult 29, 32, 46, 49, 52, 120–121, 131, 135–136, 146, 177
affiliates 2–4, 6–8, 16, 38–39, 44–45, 50, 127, 129, 165
affordability 31–32, 49, 84, 129–130, 154
agency 91, 109, 178
amenities 23, 29–31, 40–41, 45, 49, 83, 88
analysis, analytics 21, 54, 57–59, 64, 82, 86, 90, 106, 109, 119, 121, 129, 132–134, 142, 151, 153–155, 161
Anderson, Shaun 143–145, 151
announcer 15, 44–45, 69, 98
arenas 32, 88
Arizona 1, 4, 15, 30, 34–35, 46, 82, 86, 88, 98, 101–102, 115, 117
Arizona Diamondbacks 7, 30, 34, 46, 82, 88, 115
assets 155–156
athletes 9, 58–59, 62–64, 82, 121–122, 128, 130, 133, 136, 139–140, 143, 145–148, 150, 156, 162–164, 168, 173, 178
Atlanta Braves 7, 28, 33–34, 36, 64, 100, 175
attendance 2, 6, 11, 13, 19–27, 29–31, 33–49, 51, 53–54, 60, 67, 71–72, 74, 78–82, 86, 88, 93–95, 102, 116, 120, 123, 128–130, 153–156, 159, 165, 172, 174, 182–183
audiences 53, 61–62, 69–70, 107, 117, 122, 129, 131–132, 147, 161, 186

ballpark 2–3, 13–14, 19, 26, 29–32, 34, 37, 40–46, 48–50, 63, 67, 74, 76, 78, 80–83, 85–89, 91–93, 95, 104–105, 107, 122, 126, 131, 133–134, 156, 161, 167–169, 182–183, 185
ballplayers 110, 136, 170
Baltimore 1, 22, 29, 34, 45, 81, 83–84, 106, 124, 149, 162, 171, 175
Baltimore Orioles 22, 27, 29, 34, 45, 81, 83–86, 95, 98, 106, 108, 124, 128, 131, 149, 162, 166–167, 171, 185
barriers 21–22, 28, 30, 47, 109, 128, 131, 143, 145, 156, 161, 164, 173, 183–184
Baseball Almanac 4, 23, 40, 68
baseman 58, 65, 99, 106
basketball 52, 54, 70, 90, 98, 120, 122, 124, 136, 141–142, 144, 146, 157, 159, 162, 178
Bavasi, Bill 4–5, 8–9, 75, 93, 135, 140, 147–148, 182
beer 32, 54, 82, 87, 92
beverages 44, 49, 79, 86, 131, 154
billionaires 175–176, 178
bleachers 44, 54, 79, 166, 170
bobblehead 25–26, 78
Boras, Scott 28–29, 48
Boston 15, 33–36, 51, 62–64, 102, 108, 155, 158
broadcaster 11, 14, 16, 108
Brooklyn 4–5, 21, 143
Brooklyn Dodgers 4, 14, 16, 21, 23, 33–34, 36–37, 40, 63, 65–67, 71, 99, 106, 108, 115, 123, Budweiser, 132, 161
bullpen 98, 110, 126, 140

Calcaterra, Craig 10, 27–28, 38, 88–89, 98, 103–104, 116, 175, 177
California 4, 13, 15, 24, 44–45, 60, 80, 86, 137, 145, 160
Camden Yards 29, 83, 85–86, 131
camera 62, 64, 105–106
campaign 80, 116, 125, 128, 134, 151, 167–168, 187
capacities 20, 26, 29–30, 36, 79–80
career 9, 15–16, 64, 137, 139, 145, 149, 156, 163
Carter, David 24–25, 37, 72, 82, 119–120, 137, 153, 156–158, 163, 167, 170–171, 175, 180
catcher 62–63, 65, 99, 111, 118, 138, 141, 145, 186

199

Index

championship 23, 29, 33–34, 52, 63, 65, 67–68, 70, 73–74, 80, 92, 155
Chicago 1, 35–36, 40, 51, 57, 88, 90, 102, 154–155, 165
Chicago Cubs 23, 35–36, 40, 57, 88, 102, 117, 154–155, 163, 165
Cincinnati 5, 15, 25, 39, 56, 73, 78, 86, 165, 168
Cleveland 29–30, 35–36, 86, 171
Cleveland Indians 29–30
collaboration 130, 165, 179, 184
collegiate 137, 145, 164
Colorado 29, 65, 86, 148
commissioner 3, 6, 10, 28, 37, 62–64, 68–70, 74, 85, 91, 97–98, 100–101, 105, 110, 116–117, 130–131, 135, 143, 146, 148–149, 157, 161, 172–174, 176, 186–187
commitment 41, 94, 128, 133, 151
communications 5, 15, 39, 84, 89–90, 93, 98, 103, 124, 126, 133, 144, 146, 179
competition 10, 15–16, 31, 52, 66, 71–72, 80–82, 90, 121, 131, 142, 154, 157, 165, 182, 184–185, 187
concept 8, 29–30, 32, 75, 84, 110, 130, 154
concessions 20, 41, 43, 49, 86, 88–89, 92, 174
consequences 3, 10, 27, 61, 63–64, 103, 107, 169, 171, 174, 187
consumers 31–32, 53, 61–62, 72, 79–82, 94, 121, 125–128, 133, 147, 154, 158, 182
contests 46, 68, 72, 80, 93, 98, 158
Cosler, Emily 82–83, 95, 153–154
COVID 20, 33, 36, 73, 84, 91, 101, 105, 115, 172, 175–177, 179, 182
crews 39, 49, 105–107, 118
crisis 11, 24, 39, 124
customers 41, 45, 49, 78, 80–81, 93–94, 126, 154, 158, 168

demographics 119, 122–124, 126–128, 161
Detroit 26, 91, 175
development 4, 6, 8, 62, 71, 89, 101, 135, 145, 148–149, 165–168
device 13, 44, 66–67, 81–82, 89, 123–126, 143
digital 44, 48, 75, 81, 84, 90–91, 95, 101, 122–123, 161, 183
director 4–5, 93, 98, 103, 122, 124, 131, 146, 150, 163, 166
131, 142–143, 158, 160–161, 165, 171, 173–174, 176
dollars 2–3, 9, 41, 46, 48–49, 52, 66, 71, 76, 81, 132, 142, 154, 176, 182, 188
dugout 33, 63, 65, 92, 109, 138, 162, 166

education 16, 133, 150, 187
employees 6, 62, 93, 156, 167–168, 170, 187
entertainment 38, 53, 57, 73, 78, 81, 99, 124, 126, 132, 168
equipment 3, 141–143, 149
ESPN 9, 14, 19, 28–29, 60–61, 66, 79, 107, 122, 158, 170, 173, 175–176
excitement 47–48, 61, 97, 111, 116–117, 183, 185, 188
expansion 32, 58, 105, 111
expectations 22, 30, 112, 120, 169

Facebook 84, 124, 130, 167, 183
facilities 3, 6–7, 145
fame 14, 40, 55, 97, 139, 155, 180
fanbase 30, 37, 84, 86, 92–93, 95, 120, 122, 140, 153, 160
followers 127, 155–156, 162
football 51–52, 54, 61, 66, 70, 75, 81, 92, 119, 121–122, 124, 136, 144–145, 148, 162, 164, 174, 178
franchise 3–4, 7, 11, 20–21, 23, 25–26, 29, 32, 36, 39, 45, 50, 57, 64, 66, 71, 78–79, 101, 154, 157, 173–175, 185

gender 127, 165–167
generations 1, 5, 11, 13–14, 16, 30, 42, 52, 69, 75, 85, 119–134, 148, 158, 161–162, 165, 169, 171, 175, 183, 186, 188
giveaways 26, 93, 129, 162, 166
goals 3, 6, 11, 15, 50, 70, 80, 100, 102, 128, 137, 140, 149–150, 188

heroes 156, 162–163
hitters 11, 54–55, 60, 63, 94, 100–101, 103, 109, 111–115, 117–118, 138–140, 181, 186
Houston 4, 29, 33–34, 36–37, 62–65, 69, 108, 122, 163, 166

incentives 28–29, 43, 74, 81, 110, 129, 166, 175, 179
infield 55, 87, 104, 111, 146
initiatives 2, 37, 47, 86, 97, 109, 116, 126, 128, 135, 148, 151, 158, 166, 183
injuries 62, 103, 111, 137
innings 22, 45–46, 49, 54, 69, 85, 88–89, 104–105, 114–118, 123, 131, 160, 184, 188
innovate 25, 38–39, 41, 43–44, 48, 76, 78–79, 81, 85, 90, 93–94, 96, 105, 109, 116–117, 123, 133–134, 162, 182, 184, 186, 188
insights 79, 122, 127–128, 130, 134
Instagram 84, 112, 124, 127, 132, 167, 183

journalism 81, 90, 103, 182

Kansas 73, 92, 111, 114, 125, 185
Karl, Scott 28, 48, 51, 54–55, 73, 98, 108–

Index

109, 114, 118, 123, 138–139, 142–143, 172, 180, 182, 186
Krivsky, Wayne 5–6, 8, 25, 56, 73, 78, 102, 106, 110, 114, 118, 136, 141, 184, 186

leadership 3, 84, 95, 156–157, 165
leagues 1–9, 11, 13, 15–16, 19–29, 31–35, 37–57, 59–68, 70–76, 78–84, 87–95, 97–109, 111–117, 119–135, 137–151, 153–174, 177–178, 181–188
Los Angeles 1, 4, 13–17, 21, 33–34, 36–37, 40, 51, 63, 65–66, 71, 75, 80, 86, 99–100, 115, 121, 131, 135, 148–149, 160, 165, 173, 181
loyalty 6, 42, 72, 78, 80, 94–95, 151

management 35, 39, 143, 147, 156, 158, 163
Manfred, Rob 6, 8, 37, 62–64, 70, 85, 89, 91, 97–101, 110, 116–117, 130–131, 135, 143, 148–149, 172, 174, 186
Marist 52–53, 97, 136, 141, 146
matchups 14, 68, 74, 114, 160
mentality 59, 145, 165
Miami 43, 98, 111, 126, 138, 149, 165, 175, 177
Miami Marlins 43–44, 98, 108, 111, 126, 138, 149, 165, 177, 187
millennials 14, 52, 120–121, 123, 125–127, 129, 132, 186
Milwaukee 1, 33–36, 39–41, 44, 49, 82, 86, 122, 143, 164–165, 169
Milwaukee Brewers 33–36, 39–41, 44, 49, 122, 126–127, 133, 143, 161, 164–165, 169, 184
Minnesota 36, 69, 124, 140, 160
Minnesota Twins 69, 124, 160, 165, 178
MLBPA 6, 8, 76, 100, 172–173, 179

NASCAR 117, 121, 125
negotiations 6, 47, 170–173, 175–179, 183, 188
neighborhoods 13–15, 87, 133, 137, 140, 147
Netflix 31, 42, 81, 124, 127, 131
New York 1, 6–7, 20–21, 23–24, 26, 35–37, 40, 42–43, 48, 53, 59–60, 63, 66, 70–71, 74, 82, 86, 103, 106–107, 118, 131, 137, 155, 159, 163, 165, 167, 175–176
New York Yankees 5, 7, 14, 23, 25, 35–37, 40, 48, 59, 63, 67, 71, 76, 86, 99–100, 107, 131, 137, 155, 158, 163, 165, 167, 171, 173, 176, 178

Oakland 36, 42–43, 94, 132, 139
offseason 48, 60, 109, 136
organizations 3, 9, 35, 39–41, 59, 79, 84, 91, 94, 132, 149–150, 154–156, 159–160, 164–165, 168, 184–185, 187
outcomes 22, 55–56, 71–72, 89, 110, 123, 126, 141
outfield 44, 87–88, 92, 107
outfielder 64, 102, 148, 159, 171, 181
outreach 149–151, 169, 184, 186–187

pandemic 20, 24, 33, 36, 84–85, 91, 101, 107, 114–115, 172–173, 175, 182
participation 21, 128, 135–137, 139, 141, 143–145, 147–149, 151–152
passion 11, 14–15, 17, 40, 90, 140, 175
pastime 11, 19, 23–24, 51, 53, 55, 57, 59, 61, 63, 65, 67, 69, 71, 73, 75, 77, 98, 122, 146
pennants 4, 23, 27, 72, 155
percentages 35–37, 48, 55, 59, 76, 79, 147
performance 23, 26, 35, 47, 59–60, 62, 64–65, 154–156, 159
Philadelphia 35, 66, 107
Philadelphia Pirates 27–28, 34, 88, 99, 159–160, 171, 178
pitchers 22, 51, 54–55, 63, 65, 73, 80, 97–100, 102–104, 108–115, 117–118, 138–139, 146, 159, 167, 173, 180–182, 186
pitcher's mound 55, 80, 100, 111–112, 116–117, 123, 140, 188
players 8, 28, 60, 64, 70, 76, 102, 105, 113, 150–151, 158, 162, 173, 176–177
playoffs 31, 34, 64–65, 68, 73–74, 113–114
promotions 2, 26, 45, 49, 78, 93, 154, 158, 162, 166, 168, 184

Reagins, Tony 135, 148–149
recession 51, 53, 55, 57, 59, 61, 63, 65, 67, 69, 71, 73, 75, 77
regional 24, 66–67, 123, 163
relationships 2, 15, 22, 39, 79–80, 84, 94, 129–130, 143–145, 151, 154–155, 170, 173
replays 54, 62–64, 102, 104–107, 118, 158, 184
revenues 3–4, 19–20, 24–29, 32, 35, 37, 49, 61, 66–68, 74, 79, 91, 94–95, 111, 153, 155, 157, 159–161, 163, 165, 173–174, 180, 182, 185, 188
Rockies 29, 65, 69, 148
rosters 27, 34, 37, 48, 58, 71, 145–146
runners 73, 81, 103, 105–109, 111–112, 115, 139

St. Louis 7, 16, 23, 36, 69, 108, 132, 172, 174
salaries 3, 32, 70–71, 76–77, 160, 171, 175–176, 178, 180, 185
San Diego 1, 34, 36, 45, 65, 86–87, 111, 160
San Diego Padres 25, 34, 36, 45, 65, 86, 131, 160, 178

San Francisco 15, 21, 29, 34, 36, 87, 111, 166
scandals 51, 59, 62, 64, 108
Schreiber, Shavonnah 122, 133–134, 163–164, 169
scout 8–9, 57, 137
Seattle 4, 44, 66, 111
Seattle Mariners 4, 44, 66, 75, 163
Showalter, Buck 9, 24–25, 37, 55–59, 76, 98, 103–104, 123, 137–138, 173
soccer 52, 98, 117, 121–122, 124, 136–137, 139, 141, 143, 150, 156, 162, 164, 174
softball 4, 54, 116, 135, 149–150
solutions 2, 10–11, 19, 24–25, 38, 44, 47, 51, 72, 78, 91, 94, 116, 118, 127, 129–130, 136, 149, 151–152, 167, 173, 179–184, 188
spectators 22, 92, 94, 112, 140
Spokane Indians 5
sportsbook 88, 90–91
stadium 13, 17, 21, 23, 25–26, 29–32, 34, 40, 42, 44–47, 49, 61, 65, 79, 81–87, 89–91, 95, 127–129, 131–132, 134, 147, 153, 159, 172, 184
statistics 14–15, 31, 37, 54, 57, 59, 61, 90, 95, 124, 132, 153, 162, 164, 186
subscription 42–43, 46, 48, 75, 94, 96, 131, 183–185

talent 2–4, 6, 10, 15, 27, 29, 47, 71, 142, 144, 150, 157, 165, 176, 178
technology 56, 63, 94, 101, 105, 123, 125, 134, 142, 154, 161

Texas 7, 29, 34, 36, 57, 66, 82, 102, 153, 163, 176
Texas Rangers 7, 29, 34, 36, 57, 66, 176
theory 21, 76, 79, 123, 163
tradition 15, 35, 60, 105, 109, 163, 181
Turner, Justin 67, 99, 101, 106, 111, 114, 142, 160–162, 175
Twitter 84, 124, 131, 155–156, 158, 162, 167, 180, 183

umpires 99, 101–102, 105–107, 112–113, 117–118, 149, 186

viewership 67, 69–70, 75, 121, 130, 155

Washington 5, 36, 46, 54–55, 69, 73, 101, 122, 132, 175–176
World Series 2, 4, 15, 23, 25, 28–29, 31, 33–34, 53, 55, 60, 62–65, 67–71, 73–75, 81, 90, 99, 101–102, 106, 108, 120, 138, 149, 155, 158, 171, 173, 185

youngsters 13, 80, 137, 141, 151, 187
youth 14, 122, 124, 135–143, 145–149, 151–152, 186–187
YouTube 14, 76, 84, 130, 158, 167, 183

Ziedelis, Dave 6–7, 15, 45, 100, 109–110, 124, 164

www.ingramcontent.com/pod-product-compliance
Ingram Content Group UK Ltd.
Pitfield, Milton Keynes, MK11 3LW, UK
UKHW042006140426
5217IPUK00015B/1005